Do-it-yourself Supplement

Popular Science

Do-it-yourself Supplement

Popular Science BOOKS

Published by
Popular Science Books, New York, NY

Distributed to the trade by
Rodale Press, Emmaus, PA

Cover photo of A.J. Hand
by A.J. Hand

Copyright © 1986 by Popular Science Books

Published by

Popular Science Books
Times Mirror Magazines, Inc.
380 Madison Avenue
New York, NY 10017

Distributed to the trade by

Rodale Press, Inc.
33 East Minor Street
Emmaus, PA 18049

ISSN: 0733-1894

ISBN: 0-943822-85-8

Manufactured in the United States of America

introduction

You hold in your hands the fifth annual collaboration of the top workshop and how-to writers in America, and their inspiration should keep you busy in your shop and around your home for another productive year. I've been checking over the shoulder of the book's editor, Bob Markovich, as he sifted through a year's worth of my treasures from the pages of *Popular Science* Monthly; and I beamed like an approving parent each time he selected one of my favorites. It's always rewarding to see a particularly strong magazine piece printed on heavy, glossy stock and bound between hard covers. It's a tribute to the immense effort that has been lavished on the story, both by its original creator and then by the magazine staff that burnished it into an instructive, easy-to-follow printed package.

But preservation is only one aspect of this book project. Its purpose is not only to choose the best of PS how-to but to organize and augment it—by categorizing the material into logical sections (so you'll know exactly where to find it) and by adding new material from other sources especially in areas that the magazine doesn't regularly cover.

I also applaud this book because it confirms and codifies a strongly held view of mine that the very label "Popular Science" should stand for the best-available DIY instruction. In my 26-year association with *Popular Science*, I've worked hard to keep DIY a prominent part of our monthly mix. I welcome our Book Division's championing the continued quality of our home projects with this yearly anthology.

Among the projects commissioned especially for this book are:

- cherry wall paneling with built-in cabinets and fireplace mantel;
- a complete Chippendale dining room set;
- a clever shelving bridge that can embrace either sofa or bed;
- a challenging frame-and-panel oak cabinet;
- a very special picnic table constructed by means of a unique wood-epoxy construction technique featured in *Popular Science;*

- a custom-built multilevel deck that features innovative outdoor lighting.

You will also find:
- an enlarged section on home design, construction and remodeling;
- more woodworking and building projects throughout the book including step-by-step advice on both techniques and materials;
- a new separate section on wiring, plumbing, tiling and concreting;
- a beefed-up home energy section with fresh emphasis on energy-saving projects and installation procedures.

As with my how-to material in the magazine, this book focuses on practical yet innovative projects for home-owners who want to upgrade their real estate. All across the country, more money is now invested in home improvements than in new housing construction. As construction costs and home prices continue to soar, most of us have reconciled ourselves to staying put—or to buying less home than we'd hoped for. We're left with the challenge of sweat equity whether we pare down costs by taking part in the design and execution of a new home (this book shows you how) or work to bring our existing home up to the standard we can't quite afford to buy readymade.

The happy surprise is that most of us are finding satisfaction is doing it exactly the way we want it done. Whether you're building a deck, adding a dormer, remodeling your kitchen or fixing a leaky faucet, *Popular Science* Monthly and this Do-It-Yourself book are dedicated to enriching that satisfaction by offering both inspiration and practical instruction. Even as I write this, the *Popular Science* Book Division is already at work planning a similarly varied and exciting mix of prize projects from the magazine and free-lance sources.

Alfred Lees
Home and Shop Editor
Popular Science

the authors

Below is an alphabetical sampling of the authors for this issue. They include freelancers as well as members of the *Popular Science* New York and field staff.

Paul and Marya Butler are well-known to readers of last year's *Do-it-Yourself Yearbook,* where their chapter on wood-epoxy construction appeared. This year, the Butlers have incorporated those wood-epoxy techniques into a complete step-by-step "Permanent Picnic Table" project, beginning on page 104. The husband-and-wife team also contribute to a number of publications—Paul doing the writing, Marya the illustrating—and have just finished a how-to book on boating.

Bob Cerullo has over 25 years' experience as a line mechanic, service manager, and as a technical writer for such magazines as *Popular Science* and *Motor.* Owner and operator of a 23-bay auto repair shop, Bob provided five out of six chapters in this year's Car Care section. He is former vice-president of the International Motor Press Association, a member of the Society of Automotive Engineers, and a frequent guest on radio programs dealing with automotive how-to.

Richard Day, consulting editor for home and shop at *Popular Science,* has been writing in the how-to field for over 30 years. Specializing in home plumbing, electrical wiring, and concreting, he has written countless DIY articles and over a dozen related books. These include *How to Build Patios and Decks* and *How to Service and Repair Your Own Car,* in addition to his upcoming book on home wiring. Richard is also a director and past-president of the National Association of Home and Workshop Writers. His "Cookie-cutter Concrete" chapter begins on page 140.

R. J. DeCristoforo has long been one of the leading woodworking writers. Besides serving as consulting editor for tools and techniques for *Popular Science,* he is the author of numerous how-to articles—three of which are incorporated in this Yearbook. He has also written more than two dozen books, including *How to Build Your Own Furniture, DeCristoforo's Housebuilding Illustrated,* and his classic, *The Complete Book of Stationary Power Tool Techniques.* His latest book on portable power tool techniques is just off the press.

Nick Engler founded the how-to magazine *HANDS ON!* and managed Shopsmith's publishing department for over three years. During that time, he helped produce not only the magazine, but over 100 project plans, books, manuals, and a syndicated newspaper column for woodworkers. Today he writes freelance for various publications on the subjects of how-to, science, and technology. You'll find Nick's "Chippendale Dining Room Set" and "Super Shelving Unit" beginning on pages 52 and 60.

V. Elaine Gilmore, a senior editor at *Popular Science,* writes and edits stories on diverse subjects including housing technology, home heating and cooling, recreation, and tools. She began running in 1968 when running wasn't cool, and has since competed in marathons. She is also a skier and scuba diver. At home she enjoys tending her terrace garden. Indeed, the terrace planters she designed and built are the "project" alluded to in her chapter "The New Cordless Rechargeables" on page 172.

A. J. Hand began preparing for a career as a writer-photographer at age six by assisting his writer-father, the late Jackson Hand, with photo setups. A. J. later served on the *Popular Science* staff, winding up in 1975 as the magazine's home workshop editor before he began freelancing full-time. His photos have appeared on many magazine covers, and his articles appear in magazines and in his syndicated newspaper column, "Hand Around the House." He is the author of *Home Energy How-to,* as well as five of the chapters in this Yearbook.

William J. Hawkins worked for five years at RCA before joining *Popular Science* as electronics editor in 1970. While still at RCA, he won an electronics contest sponsored by *PS* and Allstate Insurance to find better auto anti-theft devices. Besides his editorial duties, Hawkins has also been responsible for installing and maintaining the magazine's computer system. He has appeared on network shows such as "Good Morning America," "Today," and "Omni." He also covers the home how-to area, as his chapter on drop-in-place patio deck squares attests.

Cathy Howard is a freelance writer and public relations consultant based in Portland, Oregon. Specializing in home improvement and related topics, she is a regular contributor to *Better Homes & Gardens, The Homeowner, 1,001 Home Ideas, McCall's,* and *Popular Science,* to name a few. Cathy has been involved in advertising and public relations with such firms as Georgia-Pacific and Louisiana-Pacific. She is married and the mother of two children. Her "Dual-storage Garden Center" chapter heads up this year's Outdoor Woodworking Projects section.

Thomas H. Jones is a full-time writer specializing in furniture making, home improvement, and woodworking techniques. Before taking up writing full time in 1970, Tom was an aerospace engineer. He has sold hundreds of articles on do-it-yourself subjects and is the author of three books, including *How to Build Greenhouses, Garden Shelters and Sheds,* and an upcoming book on building your own heirloom furniture.

Alfred W. Lees has been *Popular Science* Home and Shop Editor for nearly 20 years. He built the Lockbox leisure home as the focus of 19 feature articles during the 1970s. He also created the *PS* "Leisure Home," "Storage from Scratch," and "Room at the Top" series, as well as the national design competition for plywood projects, which he judged for ten consecutive years. Al is the author of *Popular Science Leisure Homes* and *Car Maintenance* (both with Ernest V. Heyn) and *67 Prizewinning Plywood Projects,* as well as six chapters in this Yearbook.

E. F. (Al) Lindsley was *Popular Science* senior editor for engineering before his recent retirement. He's also been a steeplejack, a semi driver, a carpenter, a meteorologist, a test pilot, an industrial engineer, and an editor with *Scientific American.* For *PS* and *The Homeowner* he continues to cover motors, engines, vehicles, house repairs, and woodworking. Al is the author of the long-time standard *Engine Installation Manual* for the Internal Combustion Institute as well as *Electric and Gas Welding* and *Metalworking in the Home Shop,* and an upcoming book on how to service and repair small gas engines.

Phil McCafferty has written countless how-to articles, five of which are incorporated in this Yearbook. His articles on woodworking, tools, metalworking, photography, and new products have appeared in *Popular Science* for more than a third of a century. He is also charter member and current President of the National Association of Home and Workshop Writers. An accomplished photographer, his color photographs have appeared on numerous magazine covers and scenic calendars.

Evan Powell, Consulting Editor for Appliances and Home Equipment for *Popular Science,* specializes in home equipment, repairs, remodeling, and energy systems. He is director of Chestnut Mountain Research, Inc., a South Carolina research and evaluation firm. He also produces the "Checkpoint" and "Road Test" TV features for Pulitzer Television, and helped design and produce General Electric's popular "Quick-Fix" program and manuals. Evan co-authored *The Complete Guide to Home Appliance Repair* (with Robert P. Stevenson) and *The Popular Science Book of Home Heating and Cooling* (with Ernest V. Heyn). His chapter on surface wiring is on page 143.

Susan Renner-Smith, formerly a senior editor at *Popular Science,* is now a freelance writer and editor. She writes on a range of topics and also edits educational texts. Sue lives with her husband and son in a 60-year-old house that serves as a proving ground for the products and projects she reports on. Six of the chapters in this Yearbook are hers.

Mort Schultz needs no introduction to DIY enthusiasts; his how-to articles have appeared in leading magazines, including *Popular Science,* since 1962. Currently a contributing editor to three magazines, Mort is also the man behind four monthly columns and 17 books. His "Insulating Louvers" and "Expensive Plumbing Repairs You Can Do Yourself" chapters begin on pages 43 and 152.

Bruce Shepherd got his start in the how-to field doing around-the-house repairs for his father, a busy country doctor. His skills broadened over the years with the purchase of his own homes, beginning with the proverbial "handyman's special." A fisheries biologist by profession, Bruce has authored several scientific articles and looks forward to seeing many more of his DIY stories in print. You'll find his chapter on three affordable backyard retaining walls on page 114.

Peter and Susanne Stevenson are the husband-and-wife team behind Stevenson Projects, Inc., a California company that supplies do-it-yourself plans for scores of projects ranging from furniture to sailboats. Many of their projects, which combine beauty and utility, have been featured in national magazines. Pete's the designer, builder, writer. Susie's the business manager and publications director. Look for their "Build a Lap Pool" chapter beginning on page 112.

Cy Wedlake— whose butcher-block carving table project begins on page 82—was brought up to be a wood craftsman from the time he was able to sweep sawdust in his father's patternmaking shop. During World War II, Cy found himself at the drawing board in an auto plant and took college engineering courses evenings for seven years. But he soon discovered that he had more fun writing about engineering than doing it—an enthusiasm that lead to numerous how-to articles and, most recently, videos. Says Cy, "I hope to live another 800 years, because that's how long it'll take me to complete all the projects I have planned."

Tom Wilkinson recently joined the staff of *Popular Science* after serving as Managing Editor of *Motor* magazine. In addition to his interests in cars, aircraft, motorcycles, military hardware, and other things mechanical, Tom enjoys photography, painting, music, and target shooting. He even has an unfinished novel lurking in the desk drawer. Tom is also a member of the American Society of Magazine Editors, the Society of Automotive Engineers, and the International Motor Press Association, where he serves as secretary. You'll find his chapter on repairing plastic autobody parts on page 156.

contents

two custom approaches to factory-built

This cedar-shingle, timber-frame Nantucket house sports traditional details such as the widow's walk. Decks on both floors help tie the home to its two-acre site.

PHOTOS BY: WILLIAM P. STEELE

Building from pre-milled factory components need not mean sacrificing individual design. In this chapter, factory-cut post-and-beam frameworks serve as the starting points for two highly personal homes—at a tremendous savings in time and at a cost about equal to what you'd spend using conventional means.

timbers frame dramatic open plan

With its weathered, cedar-shingle exterior, this vacation house looks quite at home amid the rosehips and seagrass of Nantucket Island's dunes. Behind the facade, however,

tradition takes a different form: The pre-milled structural framework of posts and beams stands open to view as a network of timbers configured into an airy, contemporary plan.

Designed by New York architect Leland L. Taliaferro, AIA, for a Manhattan physician and his wife as their weekend retreat and eventual retirement home, the 2,400-square-foot plan responds to the couple's desire for an informal living environment quite unlike their confining city apartment. Plus, it demonstrates the successful collaboration between Taliaferro and Nantucket contractor Ronald Santos in creating an exterior design that satisfies Nantucket's traditionally minded building requirements without dampening the interior's soaring spirits.

The couple searched for several years to find a "prepackaged" timber-frame design worthy of their stunning two-acre site. "Most resembled log cabins," observes the doc-

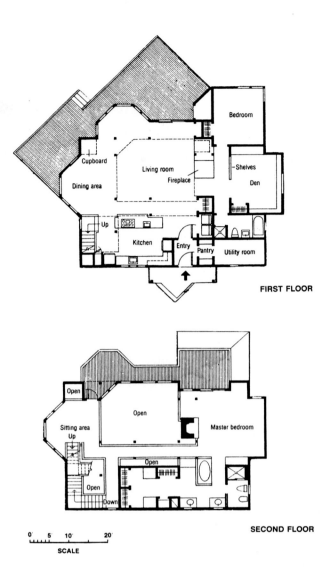

FIRST FLOOR

Bedroom
Cupboard
Living room
Shelves
Dining area
Fireplace
Den
Up
Kitchen
Entry
Pantry
Utility room

SECOND FLOOR

Open
Open
Sitting area
Up
Master bedroom
Open
Open
Down

0' 5' 10' 20'
SCALE

In New York architect Leland Taliaferro's design, the open-plan interior (photos above and below) reveals its precut structural frame in a contemporary light, showing off the intricate composition of posts and beams.

tor, "rustic and rough-sawn, with too many visible pegs and fasteners." In the end, they chose a plan from Timberpeg, a firm specializing in precut timber-frame houses, because they liked the looks of the company's smooth-planed posts and beams, sawn from eastern white pine, and the subtle joinery and custom detailing. They arranged for Timberpeg's New Hampshire plant to supply all the structural members precut to their architect's specifications.

Explains Taliaferro, "I positioned both vertical and horizontal members so that practically every point offers a sweep of the view." To accommodate the architect's spacing of posts and beams, Timberpeg supplied larger-than-average-size timbers—8 × 12s and 8 × 16s—to cover the longer spans between 8 × 8 uprights. The company also substituted blind-nailed lap joints for the usual mortise-and-tenon versions at the owners' request, and fabricated special fasteners to provide additional bracing for the massive beams. Costs for the custom-cut frame amounted to just under $20,000, including shipping by truck and ferry. Remarks Richard Neroni, Timberpeg's general manager: "Although we can provide both custom services and standard catalog designs, we most often supply a total package that includes all the components necessary for a weather-tight shell. Overall costs for our completed timber frames are about equivalent to those for a house built by employing conventional means."

Working in the dead of winter, Ronald Santos and his crew assembled the house by hand, using a crane only to hoist the rafter beams to a scaffold at roof height. Notes Santos: "The only way we could get to many of the beams was by climbing a pipe staging." Using locally supplied lumber and finishing materials, Santos and his crew completed the project on Columbus Day.

When it came to decorating, the couple brought some of their own talents to bear, the wife drawing on her interest in design to select colors and fabrics, the husband employing his woodworking skills to craft many of the furnishings. And the overall result? "It's a wonderful house," says one owner, "with the different effects of light on the wood, and the way it brings the feeling of the moors inside."

In the second-story sitting area (above, background), stairs lead to a widow's walk, which, with its partially plastic floor, is a skylight in disguise.

Specially fabricated steel plates (left) provide additional corner bracing for the beams.

Careful precutting of timbers and subtle methods of joinery add a great deal to the crisp detailing.

post-and-beam "barn" recalls colonial farmhouse

The satisfying result of a precut-timber-frame system assembled on site, this 1,700-square-foot post-and-beam structure near Norristown, Pennsylvania, is home to Marilyn and Dale Pennapacker. On the exterior, the style suggests a contemporary barn; inside, the spaces recall the homespun warmth of a Colonial farmhouse. The house was finished by Montgomery County builders Bob Bateman and John Ribble, with lots of personalizing by an energetic Marilyn working alongside them.

At the time of the project, the owner was a recently widowed young mother of three. Saddled with a large, dark 1700s-era farmhouse, she yearned to build a smaller, more energy-efficient home with plenty of light. "I needed some sunshine in my life," she says simply.

Opting for a post-and-beam frame—to be assembled on a 1½-acre site—Marilyn gathered information from a number of timber-frame companies, and finally decided on Sawmill River Post and Beam, located in Leverett, Massachusetts. To her delight, their suggested building system allowed the wood frame to remain fully exposed on the interior with walls attached to the outer surfaces of the timbers. To cut costs, Marilyn bought only the framing members plus two extras—the front door and a fanlight window for the living room.

Recalls Bateman, an industrial arts teacher who teams up with colleague Ribble to build houses during the summer months: "It was amazing to watch 36,000 pounds of New England pine go up like a giant Erector set; it took only a day and a half, and everything fit." Supplied with short timber lengths of 8 to 20 feet to keep the weight down, a four-man crew erected the frame by hand—using only a simple winch to pull the rafters into place—and connected members with simple lap joints, which were dowel-pegged or secured with invisible steel pins, and special corner bracing.

Robert Kleindienst, sales manager for Sawmill River, figures that today the Pennapacker design, frame only, would cost about $16,000; frame-plus-basics, between $36,000 and $39,000; and a customized design, carried beyond basics to include the complete insulated and finished shell but no frills, would fall somewhere in the range of $100,000 to $125,000.

The very speed with which the frame went up made the next phase seem all the more tedious for owner and builders alike: fashioning walls and ceiling from 1 × 6 tongue-in-groove pine boards nailed one by one to the timber frame. Assisted by her mother, Alma Sproul, Marilyn hand-stained every piece—including the exterior boards that were also individually nailed in place—covering some 20,000 linear feet of lumber and consuming a whopping 37 gallons of stain.

Marilyn also ordered multipane windows, traditionally

Traditional furnishings and the warmth of antiques mix comfortably with Marilyn and Dale Pennapacker's Pennsylvania post-and-beam house. The settle by the window dates from the early eighteenth century.

Dark-stained cedar enhances the barn styling. A glass-enclosed breezeway houses the laundry center, while an east-facing window welcomes sunlight indoors.

PHOTOS BY: TOM YEE

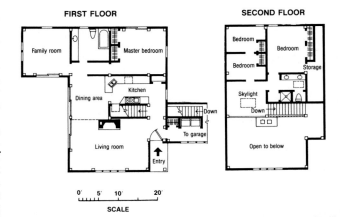

FIRST FLOOR

Family room
Master bedroom
Dining area
Kitchen
Living room
Down
To garage
Entry

SECOND FLOOR

Bedroom
Bedroom
Bedroom
Storage
Skylight
Down
Open to below

0'   5'   10'   20'
SCALE

Hanging pine cabinetry comes from the owner's previous home. The slate counter top next to the range is heat-resistant; plastic laminate on the opposite counter brightens the space.

Exposed frame and rafters flow gracefully into the dining room, where table was fashioned from an old hutch bench with a chest underneath.

styled but energy-efficient. In this atmosphere of warm woods, the owner mixed new Colonial-style furnishings with eighteenth-century pine antiques and accessorized with folk art and handcrafted items, which she collects on buying trips for her small catalog business, Country Neighbors.

Remembers new husband Dale, who brought more sunshine into Marilyn's life several months after the new house was completed: "The exposed framework, open interior, and compact layout were new to my experience; they seemed unconventional, yet aesthetically pleasing." Dale is also pleased with the affordable heating bills. And Marilyn is unquestionably satisfied with her post-and-beam project, stating emphatically, "I'd do it over again tomorrow!"—*by Christina Nelson. Photos by William P. Steele and Tom Yee. Drawings by Natalie Siegel.*

Suppliers' addresses: **Architecture** by Leland L. Taliaferro, 110 Riverside Drive, New York, NY 10024; **Contracting** by Ronald J. Santos, Wauwin Avenue, Nantucket, MA 02554, and Bateman & Ribble Inc., 3811 Sumter Drive, Collegeville, PA 19426; **Posts and Beams** by Timberpeg East, Inc., PO Box 1500, Claremont, NH 03743; **Timber Frame** (series 1700) by Sawmill River Post & Beam, Inc., PO Box 277, Leverett, MA 01054.

new kit lets you be your own architect

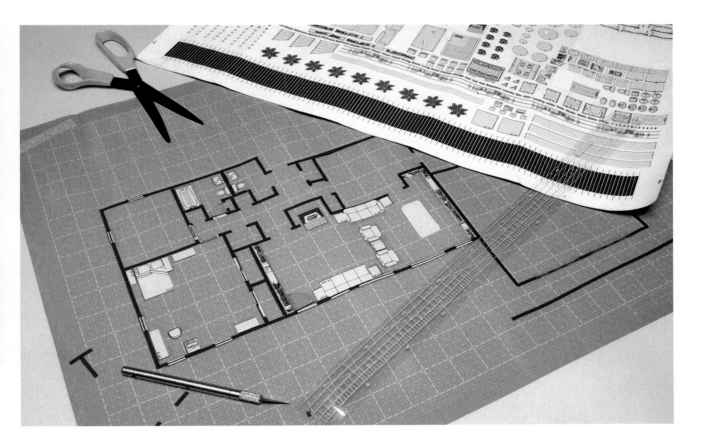

What's it going to look like when it's finished? If you've ever considered designing a house, renovating a room, or just rearranging the furniture, that's a question you've probably asked. And until recently, the only way to get an answer was to finish the project—not always an advantageous approach.

Now there's an easier way. New design kits let you repeatedly move sofas, walls, and whole rooms—just by picking up and pressing down adhesive plastic strips (or painted, detailed cardboard pieces), which represent walls and furniture, on supplied grids. These kits are like an architect in a box: They help you plan and can prevent costly mistakes. One kit even tells you how much room to leave around a bed.

I tried out three of these kits: the Plan-a-Flex Home Designer (ProCreations Publishing Co., 8129 Earhart Blvd., New Orleans, LA 70118), the Interior Design Kit, and the Professional House Building Kit (both from Design Works, 11 Hitching Post Rd., Amherst, MA 01002). For the trials, I laid out and redesigned my house. I thought I knew my home inside and out, but these kits gave me a few lessons on using space and how a house is put together, from which walls must be load bearing to why my kitchen is where it is.

Each kit provides a different view of a house—a floor plan, a perspective, or a three-dimensional model—but they're all easy to use. Scissors and glue (for the model-building kit) are the only tools required. You will, how-

ever, need an accurate drawing of your home before you start. If the original drawings aren't available, base your sketch on on-site measurements. If you're designing a dream house from scratch, work from a plan book or an architect's blueprint.

My design lesson began with the $25 Plan-a-Flex Home Designer, which produces an overhead view of a house's floor plan. One of the kit's helpful features is a concise design guide. In this 15-page booklet you'll find such useful information as the clearances needed for the comfortable use of furniture, appliances (down to optimum counter-top height), and bath fixtures.

To use the kit, tape the 20-by-26-inch plastic grid to a table top or drawing board. To transfer your di-

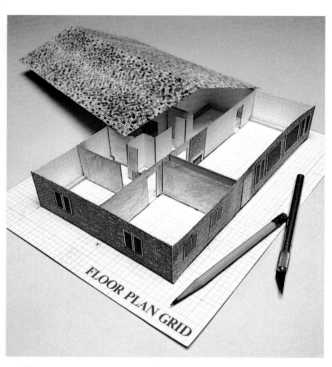

Each of these kits has a different design approach. Plan-a-Flex (preceding page) offers a bird's-eye view of a house's layout, up to 6,500 square feet. Supplied plastic strips adhere repeatedly to the plastic grid. The Interior Design Kit (left) uses a 9-by-12-inch plastic-coated grid ruled with vertical and diago- nal lines to create a perspective view. The Professional House Building Kit (right) can accommodate a model of a 63-foot-long house on a 9-by-12-inch grid in ³/₁₆-inch scale. The kit shows exterior details, including a removable roof, but you can demar- cate interior space.

mensioned drawing to the grid, you can use the supplied ruler, which has an appropriate ¼-inch scale, or a sturdier three-sided draftsman's ruler.

Laying out the floor plan—partitions, doorways, and windows—is easy. Cut and peel off ⅛-inch-wide strips of sticky plastic from a supplied sheet, then press them in place. The strips adhere repeatedly, so you can move them as often as you like.

The furniture pieces work the same way. A big plus is that these pieces come dimensioned. If you have a 20-by-24-inch end table, that's the size you lift off the supplied sheet of end tables. There are couches, tables, chairs, divans—a wide variety of furniture pieces. Be warned: There isn't a plastic strip for every furniture type or size. But even if you compromise by using a similar-size piece, this kit is a great way to experiment with various floor plans.

Getting a perspective

To put a spin on Plan-a-Flex's flat view, I turned to the Interior Design Kit, which creates a perspective view of a house's inner space.

You don't have to master complex drawing techniques to enjoy this $13 kit. Draw in the corners on the diagonally ruled ¼-inch-scale grid with a grease pencil, which wipes off easily. Then sketch lines for the walls, floor, and ceiling. The result: a box in perspective to which you affix adhesive plastic pieces representing windows, doors, and furniture. To move a couch, just peel off the plastic strip.

Adding that last feature—furniture —may cause problems. I found all the pieces I needed, but a plastic dining-room chair overlapped a plastic end table. That isn't what happens in my living room, where there's adequate space between them.

One source of trouble is that the furniture pieces are drawn to the same scale. Pressed in place, a piece at the far end of the room may dwarf other pieces. In the perspective view of my long and narrow living room, a 19-inch TV appears larger than a 78-inch-long dining-room table. In a smaller or squarer room, however, the lack of perspective would be less challenging to the eye. Still, this ingenious kit is an excellent aid in planning interior space.

Adding the third dimension

After hours spent juggling plastic pieces and shoving around two-dimensional walls and rooms, I was eager to build something. That's when I un- packed Design Works' Professional House Building kit.

This $15 kit lets you construct a three-dimensional, doll-house-scale model of your house. Pushing around sofas and interior walls may be easier with the other two kits, but this one depicts how a house's exterior looks— from the roof to the window frames.

You build the cardboard model on top of the grid. Supplied pieces have a grid on one side to make measuring easier, and architectural detail—facade (shingles or brick), windows, or doors—on the other. Pick the facade, then lay the other exterior elements over it.

Don't like the original door placement? Move it. Think you'll need more light? Add larger windows. With this kit, you can judge how alternatives look on a real house. When supplied features fall short of requirements, improvise. To get the seven casement windows I needed to replicate my house, I simply modified several other cardboard windows for the desired effect.

The kit doesn't come with material for interior walls, so I used white poster board for partitions. The result: a model of my house that's a unique planning asset—*by E.F. Lindsley. Photos by Greg Sharko.*

six unique house designs

Sweat equity is the buzzword in today's home building: Anyone planning to build a new home is well advised to pick a design that invites his participation in the construction process. So if you get involved right at the working-drawings stage, you'll find your horizon of choice greatly broadened. Commissioning an architect to draw up plans for a custom home is expensive; that's why we've included truly original designs from four sources well-

1 **Bermed courtyard house** gets its daylight illumination via skylights, sun scoops at three gable ends of the standing-seam copper roof sections, and a spacious patio bordered on three sides by stepped two-story windows. The house is ideal for either extreme of climate, where temperature swings will be modulated by the wraparound earth berm. Designed by earth-shelter architect Charles Woods on his usual 4-foot-square modules, the house is easily adjusted in size; as shown it offers 5,208 square feet of space. Its concrete-block and wood-stud walls are erected on a sunken concrete slab; the roof is supported by wood trusses. The house is superinsulated and passive-solar heated; fireplaces and wood stoves provide backup heat, however.

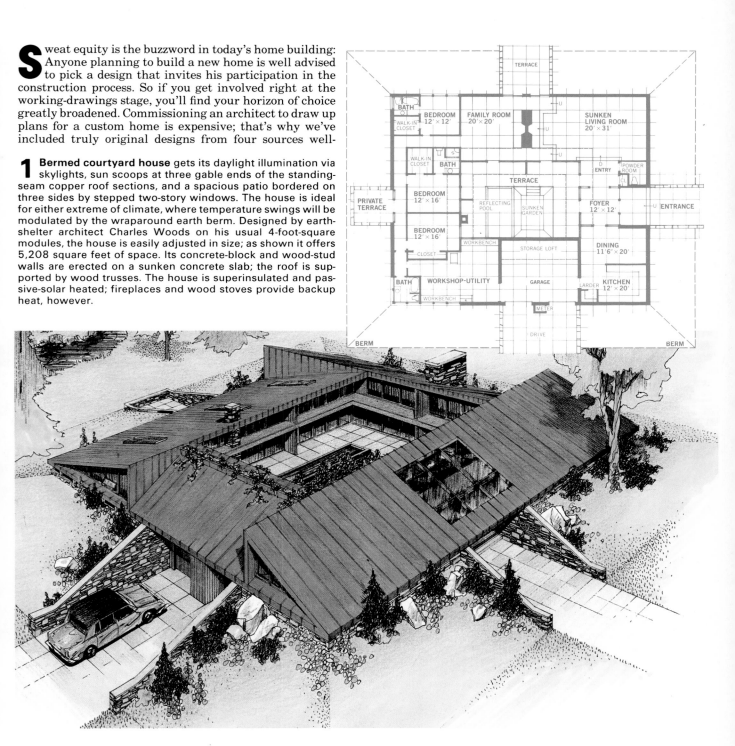

2 **Big house for a small lot** packs a full complement of amenities into a floor plan of only 30 by 32 feet, and it "stacks up" as a lot of house where property is tight. It's lifted out of the ordinary by cathedral ceilings, an eyebrow clerestory, and imaginative wood detailing. (Both this house and the one below were designed for *Popular Science* by Ken Gephart,

AIBD, in cooperation with Western Wood Products Association.) Living areas are on the second floor, oriented to a broad deck to take advantage of a view. Vertical board siding and wide board trim between floors and around windows add style. The entry door on the 390-square-foot lower level leads to a bedroom or up a stairway to the 770-square-foot main floor.

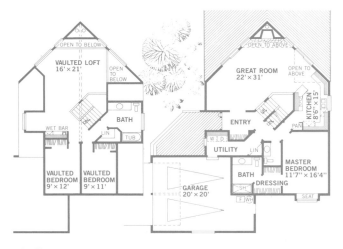

3 **Upscale A-frame** sports a large deck wrapped around the prow of its great room. Designed for enjoyment of a broad vista, the house has 1,004 square feet on the main floor and 803 on the upper level. A daylight-basement version adds 1,004 square feet of recreational and bunk space, plus storage for recreational gear. Diagonally applied 2×4 cedar decking on the entry porch establishes the pattern for the angled walls off the entry hall. Dominating the great room that occupies nearly half the main floor is a large masonry fireplace that extends two stories in the prow. All this is open to the viewing loft on the upper floor, where two bedrooms share a large bath. The master bedroom is below.

KITCHEN
8' × 8'

VAULTED MASTER
BEDROOM
12' × 16'2"

DINING

WET BAR

LIN

WOOD STOVE

BATH

VAULTED
GREAT ROOM
17' × 19'9"

RAILING

DECK

WH F

BEDROOM
10' × 12'8"

GARAGE
12' × 23'4"

W D

BATH

LIN

TUB

ENTRY

UP

DECK ABOVE

GARAGE
21'6" × 23'

DECK

ENTRY

LOFT
12' × 15'

SLOPED CEILING

SLOPED CEILING

SKYLIGHTS

RAILING

RAILING

OPEN TO BELOW

MCLURE

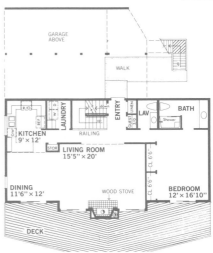

GARAGE
ABOVE

WALK

R/O

REF

D W

LAUNDRY

W D

ENTRY

RAILING

LINEN

LAV

BATH

Shower

KITCHEN
9' × 12'

STOR

LIVING ROOM
15'5" × 20'

CL 6'6"

CL 6'6"

DINING
11'6" × 12'

WOOD STOVE

BEDROOM
12' × 16'10"

DECK

4 **Hillside perch** (above) is a three-level home designed for a 20-degree slope, or a fall of 15 to 17 feet in structure length. The modest roadside facade (garage doors, entry deck) belies the spacious luxury stepped down the slope. The view of the living-dining expanse from the entry loft is impressive. A U-shaped kitchen is closed off by a snack bar. Tucked under the deck is a daylight basement (no floor plan shown).

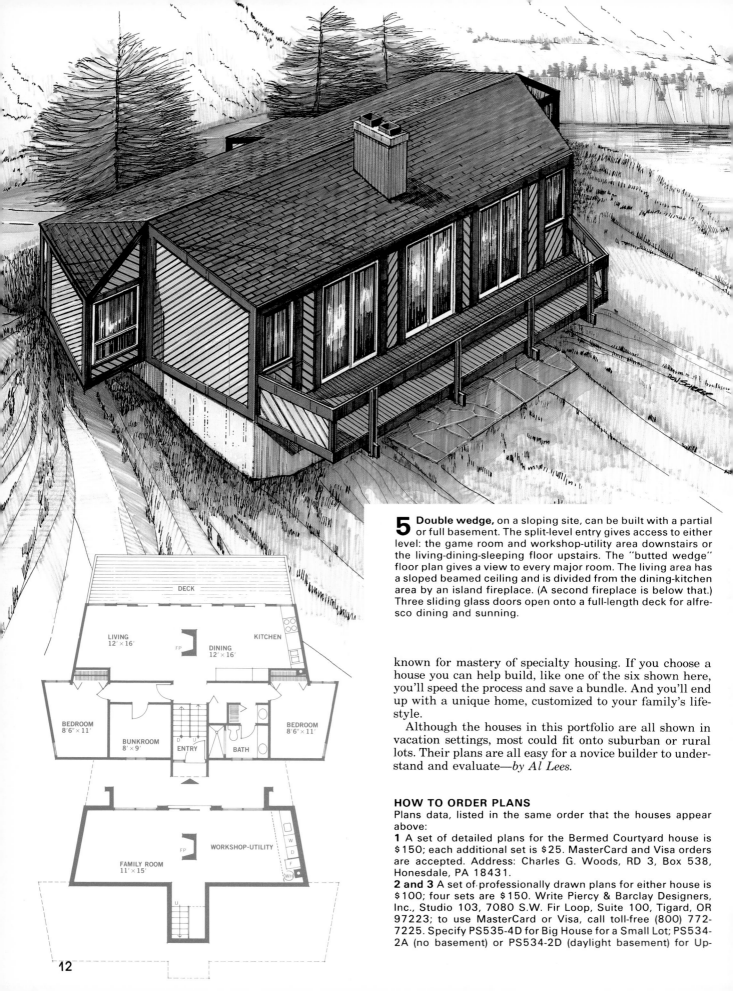

DECK

| LIVING 12' × 16' | | KITCHEN |
| | DINING 12' × 16' | |

FP

BEDROOM 8'6" × 11'

BUNKROOM 8' × 9'

ENTRY

BATH

BEDROOM 8'6" × 11'

D U

FAMILY ROOM 11' × 15'

FP

WORKSHOP-UTILITY

W
D
F
WH

U

5 **Double wedge,** on a sloping site, can be built with a partial or full basement. The split-level entry gives access to either level: the game room and workshop-utility area downstairs or the living-dining-sleeping floor upstairs. The "butted wedge" floor plan gives a view to every major room. The living area has a sloped beamed ceiling and is divided from the dining-kitchen area by an island fireplace. (A second fireplace is below that.) Three sliding glass doors open onto a full-length deck for alfresco dining and sunning.

known for mastery of specialty housing. If you choose a house you can help build, like one of the six shown here, you'll speed the process and save a bundle. And you'll end up with a unique home, customized to your family's lifestyle.

Although the houses in this portfolio are all shown in vacation settings, most could fit onto suburban or rural lots. Their plans are all easy for a novice builder to understand and evaluate—*by Al Lees.*

HOW TO ORDER PLANS
Plans data, listed in the same order that the houses appear above:
1 A set of detailed plans for the Bermed Courtyard house is $150; each additional set is $25. MasterCard and Visa orders are accepted. Address: Charles G. Woods, RD 3, Box 538, Honesdale, PA 18431.
2 and 3 A set of professionally drawn plans for either house is $100; four sets are $150. Write Piercy & Barclay Designers, Inc., Studio 103, 7080 S.W. Fir Loop, Suite 100, Tigard, OR 97223; to use MasterCard or Visa, call toll-free (800) 772-7225. Specify PS535-4D for Big House for a Small Lot; PS534-2A (no basement) or PS534-2D (daylight basement) for Up-

6 Pinwheel house, along with the Double Wedge, was designed by Robert Martin Engelbrecht for the V-PAC Council. This is one of a series of houses dubbed "Sixty Plus" because wings are placed at 60 degrees to each other. In the case of the Pinwheel, three wings radiate from a triangular core containing a spiral staircase below a pyramidal skylight. The stair is only needed, however, if the wings are built over a partial or full basement; on a level site the wings could be erected on concrete slabs. To the right of the entry hall is the living room; at one end is an open kitchen with a dining bay. Turn left from the entry, and you pass a bathroom on the way to three bedrooms.

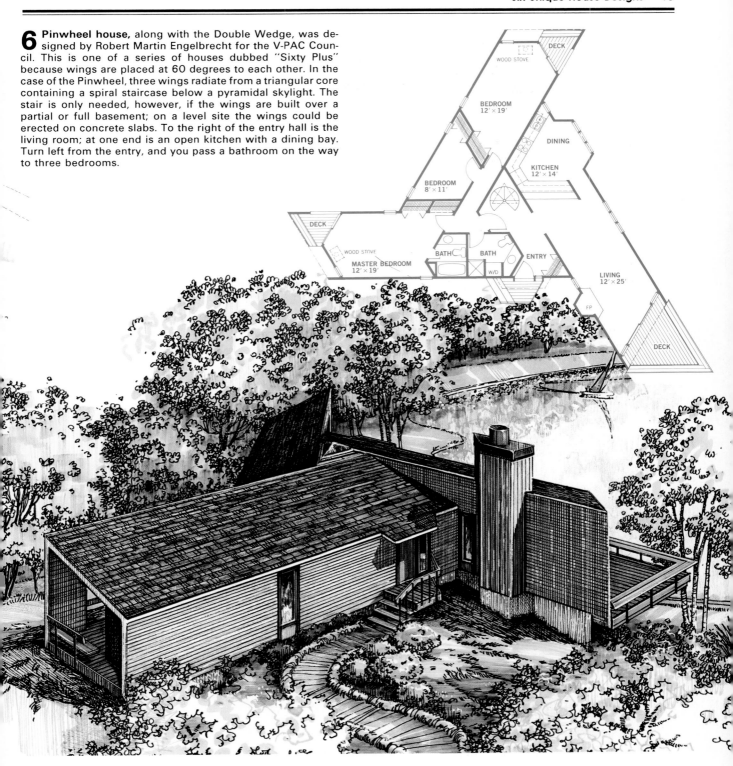

scale A-Frame. Mirror-reverse plans are available; materials list is $30; specs, $20.
4 A set of plans for the Hillside Perch is $160; four sets, $195. Write Home Building Plan Service, 2235 N.E. Sandy Blvd., Portland, OR 97232; for MasterCard or Visa orders, call toll-free (800) 547-5570. Specify plan number 966-1B. Mirror-reverse plans are $10; materials list, $30; plumbing and wiring diagrams, $7.50 each.

5 and 6 Construction plans for either the Double Wedge or the Pinwheel House are $75 a set or $105 for three. Send your check to Princeton Plans Press, Box 622, Princeton, NJ 08540; for MasterCard or Visa orders, call (609) 924-9655. A catalog of additional designs, titled "The Uncommon House Collection," is $5.
When ordering any plans please be sure to add $5 for postage and handling.

add a giant dormer

My problem was a common one: getting useful living space on the second floor of a house that was originally designed as a single-story with an attic. There was plenty of floor space up there, but much of it was useless, tucked in under the roof where the head room was less than six feet. For years, my wife and I had tolerated a master bedroom squeezed into this situation, a room so cramped I had to duck under the sloped ceiling to walk around.

The usual solution to this kind of space problem is to raise the roof into

BEFORE

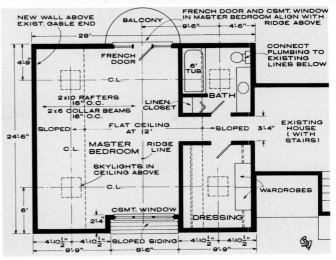

NEW WALL ABOVE EXIST. GABLE END

BALCONY

FRENCH DOOR AND CSMT. WINDOW IN MASTER BEDROOM ALIGN WITH RIDGE ABOVE

28'

9'-6" 4'-6"

4'-9"

FRENCH DOOR

CONNECT PLUMBING TO EXISTING LINES BELOW

C.L.

6' TUB

BATH

2x10 RAFTERS 16" O.C.
2x6 COLLAR BEAMS 16" O.C.

LINEN CLOSET

24'-6"

SLOPED

FLAT CEILING AT 12'

SLOPED 3'-4"

EXISTING HOUSE (WITH STAIRS)

C.L.

MASTER BEDROOM

RIDGE LINE

SKYLIGHTS IN CEILING ABOVE

C.L.

WARDROBES

6'

CSMT. WINDOW

DRESSING

2'-4"

4'-10½" 4'-10½" SLOPED SIDING 4'-10½" 4'-10½"
9'-9" 8'-6" 9'-9"

Original house (inset) had a broken-ridge roof line, split by a flat-roofed section atop which sits the giant dormer. Such an addition could also be spliced into a continuous-ridge roof. The opposite gable sports a balcony (below).

a shed-type dormer. This gives you adequate head room the full width of the attic, and opens up every inch of floor space available.

But for our house that solution didn't seem right. Like many homes, ours is stretched out over a long and narrow floor plan. I made up sketches of a shed dormer addition, and it only accentuated that length, making the house look like a stretch limousine.

To break up that long, monotonous line, architect Chris Barthlemess of RKB Associates, Westport, Connecticut used a combination of tricks:
● Turning the roof line of the attic addition 90 degrees.
● Raising the new roof on 6-foot knee walls, adding extra height to provide useful wall-to-wall head room.
● Cantilevering the face of the addition two feet beyond the existing walls to break up the long flow of the house, then adding additional texture by recessing a big arched window.

The final result was spectacular: We ended up with a true master bedroom, some 24 by 18 feet, with 12-foot ceilings and a wide-open view of the woods. The new room is so spacious we turned one corner into a family office, complete with desk and wall storage system. And that's not all. We also got a walk-in dressing room and a master bath in the bargain.

All this extra space, plus the huge increase in glass area, made me worry about energy costs, so I built the walls on 2 × 6 studs and insulated to a value of R-19, with R-38 in the ceiling.

My existing furnace was too small and too far away to handle the new space, so I decided to install a heat pump. I needed one big enough to handle the addition plus my workshop/

studio underneath, which had been heated with electric baseboards. Amazingly, I now heat both the shop and addition for less than I used to pay just to heat the shop.

I had a local contractor, Ox Bow Builders, do the basic construction. Standard framing techniques were used, as shown in the sidewall section. Things only got tricky around the recessed window (see detail).

As the "before" photo shows, the roof ridge of my house was split by a flat-roofed section that contains my workshop, so the construction crew simply erected the new story on that "platform" after stripping off the old roofing.

(With a more conventional house, the crew would have simply torn out the existing roof and rafters in the area the addition was to occupy, exposing the attic floor. This floor is just an inside version of my flat roof. Then they would have extended joists for the front cantilever and erected the framing just as it is shown in the sec-

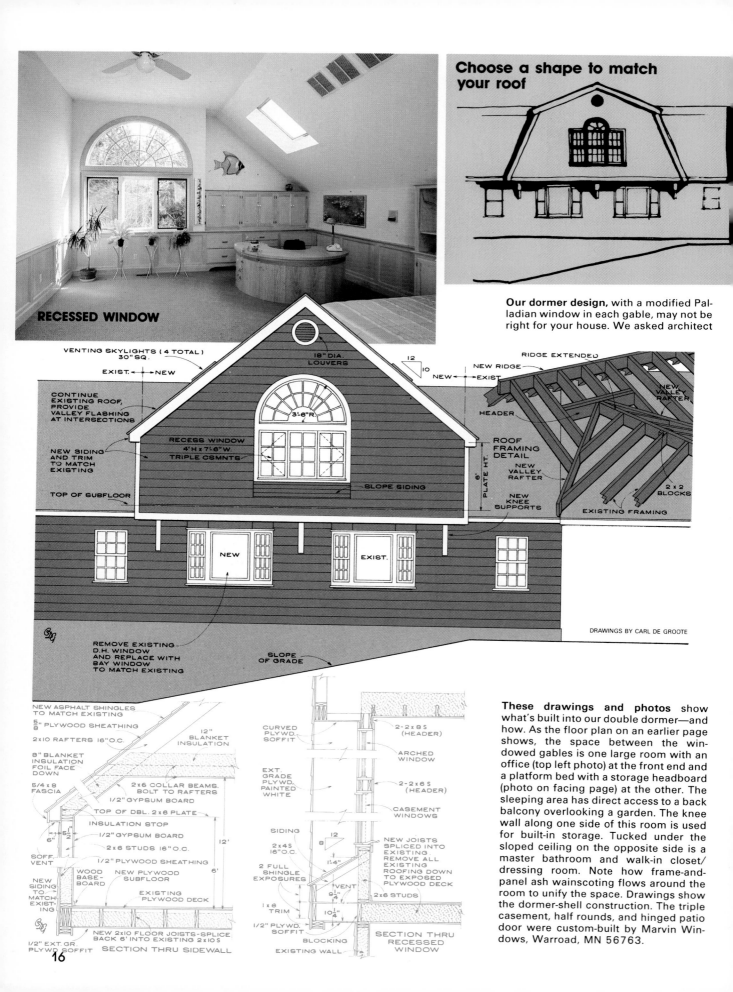

RECESSED WINDOW

Choose a shape to match your roof

Our dormer design, with a modified Palladian window in each gable, may not be right for your house. We asked architect

VENTING SKYLIGHTS (4 TOTAL) 30" SQ.

EXIST. → ← NEW

CONTINUE EXISTING ROOF, PROVIDE VALLEY FLASHING AT INTERSECTIONS

NEW SIDING AND TRIM TO MATCH EXISTING

TOP OF SUBFLOOR

18" DIA. LOUVERS

3'-6"R.

RECESS WINDOW 4'H x 7'-6" W. TRIPLE CSMNTS.

SLOPE SIDING

12

10

NEW → ← EXIST.

RIDGE EXTENDED

NEW RIDGE

NEW VALLEY RAFTER

HEADER

ROOF FRAMING DETAIL

NEW VALLEY RAFTER

NEW KNEE SUPPORTS

PLATE HT. 6'

EXISTING FRAMING

2 x 2 BLOCKS

NEW

EXIST.

REMOVE EXISTING D.H. WINDOW AND REPLACE WITH BAY WINDOW TO MATCH EXISTING

SLOPE OF GRADE

DRAWINGS BY CARL DE GROOTE

NEW ASPHALT SHINGLES TO MATCH EXISTING

5/8" PLYWOOD SHEATHING

2x10 RAFTERS 16" O.C.

8" BLANKET INSULATION FOIL FACE DOWN

5/4 x 8 FASCIA

6"

5 1/2"

SOFF. VENT

NEW SIDING TO MATCH EXISTING

1/2" EXT. GR. PLYWD. SOFFIT

12" BLANKET INSULATION

2x6 COLLAR BEAMS. BOLT TO RAFTERS

1/2" GYPSUM BOARD

TOP OF DBL. 2x6 PLATE

INSULATION STOP

1/2" GYPSUM BOARD

2x6 STUDS 16" O.C.

1/2" PLYWOOD SHEATHING

WOOD BASE-BOARD

NEW PLYWOOD SUBFLOOR

EXISTING PLYWOOD DECK

NEW 2x10 FLOOR JOISTS-SPLICE BACK 6' TO EXISTING 2x10 S

SECTION THRU SIDEWALL

12'

6'

CURVED PLYWD. SOFFIT

EXT. GRADE PLYWD. PAINTED WHITE

SIDING

2x8S 16" O.C.

2 FULL SHINGLE EXPOSURES

1x6 TRIM

1/2" PLYWD. SOFFIT

BLOCKING

EXISTING WALL

2 - 2x8 S (HEADER)

ARCHED WINDOW

2 - 2x6 S (HEADER)

CASEMENT WINDOWS

NEW JOISTS SPLICED INTO EXISTING REMOVE ALL EXISTING ROOFING DOWN TO EXPOSED PLYWOOD DECK

2x6 STUDS

VENT

12

8

1'-4"

9 1/2"

10 1/2"

SECTION THRU RECESSED WINDOW

These drawings and photos show what's built into our double dormer—and how. As the floor plan on an earlier page shows, the space between the windowed gables is one large room with an office (top left photo) at the front end and a platform bed with a storage headboard (photo on facing page) at the other. The sleeping area has direct access to a back balcony overlooking a garden. The knee wall along one side of this room is used for built-in storage. Tucked under the sloped ceiling on the opposite side is a master bathroom and walk-in closet/dressing room. Note how frame-and-panel ash wainscoting flows around the room to unify the space. Drawings show the dormer-shell construction. The triple casement, half rounds, and hinged patio door were custom-built by Marvin Windows, Warroad, MN 56763.

16

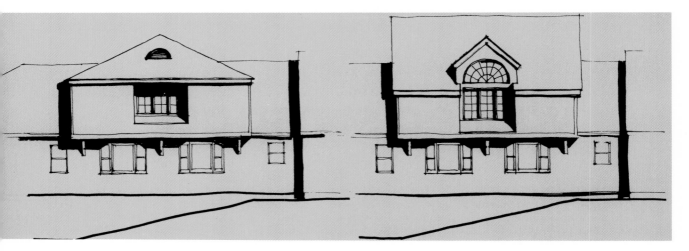

Chris Barthlemess to draw variations for different roof lines. In his first drawing, he's designed a dormer to be spliced into a gambrel roof. In the second, the dormer has a hip roof to match one on the house. The third addition has its ridge parallel to that of the existing roof. This treatment also has its own dormer, complete with a recessed window.

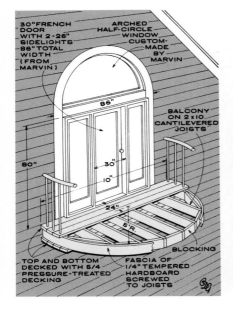

BALCONY DOOR

tions. Once the full-length rafters and ridge of the new structure were in place, the crew would have extended the old ridge on both sides to butt against a new doubled header, as shown in the framing detail, added new valley rafters on each side—a total of four—and then filled in with short rafters as shown, just as they did for my house.)

My crew nailed roof decking over all new rafters and applied asphalt shingles to match those on the existing roof. All exterior walls of the new framing were then sided with the same material used on the first floor of the house.

Splicing into one of the roof styles drawn above may involve modifications in the framing. A gambrel roof, of course, will require more complex valley rafters, as you'll need a separate one for each roof plane. (This type of an addition to a gambrel or mansard roof may not be economically justifiable because head room under the existing roof is less of a problem.) Splicing into a hip roof is much the same as shown because you're tying into the part of the roof with no hip.

Several details shown in my architect's drawing hadn't been added when I took the lead photo: three knee braces, the second bay window, and the snap-in muntin grids for the casement windows. I was too busy finishing off the inside, applying drywall to the studs and across the collar beams after all the fiberglass-batt insulation was in place. I did all the trim work, building in a platform storage bed that flows out of frame-and-panel wainscoting, and finishing off the dressing room and bath—*by A.J. Hand. Drawings by Carl De Groote.*

Dressing room is compartmented and lighted by its own skylight, as is the bathroom directly across the hall.

vaulted sunspace

When the owners of a Cape Cod cottage-style house decided to make an addition to their Ohio home, their primary goals were creating more living space and letting in more light. In the sun porch I designed for them, they have the additional room they needed. And the light is provided in abundance by a continuous bank of double-hung windows combined with a row of low-profile bronze-tinted skylights.

Integrating the new 12-by-25-foot structure so that it appears to be part of the home's original design was accomplished by maintaining the same roof slope, shingles, and exterior siding used on the rest of the house. In-side, the south-facing porch is finished in natural yellow pine and redwood siding. The latter covers what used to be the exterior wall of the living room, as well as the unglazed portions of the new walls.

The addition incorporates a passive-solar design using a rock heat-storage zone located under the tile-

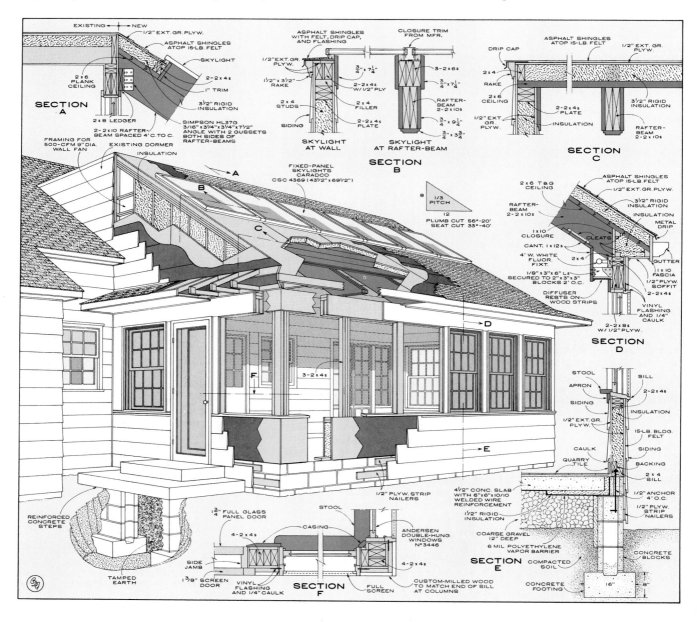

Porch addition (top) blends in admirably with the house's original lines (left). Bar top (middle), sink, and under-counter storage are built under the old windows, which now serve as a pass-through. Tile floor stores solar heat.

faced concrete floor slab. In winter the slab absorbs and slowly radiates solar heat passing through the leafless trees above. So far, the owners haven't had to use the backup electric baseboard heaters.

In summer the porch is shaded by trees and the roof overhang running around its perimeter. When the porch, dormer, and first-floor north-side windows are opened, as well as the doors between the porch and living room, a convection loop is established that considerably reduces the need for air conditioning. Ceiling and gable fans moderate porch temperatures year-round.

The handsome roof beams are made by spiking pairs of 2×10s with staggered 10d nails, then casing the assembly in $\frac{3}{4}$-inch pine (see section C in drawing). Yellow pine 2×10s were chosen because the lumber has a high fiber-stress rating, which allows it to carry the weight of the roofing and skylights on 4-foot centers.

Reinforced concrete steps are placed outside the porch doors. The east-facing step's apron provides terra firma for an outdoor gas grill—*by Jack Hillbrand, A.I.A. Photos by Susan Hillbrand. Drawing by Carl De Groote.*

Lofty cathedral ceiling gives the sun porch a bright, airy feeling. Sunlight reaches the original windows via skylights.

luxurious light deck

Day or night, a deck extends a home's living space into the outdoors. Elegant furniture and soft, glare-free lighting enhance the woodsy effect.

Bringing the feel of the woods closer to home was a key design idea for this northern Illinois backyard deck. By using treated lumber and installing outdoor lighting, Marc and Barb Posner now have durable, year-round relaxation space in which to enjoy the beauty of nature night or day.

The Posners chose Wickes Lumber for the design and materials used in this project. An advantage the couple found in a large building-supply center such as Wickes was that it had on hand entire series of well-designed deck plans, buildable as offered or easily modified to fit their needs. Then, when they were ready to build, both materials and construction advice were readily available—in their case, from the same person who helped with the initial project plans.

Before the first rough sketches were drawn, the homeowners wrote down all the reasons they wanted a deck; this helped determine what features needed to be designed into it. The most important concern was appearance. For that reason, they chose Deck Plank Wolmanized lumber for the decking, available exclusively from Wickes.

The specially-milled, pressure-treated lumber is 6 inches wide and comes in lengths of 8 to 16 feet. This "5/4 -inch" (1¼-inch thick) decking is lighter and more economical than traditional 2-inch lumber, yet strong enough for spans up to 24 inches on center. The Posners also found that Deck Plank's distinctive size and shape made it easy to handle, cut, and nail, while its rounded edges lent themselves easily to tables, benches, and steps, virtually eliminating splinters and wane. In addition, the lumber can be

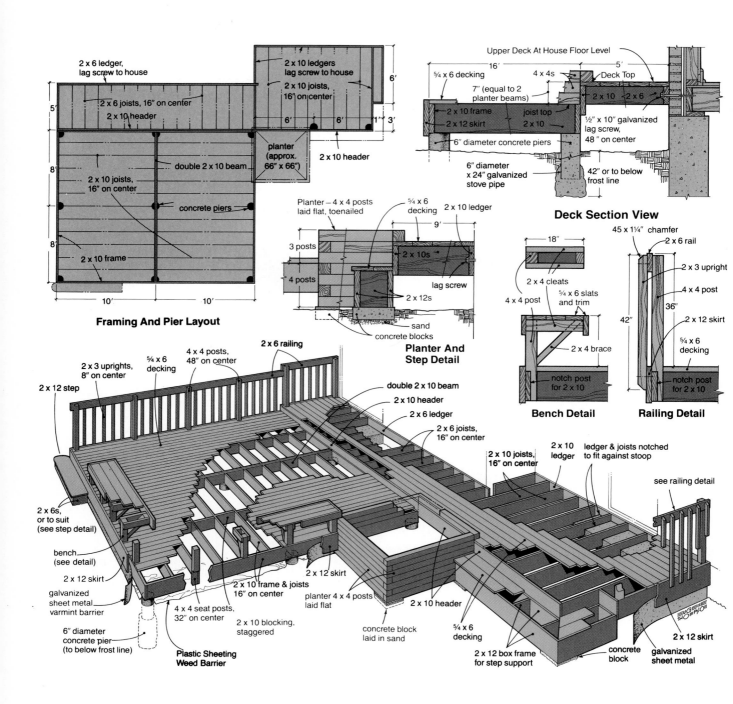

Framing And Pier Layout

Deck Section View

Planter And Step Detail

Bench Detail

Railing Detail

nailed tightly together. One-eighth-inch gaps between boards, necessary for water drainage, appear when the lumber dries out after installation.

Sanibel patio furniture from Samsonite provides seating for smaller groups. Because the homeowners also needed to accomodate larger groups of family and friends, they built integral benches into the deck. A variety of hardy native plants, shrubs, and trees fulfilled the couple's desire to integrate the deck into its natural surroundings. And as a final touch, Malibu low-voltage outdoor lighting from Intermatic was installed on the deck and around the per-

imeter at ground level. The 12-volt lights cast a soft glow over the area—a welcome relief from the harsh glare often encountered with standard floodlights.

Building the deck

The basic structure is a straightforward design, as shown in the working drawings. However, several unique construction methods were used to make the deck extra-sturdy and ensure years of maintenance-free use.

A total of 11 concrete piers support the deck off the ground. Once the perimeter of the deck area was staked

out, the pier holes were drilled with a power auger to the 42-inch depth required by local building codes (fig. 1). This distance is below the frost line, a necessary concern in northern states.

Standard premixed concrete was used according to the package instructions and shoveled into the holes. Then, as the mixture reached the top, a 2-foot length of 6-inch-diameter galvanized stove pipe was inserted and adjusted to the height for each pier (fig. 2). The rest of the mix was then shoveled into the stove pipe, which became a permanent retaining form.

The pressure-treated box frame of the deck rests on the flat tops of the concrete piers (fig. 3). There was no need to attach the boards to the piers since one side of the deck was anchored to the house to keep the deck from shifting. To do this, the height of the deck was first determined. Then the distance was marked along the exterior wall. Holes were drilled at 4-foot intervals through the brick wall and into the home's wooden box frame (fig. 4). Corresponding holes were also predrilled along the centers of 2×10 nailer boards, after which 10-by-½-inch galvanized steel lag bolts were inserted through the nailer boards and screwed directly into the house frame (fig. 5).

As you build the deck box frame, be sure to check the level of the boards that rest on top of the concrete piers. The Posners used 2×10 lumber for the frame, and 2×10 boards for the joists, which were hung and secured with metal hangers (fig. 6). For extra rigidity, 14½-inch lengths of wood cut from 2×10 boards were used to form bridge

beams between each joist. The beams were staggered so that they could be nailed in place (fig. 7). By the way—if electrical, natural gas, or other connections with the inside of the house are needed, now is the time to drill. Note also how, in figure 8, the joist at right has been notched around the existing vent in the exterior wall.

Corner posts and other details

Since the corner posts were not inserted into the ground, they can be worked on easily before installation. Figure 9 shows a radius edge being put on the sides of a corner post to match the edges of the Deck Plank lumber. Posts are then attached to the box frame with L-brackets (fig. 10).

Height of the deck was carefully measured before construction so that certain obstacles could be worked around. One of these problem areas was a back-door stoop, so the nailer board and joists were carefully cut out to accomodate it (fig. 11).

Decking

Figures 12 and 13 show two views of the completed framing and joists. That plastic sheeting peeking out around the deck's perimeter was put down to keep weeds and plants from growing beneath the structure. The Deck Plank lumber that goes on top is laid down and nailed to the joists in the usual manner (fig. 14). Once all decking is installed, the edges are trimmed with a circular saw (fig. 15). As an added touch, the sawed edges can also be

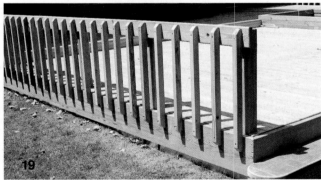

finished with a router to match the rounded edges of the planking.

To protect against nesting animals, lengths of galvanized sheet metal were nailed to the bottom of the box-frame boards and then covered over with the 2 × 12 skirt boards (fig. 16).

Planter and railing

An attractive planter will do a lot to bring a lush, woodsy atmosphere to any deck. This one was built from 4 × 4 beams, with interlocking ends toenailed together from the inside. Edges were then radius-cut with a router to match the rest of the treated lumber (fig. 17). Alternating edges (fig. 18) not only provide a striking corner treatment but also reinforce the structure.

The railing Marc and Barb chose for their deck is similar to the standard precut component system available at all Wickes stores (fig. 19). Figure 20 shows the posts where integral benches will be positioned and permanently connected to the deck.

Even as the Posners stood back to admire the finished project, they were already thinking of add-ons. Perhaps the real beauty of this design is that it will let you put in such items as a hot tub, gazebo, walkway, or trellis at your convenience, without having to redo the basic structure—
by Mike Bruening. Construction by Henry Johnson. Photos by Ken Oakes and Allan Weick. Drawing by Eugene Thompson.

MANUFACTURERS' ADDRESSES

Intermatic Inc., Malibu Division, Intermatic Plaza, Spring Grove, IL 60081 (Malibu low-voltage outdoor lights); **Samsonite Furniture Co.,** Samsonite Blvd., Murfreesboro, TN 37130 (Sanibel patio furniture); **Wickes Lumber,** P.O. Box 2030, Dept. 988, Vernon Hills, IL 60061 (Deck Plank pressure-treated lumber, building materials, and plans).

self-sufficient sun room

Old screened porch above was replaced with the expanded structure at right, and the tiled patio was added.

The owners of this Illinois home knew they wanted more space for entertaining and relaxing. They also knew they weren't willing to put up with higher heating bills to keep a new addition warm during winter.

The solution? A passive sun room that can replace a south-facing porch on virtually any home. It boasts a quarry-tile floor that absorbs and radiates warmth from sunlight streaming through sliding glass doors facing south and east. The miniblinds behind the glazing are fully raised on sunny winter days but closed at night to conserve the warmth soaked up by the dark masonry flooring (Lava Red quarry tile, available at Color Tile outlets). On such days, the sun room remains comfortable well into the evening, without any backup heat. Beyond this self-sufficient corner, extra space was added to an existing family room by knocking out most of a wall. The house's existing heating system was adequate to keep the expanded room cozy when the sliding door between it and the sun room is kept closed. (Note that on the floor plan, all four walls of the sun room have a sliding glass door.)

The homeowners began by dismantling the old screened porch shown in the "before" photo. The material was left at the site so lumber could be salvaged to reduce costs.

A trench for footings and foundation was dug beyond the perimeter of the existing porch slab. Because the sun room was to be independent of the home's heating and air conditioning, that part of the extension was insulated with rigid foam, as shown in the section below. The sun-room slab was poured over 2 inches of foam so that the heat it absorbed wouldn't be lost to the earth beneath. Once the forms were removed from the extension floor slab, a stepped-down patio slab was poured, with simpler footings pitched slightly away from the house for drainage.

After the walls were raised, a new roof was added—spliced into the cutaway existing roof—with both new and cutaway rafters butting against an added support beam. The roof over the sun-room section ties into the house's second story, with the rafters notched over a ledger lag-screwed into existing

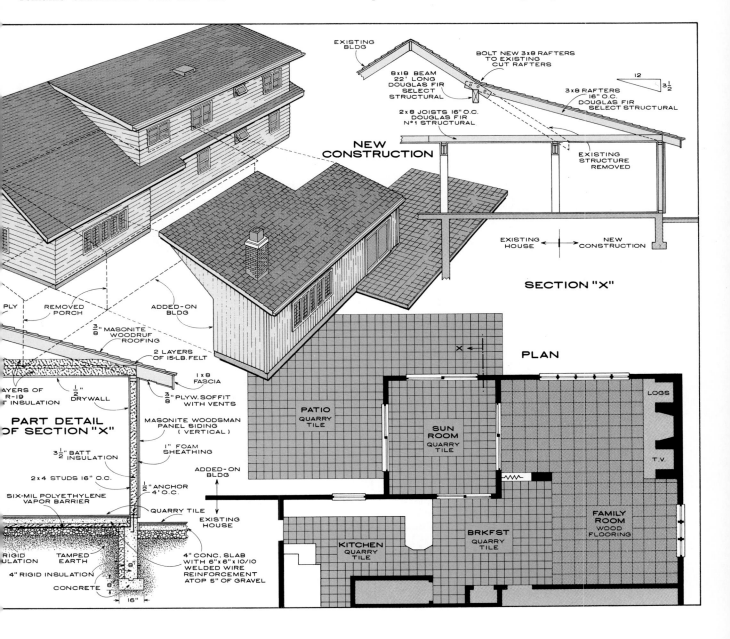

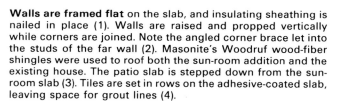

Walls are framed flat on the slab, and insulating sheathing is nailed in place (1). Walls are raised and propped vertically while corners are joined. Note the angled corner brace let into the studs of the far wall (2). Masonite's Woodruf wood-fiber shingles were used to roof both the sun-room addition and the existing house. The patio slab is stepped down from the sun-room slab (3). Tiles are set in rows on the adhesive-coated slab, leaving space for grout lines (4).

Cut the tiles with a tile cutter to fit along walls by scoring the tile and snapping it in half. When applying grout, work it thoroughly into joints. Remove excess grout first with a wet sponge and later with a dry abrasive cleaning pad. The same tiling technique was used on the outdoor slab. A 3-inch step-down and slight pitch prevents puddling or freezing against the glass-door sills. If other than quarry tiles are to be used outdoors, be sure they're frost-proof.

studs. For efficient solar heating, the homeowners dropped the ceiling of the sun-room area and packed the space above with insulation. Over the adjacent family room, the owners decided to nail the drywall ceiling directly to the bottom of the new rafters for a visually pleasing cathedral effect. (R-19 fiberglass batts were stapled between the rafters first, however, for even greater energy efficiency.)

Masonite wood-fiber shingles were chosen for the roofing, and because these 12-by-48-inch strips nail up quickly, it was no chore to reshingle the existing roof to match. To complete the exterior, Masonite's Woodsman textured panel siding was applied to the walls. In addition to complementing the appearance of the roof, the high-density siding material adds somewhat to the insulation rating of the walls.

Energy efficiency was of prime importance in the selection of materials for the sun room's interior. The walls were insulated with 3½-inch batts, which were then covered with a vapor barrier of 6-mil polyethylene stapled across the studs. The quarry tiles are thermally coupled to the heat-storing masonry mass beneath.

Installation of the ½-inch-thick tiles is simple; all the tools necessary are available from tile specialty outlets. After grouting, coat the surface with silicone sealer to prevent dirt and moisture penetration—*by Al Lees. Drawing by Carl De Groote.*

installing "smart" skylights

One afternoon I'd been too busy making lunch to notice that the light streaming through my newly installed kitchen skylights had changed from golden yellow to somber gray. By the time I sat down to eat, the first heavy drops of a summer cloudburst were thumping down on the roof. Immediately, motors whirred overhead, and the skylights swung themselves shut as the rain started to pound. The amazing thing was that I never got up from the kitchen table; a sensor on the roof had detected the rain and closed the windows.

Let there be light—and air. Remotely operated power roof windows (left, bottom) illuminate and ventilate a formerly dark kitchen (left, top). Andersen's awning windows (above), which also ventilate efficiently while sheltering window openings, can be fitted with the power operating units, making them an attractive feature for inaccessible windows, and for homes occupied by the handicapped or elderly.

This useful feature is just one of many found on the new remote-control power-operated skylights available from Andersen Corporation (Bayport, MN 55003). Before selecting them to brighten my formerly ill-lit kitchen, I had been wary of skylights because I had notions that they might leak water and heat. But these watertight, energy-efficient roof windows were just what I needed: I could not only increase the amount of natural light in my kitchen, a simple touch of a button would ventilate it as well. That's a lot better than having to bother with a long, clumsy pole to operate a hard-to-reach crank.

In addition to the full-contact double gasket and excellent step flashing to prevent water and heat leakage, the Andersen system is smart. The double-pane tempered windows have a thin, transparent metallic coating permanently bonded on an inside surface to bounce back part of the radiated heat. So in summer less heat gets in, and in winter less heat gets out. Andersen claims that its low-emissivity glass system retains 42 percent more interior heat in winter and rejects 28 percent more exterior heat in summer than uncoated double-pane windows.

The power window-opening system may be added during window installation or later. (The retrofit parts work only on operable Andersen roof and awning windows up to about two decades old.) Among the system's more significant features:

● A power supply with a plug-in extension cord that reduces 110-volt power to 16 volts and distributes it to up to four window operators via low-voltage wiring.

● A power window-operating unit that houses an electric motor and gear train to rotate a window's sash-operating mechanism. A small folding crank on the unit—much like the film rewind on a 35-mm camera—lets you release the gear train's clutch and manipulate the window manually in the event of a power failure.

● A four-window remote-control module on a 10-foot cord that can be set to open to any desired degree. A microprocessor in the system lets the homeowner open the windows in sequence or back off on the gear train just a bit when the windows close, to reduce strain on the mechanism.

● A circuit-breaker safety switch that prevents a roof win-

You needn't have a cathedral ceiling

The drawing shows typical installation details for a roof window in a room with an attic above the ceiling. The skylight sits atop a box made of drywall or plywood that directs light and air down through a hole cut in the ceiling. The sides of this shaft may be parallel, as shown, or flared for broader distribution. If the shaft passes through an unheated attic, it should be wrapped with a vapor barrier and insulation. Because the author's kitchen has a cathedral ceiling, installation is simpler: Carefully lay out the hole location and dimensions, then cut the rough opening in the roof (below left). Remove the sash before installation. Install brackets that fasten the frame to the roof. Step flashing (below, right) fits under the shingles. When caulking and flashing are completed, reassemble the sash.

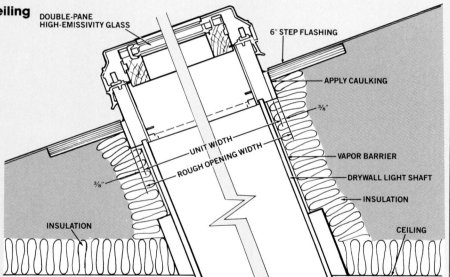

DOUBLE-PANE HIGH-EMISSIVITY GLASS
6" STEP FLASHING
APPLY CAULKING
3/8"
VAPOR BARRIER
DRYWALL LIGHT SHAFT
INSULATION
CEILING
UNIT WIDTH
ROUGH OPENING WIDTH
3/8"
INSULATION

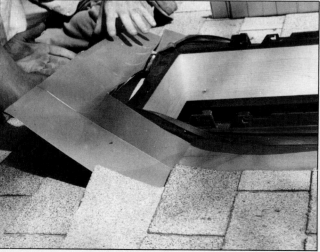

dow from closing when its insect screen is not in place, to avoid clamping down on an arm or hand—during washing, for instance.

● A rain sensor mounted on the window that closes it if precipitation is detected. Any of the circuits that detects water will close all the windows.

Andersen sells the roof windows in six sizes: 21 by 33, 21 by 44, 29 by 44, 41 by 44, 29 by 57, and 41 by 57 inches.

One procedure that requires particular attention is the flashing installation. I suggest that you read and reread the instructions, then lay out all the pieces so you fully understand how the system works before you install it.

Aside from the wiring, which may take some time, installing the power operator is a quick, simple job. The low-voltage wiring from the window to the power supply can be hidden in the ceiling and wall if you want to remodel, placed in surface channels, or simply clipped unobtrusively along moldings, behind curtains and drapes, or along baseboards—*by Phil McCafferty.*

A drop of water on the rain sensor will cause roof windows to close automatically, as in test above. The best place to mount the sensor is atop the curb.

You can retrofit existing windows and skylights, too

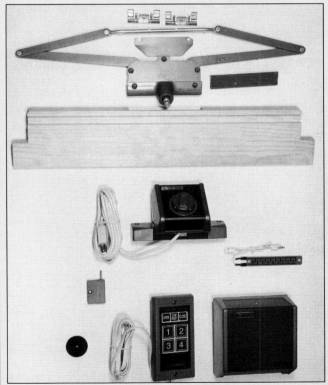

Installation of the power operator differs with window type because awning windows have a crank mechanism, whereas many roof windows must be adapted. Parts at top in the photo above convert a latch-handle-operated roof window to crank operation ($36 per window). Power operator system (above, center) is composed of an insect screen safety switch, motor unit, and rain sensor. Control system (above, bottom) consists of a command module and power supply. The first window requires a $230 "starter package," which includes power operator, power supply, and command module. Each additional window operating off the same control requires a $96 power-operator package.

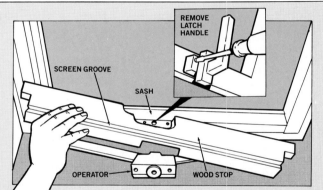

REMOVE LATCH HANDLE

SCREEN GROOVE

SASH

OPERATOR

WOOD STOP

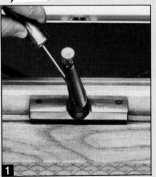

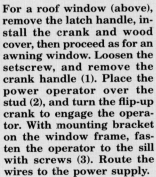

For a roof window (above), remove the latch handle, install the crank and wood cover, then proceed as for an awning window. Loosen the setscrew, and remove the crank handle (1). Place the power operator over the stud (2), and turn the flip-up crank to engage the operator. With mounting bracket on the window frame, fasten the operator to the sill with screws (3). Route the wires to the power supply.

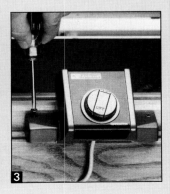

redwood platform bath

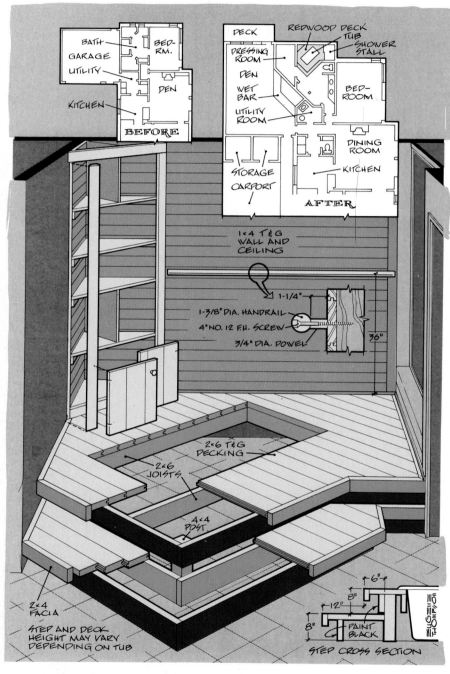

In addition to redwood paneling, other design elements of the bathroom include a 3-by-5-foot skylight, recessed lighting, a 3-by-5-foot sunken tub, a redwood cabinet, and redwood corner shelving. The area borrowed space from the former garage, which was redone to become a family room.

The next-best thing to bathing in a redwood forest is bathing in a luxurious redwood chamber. That's what designer Frank Marsters, from the Houston, Texas, area, created with this bathroom renovation. By extending a couple of walls and adding a platform for the tub, he built an elegant spa just off the master bedroom.

The bathroom was doubled in size by borrowing from the adjacent garage space and extending both the garage and bathroom walls. The project, which was sponsored by the California Redwood Association (591 Redwood Highway, Suite 3100, Mill Valley, CA 94941), features an accent wall and sloping ceiling that are covered with horizontal 1×4 tongue-and-groove clear-grade redwood paneling. The angled, multilevel deck and tub surround is covered with clear-grade redwood 2×6s applied diagonally.

The paneling was specially milled for V-joint tongue-and-groove joints. It was installed—glued and nailed—over Sheetrock. Because the area is frequently exposed to water, all the wood was covered with multiple coats of clear polyurethane finish.

Before the bathroom could be renovated, it had to be completely gutted. Many of the structural members were removed, and the walls were temporarily braced so they wouldn't bow. The flat ceiling had to be reframed to achieve the cathedral effect; it now follows the slope of the roof. A 3-by-5-foot skylight was framed between new rafters. When the reframing was completed, the structural design was probably stronger than the original.

All the plumbing had to be redone, but it was easy to run beneath the platform. This sort of step-down installation is the simplest for a whirlpool tub, where multiple pipe connections must be made.

The tub deck is framed with 2×12s on 4×4 posts and covered with $\frac{3}{4}$-inch plywood, over which the redwood is nailed. The shower pan is at the same platform height as the tub rim—*by Charles A. Miller. Illustration by Eugene Thompson.*

tiled tub deck

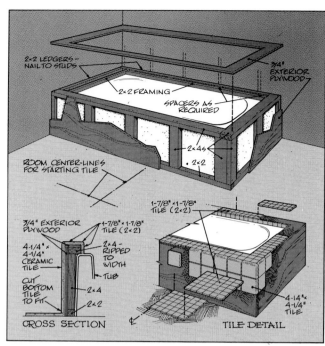

You're tired of your boring bathroom with its (pick one) tacky plastic tiles; ersatz wallboard tiles; 1950s-style, pink-and-gray ceramic tiles.

You'd like to bump out the walls and create a spacious spa-bath, complete with redwood sauna and sunken whirlpool. But you can't spare the space—or the cash.

Building a tiled deck around your tub can transform your bathroom without the need to relocate plumbing, tear down walls, or buy new fixtures. Keeping the old fixtures means you can afford to invest in a lavish display of elegant tile. You may even choose to retile walls and floors, as the homeowners did for the bathrooms shown here.

If your walls are covered with old plastic tile, it's a simple matter to pull it down and retile. If you've got well-anchored wallboard, you can roughen the surface and tile right over it. If you have ceramic tile you want to keep, you may be able to find a match. Or you may choose to replace the tile closest to the tub with a patterned feature tile that you can then lay on the upper tub deck.

Each bathroom has its own design potential, but you can glean some ideas from the portfolio of tub decks presented here. One option not shown is decking out a tub that's surrounded by walls on three sides. You're limited there, of course, to building out from the one open side. As in the decks shown, you frame with 2 × 4s and cover with ¾-inch exterior plywood.

No matter what type of deck you plan, the design experts at Color Tile Supermart, Inc. (515 Houston St., Fort Worth, TX 76102, with stores in most cities), suggest the following guidelines:

● To minimize tile cutting, coordinate deck size with tile dimensions. You'll still have to do some fitting around corners and against walls, but careful planning will reduce the amount of cutting needed.

● Be sure to use at least a ¾-inch plywood deck in any built-out structure. A lesser thickness might result in deck "give" that could cause tiles to loosen.

● Before you start work, line the tub bottom with cardboard to protect it from any dropped tools or tiles.

● Finally, dry-lay the tiles over the deck surface before you apply adhesive. This gives you an accurate idea of how the tiles line up, and you can shuffle them around to determine the layout with the fewest cuts—*by Susan Renner-Smith. Drawings by Eugene Thompson.*

Simple box frame built around a corner-anchored tub produces a built-in look (right), dramatized by the mix of mosaic and patterned tiles. The Color Tile mosaics come on prespaced backer sheets, easing installation. Space between existing tub and both walls was closed as shown (top sketch), and front and foot of tub were capped (section) to support frame of plywood. At least 1½ to 2 inches of tub edge should be left exposed around tub perimeter. Fill tub before running caulking bead where tiles and tub top meet.

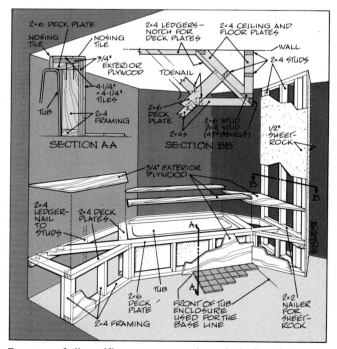

Expanse of tile unifies a corner-turning tub deck and triangular stud wall (right). The stud wall creates a private alcove for the tub, separating it from the toilet. (All studding should be 16 inches on center or less.) The built-out deck makes the 8-by-10-foot bathroom seem larger and converts waste space into ledges for bathing supplies and houseplants. Using the front of the angled tub as the floor-tile baseline gives a neat look and minimizes tile cutting. Matching vanity tile extends the seamless look.

Angled tub deck (above) adds to the elegance that new tiles bring to this vintage bathroom. The deck, a simpler version of the one below, was scaled to minimize tile cutting. Deck's top (front) edge is exactly the width of two tiles plus grout lines. Deck height equals height of four tiles plus grout.

four great ideas for fireplaces

When *Popular Science* Art Director Dave Houser picked up his sketchbook to plan a fireplace wall, he aimed for architectural drama and structural efficiency. The zero-clearance fireplace Houser planned to install in his new wing—shown in the *1986 Popular Science Do-it-Yourself Yearbook*—required no extra floor supports, only a noncombustible hearth, according to the manufacturer (Heatilator, 1915 W. Saunders Rd., Mount Pleasant, IA 52641).

But Houser had more in mind. He envisioned a stunning ceramic-tile mural. "I wanted a vertical sweep of color that would lift your eyes to the roof peak," he says. And he wanted a raised tiled hearth that would double as a seat. But he worried that a platform hearth might not withstand the inevitable settling.

Houser also wanted outside-air intakes for efficient combustion. But the fireplace is on the end wall. "I didn't want those louvered vents right by the pool," he says. And he fretted that he'd have no way to check the system once the surround wall was closed.

The solutions to these problems are visible in the accompanying drawing. They include:
- Bands of ever-lighter ascending colors in the tile facing, from brown through red to orange.
- A ruggedly framed, cross-braced platform hearth.
- Outside-air intakes ducted through the floor.
- Removable wall panels for air-vent access.

Once Houser planned it all, the installation went smoothly. First, he framed the platform hearth that doubles as a fireplace support. He tied it into a ledger on the back wall and added an extra joist under the floor, at the center, which rests on a block wall at one end and its own concrete pier at the other. "Everything ties together, so the weight is distributed throughout the entire structure," he points out. "There won't be any sag."

After framing the hearth and installing its plywood floor, Houser and two helpers lifted the fireplace into position. Then he installed Heatilator's outside-air kit as directed, except that he drilled holes for the duct through both the platform and floor (see drawing). "It was uncomfortable lying on my back under the house," he reports. "But this way, the ducts don't show."

Next, Houser put together the sections of Heatilator's double-walled air-cooled chimney, figuring out from his roof pitch how high to go for a proper draft. The height also conforms to local code.

Finally, he erected the studding for the surround wall, leaving two cavities on the front, as shown in the drawing. He closed the holes with panels made of the same redwood siding used on the rest of the wall, and used magnetic touch latches for a seamless-seeming fit. "The access panels let me come in behind the fireplace to check on the air kit and flue," he says. "The panels also give me hidden storage for valuables."

Houser fastened plywood to the studding over the fireplace to serve as a base for the tile. For the mural, he chose 3-by-6-inch Caribbean II tile from American Olean (Lansdale, PA 19446-0271), partly because all the vibrant colors were available with a glazed, rounded "bullnose" edge on either a long or short side. This let him use butting bullnose edges to attain a vertical grooving effect in the mural and get finished edges on his hearth. "I wanted to create a design using the shape as well as the color of the tile," he says.

The mural was planned to minimize cutting, though it

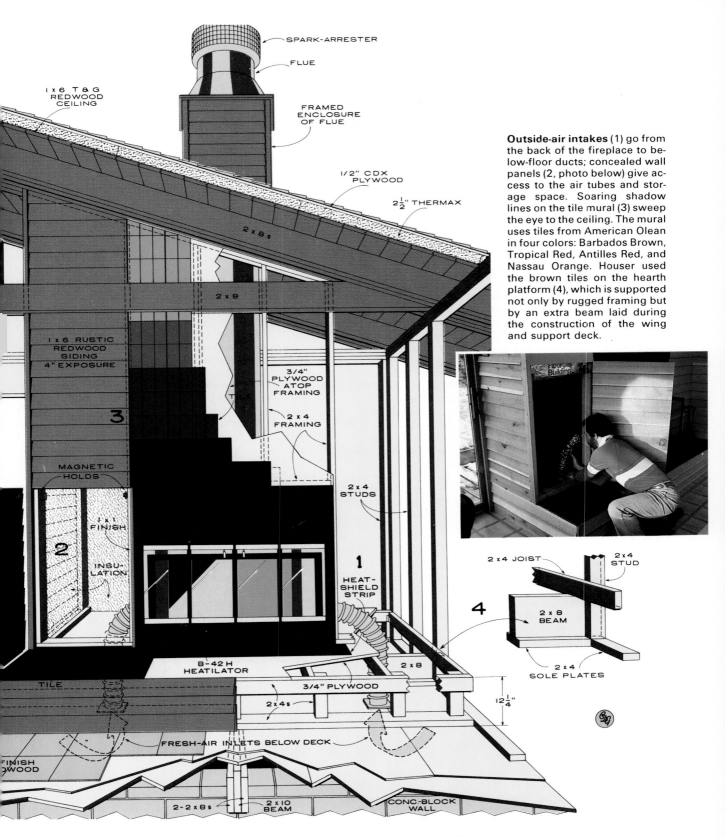

SPARK-ARRESTER

FLUE

FRAMED ENCLOSURE OF FLUE

1 x 6 T&G REDWOOD CEILING

1/2" CDX PLYWOOD

2½" THERMAX

2 x 8s

2 x 8

1 x 6 RUSTIC REDWOOD SIDING 4" EXPOSURE

3

3/4" PLYWOOD ATOP FRAMING

2 x 4 FRAMING

2 x 4 STUDS

1

HEAT-SHIELD STRIP

MAGNETIC HOLDS

1 x 1 FINISH

2

INSU-LATION

B-42H HEATILATOR

TILE

2 x 8

3/4" PLYWOOD

2 x 4s

12¼"

Outside-air intakes (1) go from the back of the fireplace to below-floor ducts; concealed wall panels (2, photo below) give access to the air tubes and storage space. Soaring shadow lines on the tile mural (3) sweep the eye to the ceiling. The mural uses tiles from American Olean in four colors: Barbados Brown, Tropical Red, Antilles Red, and Nassau Orange. Houser used the brown tiles on the hearth platform (4), which is supported not only by rugged framing but by an extra beam laid during the construction of the wing and support deck.

2 x 4 JOIST

2 x 4 STUD

4

2 x 8 BEAM

2 x 4 SOLE PLATES

FINISH REDWOOD

FRESH-AIR INLETS BELOW DECK

2-2 x 8s

2 x 10 BEAM

CONC-BLOCK WALL

jumps a wall beam. Measuring for the triangle above the beam was critical. Houser marked the cut lines on each tile, then took them to a retail tile shop for cutting. He installed the hearth tiles in a conventional manner with a latex mortar bed. "But I realized in the middle of the job that I couldn't put the wall tiles up the same way," he recalls. "It's too messy a job. And the tiles would fall off since the mortar takes 24 hours to set up."

So Houser used Scotch-Grip industrial adhesive, made by 3M Company. He put five little dabs on a tile and placed it on the wall, holding for a second or so. "It has great grab and sticks to the wall right away," he reports. "But I had 15 minutes before it finally set, so I could wiggle the tile a bit if it needed alignment." To finish the job, he applied a brown grout on both hearth and wall tiles—*by Susan Renner-Smith. Drawing by Carl De Groote.*

install a fireplace insert

If there's one thing the wood-stove boom of the 1970s taught a lot of homeowners, it's that the traditional open-front masonry fireplace can often be an inefficient heater. Beautiful and charming as they may be, many fireplaces let most of the heat go up the chimney along with the smoke. Even a well-designed, continuously burning fireplace delivers only about 10 to 15 percent of the firewood's available heat energy into your home.

This isn't news to heating engineers, but their advice on efficient fireplace construction has far too often been ignored. A prime example: the "contractor's specials" found in many contemporary tract houses and condominiums are likely to have less-than-ideal proportions from an efficiency standpoint. Typically, these fireplaces are too deep, have sides at right angles to the back, and have a large-section flue positioned at the rear of the fireplace cavity. They're built this way because it simplifies construction and makes it unlikely that the fireplace will ever smoke.

Perhaps you're the owner of one of the 25 million traditional masonry fireplaces in the nation. If you want to convert it from an energy waster into an efficient heating appliance—without losing any of its cozy charm—there's only one effective and cost-efficient way: Install a fireplace insert.

Progress in design

Fireplace inserts aren't a new idea, but units as thermally efficient as freestanding stoves are a recent development. Most of the fireplace inserts of five to ten years ago claimed unparalleled efficiency, but few actually delivered it. And as far as appearance was concerned, the majority were downright ugly.

This has now changed. The current generation of fireplace inserts is much improved in terms of design, performance, and appearance. Though the primary goal—to provide stovelike woodburning efficiency without compromising the allure of an open fireplace—has not changed over the years, engineers have found technical solutions to several of the earlier inserts' shortcomings. These advances include:

- Built-in baffle systems.
- Fan-assisted air-circulation systems.
- Secondary combustion chambers.
- Catalytic combustors.

Baffles slow down smoke and gases as they pass from the firebox to the chimney flue, allowing more time for the heat to be captured by the metal body of the insert. This increases heat-transfer efficiency as well as secondary (wood-gas) combustion efficiency. Most baffled inserts have a bypass damper, which allows smoke to go directly up the chimney when you're lighting a new fire and prevents smoke spillage when fuel is loaded. Some units even have bypass dampers that open automatically as you unlatch the fuel-loading door.

Blowers are another common feature of late-model inserts that can increase effective heat output while enhancing heat-transfer efficiency. Because most fireplace inserts are flush mounted or protrude only slightly from the fireplace opening, getting the heat out of the masonry surround and into the room isn't always easy. Fans are a great help, although there are fanless passive-circulation systems based on natural convection that also work well. Both systems typically draw cool air through a duct near the bottom of the insert, pass it around the back of the

Installing your insert

1 Remember to check the dimensions of your fireplace before purchasing an insert. Photos above and at right show installation steps for author's Vermont Castings insert. A cardboard template, same size as the insert exterior, is supplied with the unit. Use it to measure clearance (1). Remove the damper, or secure it in the full-open position. Measure and trim the sealing plates supplied to hold the flexible connector on top of the damper frame. Bend the con-

2 nector to the proper contour to pass through the throat, and feed it up through the plates and into the chimney (2, drawing opposite). Assemble the surround panels (3), following the maker's instructions. This includes gluing glass-fiber strips onto the back of the surround (4) to seal it against the fireplace opening. Roll the insert into place, reaching in through the front and up the flue collar to pull the connector's slip piece into place.

inner firebox to be heated, then exhaust the warmed air through grates or louvers near the top of the front section.

Blower-assisted units deliver warm air faster and more controllably than passive systems; most blowers are regulated by a rheostat or controlled by the insert's heat-output thermostat. A pointer: There are still some inserts on the market with noisy blowers, so listen before you buy. Passive systems don't circulate hot air quite as rapidly as do blower systems, but they're utterly silent and require no electricity and little maintenance.

Burn it twice

Another stove-inspired feature found in several of the new high-efficiency inserts is a secondary combustion chamber

—usually located atop or in back of the main firebox—that is designed to burn combustible wood gases, or volatiles, before they reach the flue. Because these gases account for nearly one-half the energy content of dry, seasoned hardwood, inserts that can burn them more completely are likely to be much more efficient. Inserts that are efficient gas burners will also generate less creosote and, consequently, less air pollution.

The fact that an insert may have a secondary combustion chamber or a secondary air inlet, though, doesn't automatically make it a good wood-gas burner—only testing can determine whether these features are really effective. In fact, any insert that promotes high temperatures (1,200 to 1,500° F) and provides sufficient oxygen in the presence

Vermont Castings insert (right) features thermostatically controlled inlets, variable-speed fans, a firebrick-lined secondary combustion chamber, and large fire-view windows.

Consolidated Dutchwest's Federal Convection insert (below, right) uses a catalytic combustor and converts for coal burning. Cooking plate has an inset thermometer.

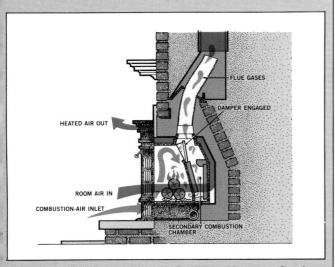

Drawing shows convection airflow in a Vermont Castings insert. Damper opens to exhaust smoke while the fire is tended. Flexible connector links insert to chimney flue.

of large concentrations of combustible gases will be an efficient wood burner, even if it doesn't incorporate any special features.

How can you tell, amid a welter of advertising claims, whether an insert provides good primary (solid-fuel) and secondary (wood-gas) combustion? One indicator is whether it's passed the Oregon Department of Environmental Quality (DEQ) standards. Because the Oregon DEQ test results also list power output and overall efficiency obtained under standard conditions, they're a good source of independent information for the consumer. Bear in mind, however, that many good inserts have not yet been tested according to the Oregon DEQ standard, so you can't assume an insert is substandard merely because it isn't listed.

An even more effective secondary combustion device has found its way into some of the latest inserts—the catalytic combustor. Justly hailed as this century's most important contribution to efficient woodburning, the typical combustor is a short ceramic cylinder, 4 to 6 inches in diameter, laced with perforations in a honeycomb pattern. A platinum or palladium coating on the ceramic material reacts chemically with the wood gases to lower their combustion temperature from about 1,200° F to between 500 and 600° F. As a result, combustion efficiency markedly increases while pollution and creosote formation decrease. Indeed, catalytic inserts have earned thermal-efficiency ratings that are higher than those of the best of the noncatalytic inserts, and superior to those of freestanding wood stoves.

There are some disadvantages to catalytic inserts: They're often more expensive than conventional models, and the catalytic combustor itself must be replaced every three to six years, depending on how much wood you burn. Replacements cost $80 to $150. Also, you must get used to running your fireplace at high output when lighting a new fire to bring the catalyst up to its operating temperature. Then you can close the bypass damper and adjust the output control to the desired setting. Catalysts should also be checked a few times each heating season for deterioration and clogging.

Despite these drawbacks, the performance of the catalytics is impressive. They burn efficiently with little pollution at low output settings; noncatalytics can achieve efficient combustion only at medium or high output.

Safe installation

Here are three key installation rules that will help you make sure your insert isn't a fire hazard:
● A stainless-steel "flex vent" connector must extend from the smoke-outlet collar of the insert to the flue liner of the chimney. This prevents overheating of the fireplace header beams.
● The area of the chimney flue must be no more than three times the cross-sectional area of the insert's flue collar to ensure a proper draft. If the flue's area is larger, it should be relined with a smaller stainless-steel liner surrounded with vermiculite insulation.
● The installation must be easy to inspect and clean. Every fireplace insert should be checked for creosote buildup at least twice a year—*by Jason D. Schneider. Drawing by Gerhard Richter.*

SELECTED MANUFACTURERS OF FIREPLACE INSERTS
Capitol Export Corp., 8825 Page Blvd., St. Louis, MO 63114; **Citation Stoves,** 3 Beacon St., Marblehead, MA 01945; **Consolidated Dutchwest,** Box 1019, Plymouth, MA 02360; **Kent Heating Ltd.,** Box 40507, Portland, OR 97240; **Vermont Castings,** Box 3000, Randolph, VT 05060.

Kent Heating's Log Fire insert (top), imported from New Zealand, features contemporary styling. Firebrick-lined Citation Stoves insert (middle) is shown with optional soapstone top and brass trim. Unit burns wood or coal. Capitol Export's Rembrandt insert (above), also from New Zealand, is available with a water booster for preheating water.

add-on solar greenhouse

Several years ago I built a garage with the intention of making it into a multipurpose workshop. I planned for power tools, workbenches, and a second-floor artist's studio with skylights. But when winter came and the high cost of electric heating kept me from enjoying what I had built, I decided to add on a solar greenhouse to help keep the shop areas warm.

Living in southeastern Massachusetts, I have to contend with severe winter storms that batter my house with driving rain and wet snow. I knew I needed glazing that would neither leak nor buckle under the combined weight of ice and slush. And because the house is situated beneath several large oak trees, the glazing had to be shatter-resistant to withstand the impact of foot-long falling icicles.

My greenhouse would be expected to heat not only itself but the entire workshop area, without ever freezing or overheating. I also wanted to use it for growing winter vegetables, raising seedlings, and sunbathing. Above all, I wanted a greenhouse that would be handsome and inconspicuous—a complement to my New England–style house. It had to be simple and inexpensive, and something I could build myself.

By using rugged wood-frame construction for the south, east, and west walls, and by glazing the roof with prefabricated Sunlite solar panels (supplied by Solar Components, Box 237, Manchester, NH 03105), I built a good-looking, sturdy greenhouse. Its matching roof line, trim, and siding make the addition look well integrated into the design of the garage-workshop.

Natural convection loops, which complement my woodstove forced-air heating system prevent overheating. The result is an effective solar heating system that doubles as a sun room and triples as a gardener's greenhouse.

When I built the greenhouse addition, I spent what would now amount to about $2,400 for materials, and I provided the labor myself. I calculate that the greenhouse has saved me $400 to $500 annually compared with the cost of electric heat; the project's payback period is surprisingly short. And it's hard to put a price tag on the year-round pleasure of having a plant-filled sun room—*by Larry Pina. Drawing by Adolph Brotman.*

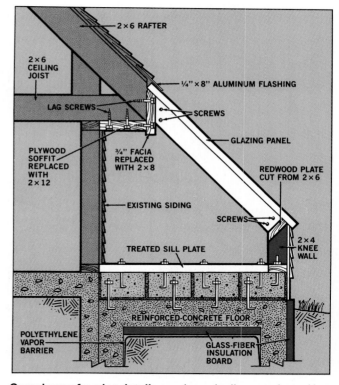

Greenhouse framing details are shown in diagram above. Use of lag bolts and screws is recommended because they are less likely to work loose due to heat-induced expansion and contraction. Greenhouse foundation is dropped 7 inches below garage level, providing extra head room and eliminating the difficulty of matching the existing floor grade. No structural modifications to the garage wall are needed. Except for the removal of corner boards, no siding or roofing need be disturbed. The end walls, which are nonbearing, are framed 16 inches on center. Load-bearing knee-wall studs are spaced 12 inches apart. Roof rafters are spaced 24 inches on center. The solar panels are held by 1-by-3-inch aluminum angles at corners and bottom. Center joints between panels are secured by 2-inch aluminum double battens. The lower piece of each batten is attached to the roof rafter with screws. The top piece of the batten sandwiches the glazing edge and attaches with lag screws. Both of these aluminum hardware items were supplied by the panel manufacturer.

Greenhouse addition (left) keeps the author's garage-workshop warm enough in midwinter to permit use of work areas without additional electric heat. On a sunny January afternoon, temperatures reach 65° in the garage, mid-70s in the upstairs studio, mid-90s in the greenhouse. Summer heat escapes through second-floor windows. The project required 100 hours of work.

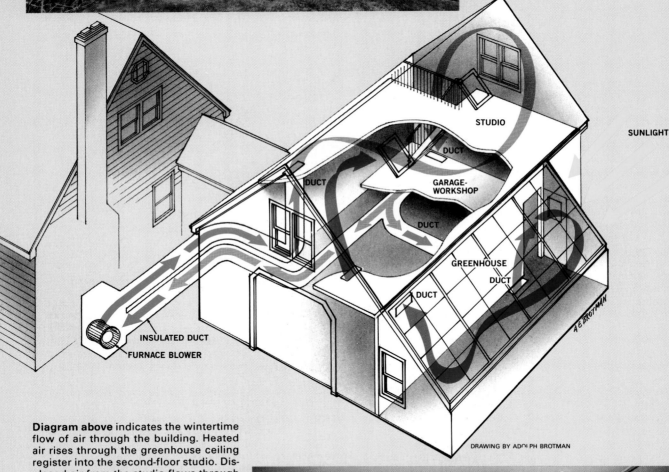

STUDIO

SUNLIGHT

DUCT

DUCT

GARAGE-
WORKSHOP

DUCT

GREENHOUSE

DUCT

DUCT

A.E. BROTMAN

INSULATED DUCT

FURNACE BLOWER

DRAWING BY ADOLPH BROTMAN

Diagram above indicates the wintertime flow of air through the building. Heated air rises through the greenhouse ceiling register into the second-floor studio. Displaced air from the studio flows through a duct into the cooler garage below. When the workshop temperature exceeds the household temperature, the forced-air furnace fan engages, tempering the cooler house air with warmer shop air. Similarly, when the wood-stove-heated house temperature exceeds the shop temperature, the furnace fan mixes house air with cooler shop air. The workshop acts as a heat sink for the house, preventing it from overheating at night. The house performs the same function for the workshop during the day. House-to-workshop ducts are closed during the summer, however.

insulating louvers

"Let the sun shine in"—that refrain from the popular 1960s song could pass as a slogan for today's houses. An ever-increasing number of homes are being outfitted with skylights, which provide daylighting and a sense of openness. But they also provide a prime escape route for heat in winter.

Until recently there were few easy ways to block that heat loss. Now there's InsulLouver, from InsulShutter (Box 888, 69 Island St., Keene, NH 03431). InsulLouvers are energy-saving insulating louvers that fit into a skylight cavity or the frame of a recessed window. The custom-made louvers are available with a power option: Hit a switch, and they swivel shut to seal in heat in winter and shut it out in summer. And they open at a touch to admit light and heat when you want them.

InsulLouvers are made of polyisocyanurate foam sandwiched between hardwood panels. The louvers have an insulating value of R-6.9. Install a louver behind a single-glazed skylight, and the R-value of the unit jumps to 9.1, says the maker—almost three times the R-value of a triple-glazed window. That's enough to cut unwanted heat loss or gain from energy-inefficient skylights and help trim your energy bills year-round.

A standard InsulLouver features louver panels of birch—other types of wood are available—with a white vinyl exterior (for maximum reflectivity) in a 1 × 4 basswood frame. The basic louver bank comes unpowered—you have to use a long-handled crank to open and close the panels.

But spend an extra $170 per bank, and you can enjoy the convenience of automation. A motorized louver comes with a factory-mounted 12-volt DC motor that's connected to one panel. When it moves that panel, the others also swivel. To step down a house's 110-volt AC, there's a power supply that plugs into a standard electrical outlet; a three-way toggle switch controls the louvers. If you're installing two or more louver banks, you can connect each to its own switch or wire them to a single switch.

How easy are the louvers to install? When I asked InsulShutter's Joe Harvey that question, he invited me to watch an installation. As he unpacked the unit, he bragged about what a fast job it would be. Did I want to give it a try? I certainly did.

There are two ways to install the louvers, Harvey explained. One is to nail the frame right into the skylight cavity or window opening. If the cavity isn't square, you'll have to add shims, then tack up trim to hide them. A second option, the one I chose, eliminates the need for shims and trim. Nail up a ridge of stops—1-inch-thick pieces of wood that are supplied with every set of louvers—in the cavity, and then rest the louver unit on top of these. Because an electrical outlet was handy, I had the louvers in place and the wiring completed in an hour.

To order InsulLouvers from dealers or the manufacturer, you'll need to supply the following information:
● The cavity's width, length, and depth, in inches. The louvers come in lengths up to 12 feet; there's no width limit.
● The number of louver panels you prefer in each bank. Panel widths run from 8 to 24 inches. If you don't specify a number, the manufacturer will make that decision for you.
● Whether you want the louvers to pivot on their horizontal or vertical axis.

The cost varies with size. But to give you an idea, outfitting the two 44-inch-square skylights on my enclosed porch would cost about $480 ($240 per unit), without automation—*by Mort Schultz. Drawing by Gerhard Richter.*

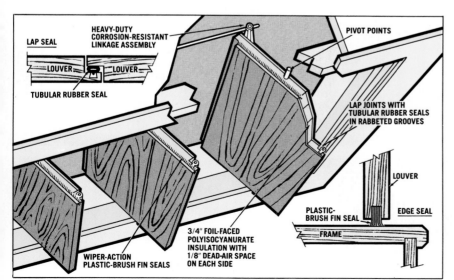

Louvers shut tight in a tongue-and-groove design. Compressive-rubber-tube seals and plastic-film-and-brush fin seals prevent air from escaping.

Insulating louvers can be installed inside any window frame deep enough to let them pivot. They let you avoid the space problems of hinged shutters.

Custom-made insulating louver (1) comes pre-assembled and sized to fit the skylight cavity. Begin installation by cutting and inserting supplied seals between panels to make them airtight on closing. Then wire the 12-V DC motor (2) according to the supplied wiring diagram. To install the louver, nail up supplied stops on two sides of the cavity. Then set the louver unit on top of them. Hold the unit in place, and nail up the last two stops (3). Secure the power supply, which is plugged into a wall outlet, in a remote spot (4), and install the on-off switch. I also recommend snaking the wire that runs from the power supply to the switch and to the banks through the wall so that it's hidden. Louvers can be stained, laminated, or varnished to match decor (5).

setback thermostat —step-by-step

NEW

OLD

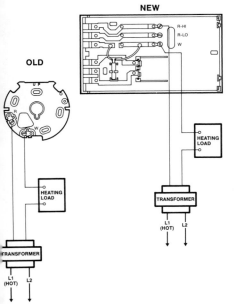

R-HI
R-LO
W

HEATING LOAD

TRANSFORMER

L1 (HOT)   L2

HEATING LOAD

TRANSFORMER

L1 (HOT)   L2

R

W

1. Disconnect power and remove cover of old thermostat by tugging firmly from bottom. If it resists, check for a screw that locks the cover on. Loosen screws holding thermostat base to wallplate or wall and lift away. Disconnect wires from old subbase, tape ends, and label with the letter of the terminal designation. You can slip a large paperclip over wires to prevent them from falling back into wall opening.

2. Pull wires through Fuel Saver thermostat wallplate. Connect to proper terminals using drawing as a guide. Use a level to properly position wallplate. Mark and drill holes for anchors, then gently tap anchors into holes until flush with wall. Reposition wallplate, then insert and tighten mounting screws.

3. Align thermostat with wallplate and press gently, but firmly, into place.

4. Now you're ready to program the new microelectronic Fuel Saver thermostat for one or two energy-saving periods a day. Change as desired to accomodate any changes in schedule.

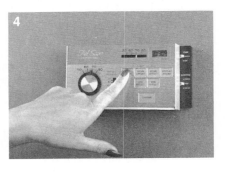

Why pay extra to maintain a comfort level during those long hours when no one is home to enjoy it? Seems rather silly. Yet for years the only alternative was to manually adjust your old-style thermostat up and down, several times a day, in an effort to blend comfort with economy. Well, now you can choose from an array of affordable new thermostats that'll keep you as warm or as cool as you like—then lower or raise your home's temperature *automatically* to trim costs while you or your family are out during the day or asleep at night.

This chapter shows how to replace conventional thermostats with the new setback models. Featured here is the Honeywell Fuel Saver CT350, their latest offering. Designed for easy installation, the unit can save from 9 to 30 percent on heating costs and 7 to 25 percent on cooling costs, according to Honeywell. Just tap CT350's touch-pad keyboard to program in up to two energy-saving periods a day. At bedtime, the thermostat sets back temperature to, say, 62°, automatically raises it to a balmy 72° while you prepare for work the next morning, then lowers it back to 62° until you return home that evening. A digital LCD clock displays the time and indicates when the selected energy-saving mode is operating.

The Honeywell CT350 line consists of three setback thermostats: one compatible with heating-only gas or oil systems; one for heating and cooling, gas or oil systems; and one for heating and cooling, electric systems. Prices are $74.95 for the heating-only model, and $79.95 for the heating/cooling model. For more information contact Honeywell's Residential Controls Division, 1985 Douglas Drive North, Golden Valley, MN 55422-3992—*by Bob Markovich. Photos and drawing courtesy Honeywell, Inc.*

cherry paneling with mantel and cabinetry

Cherry frame-and-panel wall paneling and fireplace mantel (right) were created by layering frames and moldings atop a base of cherry plywood. Built-in cabinets (left) flow out of the paneling and provide storage for books and hi-fi equipment, plus a display area for pressed wildflowers in frames.

There's just no better way to give a room a rich, dramatic look of luxury than with built-in cabinetry surrounded by cherry frame-and-panel. Even so, you don't see many rooms done that way these days. One reason is that there aren't many craftsmen around who know how to do the work. Another is that few people could afford to pay for all the man-hours such a job requires.

In the next few pages, we'll show you how to simulate the custom-carved look of frame-and-panel and build those cabinets, without the skills of an Old World craftsman. Then, once you know how to do the job yourself, you won't have to come up with all that money to pay for all those man hours.

We'll be using simple techniques throughout: glue and nails, butt and miter joints. Although these techniques do not require a tremendous amount of skill, they do require time, and lots of it. I'd estimate my brother and I put in well over 550 hours paneling my living room and building in the matching cherry cabinetry. If the results are worth it to you, then let's get started.

Where to begin

Your first step is to make simple sketches, to scale, of every wall you intend to panel. Then plan your panel layouts. You'll be working with 4 × 8 sheets of plywood, so your

maximum panel width will be 4 feet. If you have a wall 12 feet long, you can cover it perfectly with three panels. If, however, a wall is 15 feet long, you'll have to use four panels and juggle panel widths so that they're all the same. In this case, divide 15 by 4 to find the width of each panel (3 feet, 9 inches), and then draw your panel layout to scale.

You may also have to juggle your layout to cope with windows and doors, as I did. If so, it's easiest to plan your layouts so panel frames run alongside the openings and double as window or door trim (fig. 1). I also had a pair of windows so small they would fit into the center of my panels, so I paneled around them and then made special casings to trim them out (fig. 2).

After you lay out your panels, draw in the frames and baseboard. Then plan the moldings that line the frames, plus the details of your crown molding along the ceiling. The sketches show the moldings I used. Many of these are quite complicated and were created with custom molding cutters I ground myself. Please feel free to use simpler moldings. We'll talk more about making your own moldings in a little while.

For the plywood that makes up the panels, get ¼-inch veneer grade plywood. I used cherry, but other woods will work as well. If possible, get "flitch-cut" plywood sheets that have been cut in sequence from the same log. This will allow you to create matched panels because the grain patterns in each sheet will be nearly identical.

For your trim, get ¾-inch solid hardwood to match your plywood. Ordinary lumber yards usually don't carry veneer grade plywoods or hardwoods. Your lumber yard may be able to order the plywood for you, but you will probably get a better deal on the solid stock if you hunt up a local mill or hardwood dealer. *Get at least 20 percent more hardwood than you think you will need.*

Putting up the paneling

Begin by removing all your existing trim. Then, draw your panel layout right on the wall with a heavy pencil. This will help you visualize your layout full-size and point out any mistakes before you start cutting up valuable wood.

If you are happy with your layout, put up the plywood. Cut the sheets to size, if necessary. Pay attention to the grain patterns to achieve a grain match from one panel to the next. To install the plywood, use panel adhesive and finishing nails. You can put the nails along the edges of the panels, to be hidden by your trim, and behind where the center rail in your frames will go.

Panels up? Now rip out your stock for the baseboards and top rail. Install the baseboards with finishing nails, then snap a chalk line marking the lower edge of the top rail. If you follow my layout exactly, this should be 4½ inches down from the ceiling. Then fasten in the top rail, using finishing nails near the top edge of the rail.

Next, cut out and install the full-length stiles that cover the panel edges. Glue and nail these in place, centering them over the seams between panels. Then put up your center rails, and then your short center stiles. Each frame piece should be custom-cut to fit its space snugly.

Now it's time for your moldings. Best way to get the moldings you need is to make your own. You can use a router, a shaper, a molding head, or (for big coves) a table saw with crosscut blade. I used a router for some of my moldings, the molding head for some of the more intricate moldings, and the saw for my coves (fig. 3).

The router is fast and easy for small, simple moldings. That's why I'd advise most people to stick with router-made moldings for every part of the job except the big ceiling cove. To make router moldings, select one or two bits you like. My favorites are the "classical" and ogee with fillet. The classical combines a bead and cove with some square fillets to produce a nice intricate design with lots of lines and detail. The ogee is more open and flowing, but still creates plenty of interest.

Just rout the edge of a nice straight board, then rip off the edge to the desired width. Then rout and rip again. Keep up this rout-and-rip operation until you have all the molding you will need—again, *plus about 20 percent.* Cutting to length will create some waste, and there is always the chance you will make a mistake.

Putting up the moldings

Before you install your moldings, go over your frames with a sander. Smooth them out and pay special attention to all joints, making sure they are all even. If they aren't, I like to hit them with a belt sander and 120 grit belt to "plane" all members down to the same level. Then touch up with an orbital sander to remove any crossgrain sanding scratches.

Now put up your moldings. Use miters at all joints and aim for perfection. The best way to cut the miters is with a power miter box, right at hand in the room you are

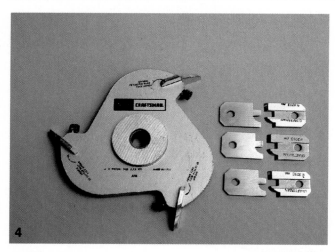

4

5

6

paneling so you can cut and fit until your joints are just right. Put moldings up with small finishing nails and a bit of glue. Keep nails to a minimum. Every one you drive will have to be set and filled over later on.

Built-in cabinets

These are built in two sections. The upper cabinets are built separately from the base cabinets, and simply fasten in place atop the base unit countertop. A boxlike soffit connects the upper cabinets and houses eyeball fixtures to light the center display area. The soffit is finished off with the same ceiling moldings used with the paneling.

The plans show you what you need to know, and all construction is pretty simple. One part that might be new

to you is the door construction, so let's take a look at that in detail.

Like the paneling, the doors are a frame-and-panel design. The frames are made on the table saw, with a molding head and a special double set of cutters sold by Sears. You need set 9-3210 and set 9-3213 (fig. 4). Set 9-3210, at left in photo, cuts the dado for the door panels and, at the same time, cuts a bead molding. You use this cutter along the inside edges of all frame parts.

Set 9-3213, shown at right in photo, is the exact opposite of the first. You use it to cut both ends of all the horizontal frame parts, or rails. When you do so, you profile (or cope) the ends of these so they fit perfectly into the cuts along the inner edges of the vertical frame parts (the stiles). This creates a strong, interlocking glue joint.

There are a few tricks to using this cutter set:
● Cut a few "dummy" frame parts at the start to get things right. These needn't be the right width or length, but they must be the same thickness as your frame parts.
● Be sure to cut your rails ½ inch longer than the frame opening of your doors. This allows for the part of the rails that sticks into the stiles.
● Alignment is critical. Make all your dado/bead cuts on all parts first, using the fence protector and hold-downs shown in figure 5. Then switch over to the 9-3213 set of cutters. You use these with the special end-milling jig shown in the sketch and photos. This jig fastens to an extension screwed to your miter gauge.

Jig position is also critical. To set it, take one of your dummy parts and clamp it in the jig. Unplug your saw and rotate the molding head so one of the cutters is up. Slide the jig left or right until the groove in the cutter that forms the "tongue" on your stock aligns perfectly with the dado already cut in your stock. Clamp the jig to your miter gauge extension (fig. 6) and check again to see that it hasn't moved. If alignment is right, fasten the jig permanently in place with two screws into the miter gauge extension.

Make a test cut and check it for depth. It should make a complete cut across the end of the stock, but shouldn't cut so deeply that it reduces the length of the stock. Adjust depth if necessary and make another test cut.

When you get the right depth, check the part for fit in one of your frame parts. If you have good alignment, the faces of both pieces should be flush. If they aren't you'll have to adjust the jig slightly left or right. One you get your jig set up properly, put a fresh stop on the jig. The "kerf" in this stop created by the cutter head must align perfectly with the cutters. If it doesn't, the stop won't back up the stock adequately, and the cutter will tear chips off the trailing edge of your rails.

Once you have the jig set right, cut all your rail ends using a smooth, steady pass. You can then cut the plywood door panels (aim for grain matches whenever possible), and glue the doors up.

Door edge moldings

Cabinet doors are of the ⅜-inch overlay type. In other words, a ⅜-by-⅜-inch rabbet around the door edges forms a lip that overlaps the door openings. Normally, you would cut this rabbet out of the door with a router, or a door-edge cutter in a molding head. We created the rabbet by adding on a special molding instead (fig. 7).

Why? Because we goofed and made the doors too small. The moldings brought the doors out to the proper size, gave us the rabbet we needed, and actually enhanced the look of the doors in the process. The point is, all woodwork-

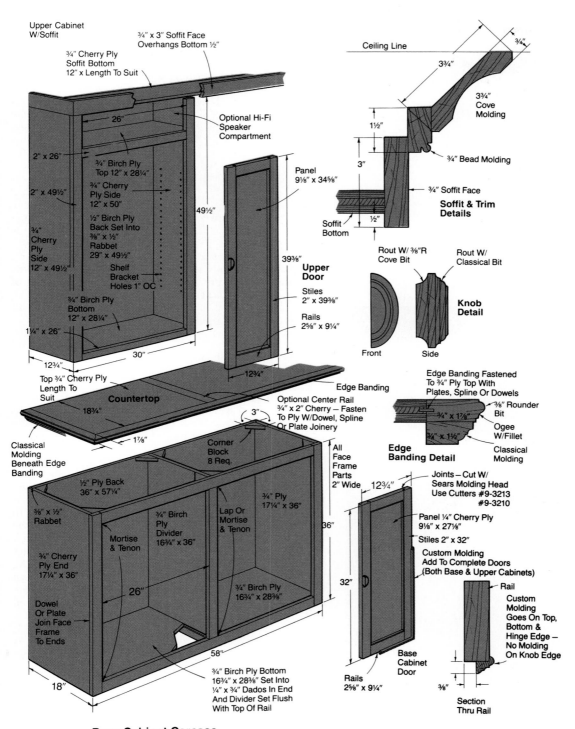

Upper Cabinet W/Soffit

¾" x 3" Soffit Face Overhangs Bottom ½"

¾" Cherry Ply Soffit Bottom 12" x Length To Suit

Optional Hi-Fi Speaker Compartment

26"

2" x 26"

¾" Birch Ply Top 12" x 28¼"

2" x 49½"

¾" Cherry Ply Side 12" x 50"

½" Birch Ply Back Set Into ⅜" x ½" Rabbet 29" x 49½"

¾" Cherry Ply Side 12" x 49½"

Shelf Bracket Holes 1" OC

49½"

¾" Birch Ply Bottom 12" x 28¼"

1¼" x 26"

30"

12¾"

Top ¾" Cherry Ply Length To Suit

Countertop

18¾"

12¾"

Panel 9⅛" x 34⅝"

39⅜"

Upper Door

Stiles 2" x 39⅜"

Rails 2⅝" x 9¼"

Edge Banding

Optional Center Rail ¾" x 2" Cherry — Fasten To Ply W/Dowel, Spline Or Plate Joinery

3"

1⅞"

Classical Molding Beneath Edge Banding

½" Ply Back 36" x 57¼"

⅜" x ½" Rabbet

¾" Cherry Ply End 17¼" x 36"

Mortise & Tenon

¾" Birch Ply Divider 16¾" x 36"

Lap Or Mortise & Tenon

¾" Ply 17¼" x 36"

26"

¾" Birch Ply 16¾" x 28⅜"

Dowel Or Plate Join Face Frame To Ends

All Face Frame Parts 2" Wide

Corner Block 8 Req.

58"

18"

¾" Birch Ply Bottom 16¾" x 28⅜" Set Into ¼" x ¾" Dados In End And Divider Set Flush With Top Of Rail

Base Cabinet Carcase

Ceiling Line

¾"

3¾"

3¾" Cove Molding

1½"

3"

¾" Bead Molding

¾" Soffit Face

Soffit & Trim Details

Soffit Bottom

½"

Rout W/ ⅜"R Cove Bit

Rout W/ Classical Bit

Knob Detail

Front

Side

Edge Banding Fastened To ¾" Ply Top With Plates, Spline Or Dowels

⅜" Rounder Bit

¾" x 1⅞"

Ogee W/Fillet

¾" x 1½"

Classical Molding

Edge Banding Detail

12¾"

Joints — Cut W/ Sears Molding Head Use Cutters #9-3213 #9-3210

Panel ¼" Cherry Ply 9⅛" x 27⅛"

Stiles 2" x 32"

Custom Molding Add To Complete Doors (Both Base & Upper Cabinets)

32"

Base Cabinet Door

Rails 2⅝" x 9¼"

Rail

Custom Molding Goes On Top, Bottom & Hinge Edge — No Molding On Knob Edge

⅜"

Section Thru Rail

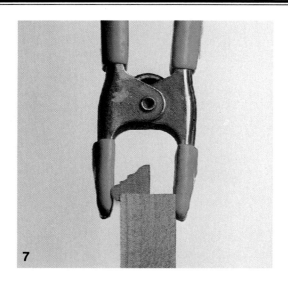

7

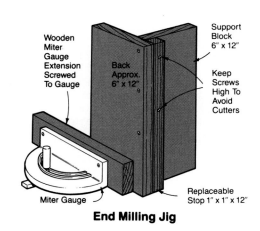

Wooden Miter Gauge Extension Screwed To Gauge

Back Approx. 6" x 12"

Support Block 6" x 12"

Keep Screws High To Avoid Cutters

Miter Gauge

Replaceable Stop 1" x 1" x 12"

End Milling Jig

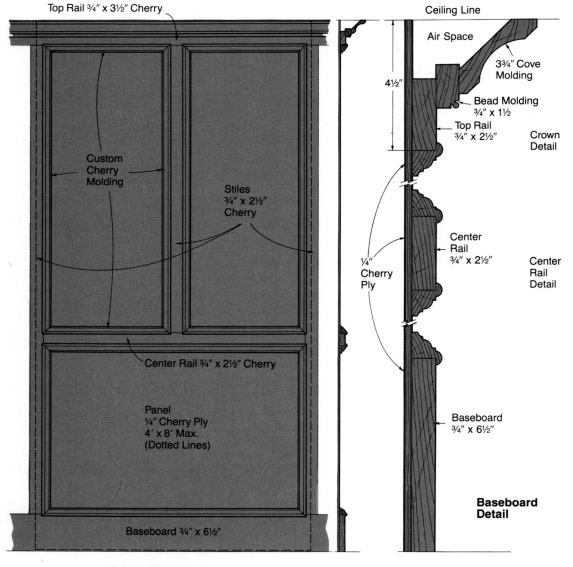

Top Rail ¾" x 3½" Cherry

Custom Cherry Molding

Stiles ¾" x 2½" Cherry

Center Rail ¾" x 2½" Cherry

Panel ¼" Cherry Ply 4' x 8' Max. (Dotted Lines)

Baseboard ¾" x 6½"

Basic Panel Layout

Ceiling Line

Air Space

4½"

3¾" Cove Molding

Bead Molding ¾" x 1½

Top Rail ¾" x 2½"

Crown Detail

¼" Cherry Ply

Center Rail ¾" x 2½"

Center Rail Detail

Baseboard ¾" x 6½"

Baseboard Detail

ers make mistakes. What separates the men from the boys is the ability to correct those mistakes.

The mantel

The mantel itself is just a sandwich of plywood, built up to create the required thickness. The edge is then finished off with three different moldings, stacked to look like a single big one (fig. 8).

The mantel rests on columns that are equally straightforward. At heart, they are nothing but channels of cherry plywood standing on end. The base, capital, and frame are appliqued on top, and a few moldings are thrown in to give everything a smooth, carved look.

Finishing

The cherry, especially the plywood, began as a lifeless grayish, pinkish brown. Rather than stain it, I gave it all a coat of Watco Danish Oil, brushed on and wiped off after 20 minutes.

As soon as oil hit wood, the cherry took on a deep, warm tone. I left it that way for several months, allowing oxygen and light to age the wood even more. As time passed, the cherry got even mellower. Finally I gave everything three coats of alkyd varnish, sanding between coats (see my Frame-and-Panel Oak Cabinet chapter on page 65 for details). The lustrous patina made all that work worthwhile —*by A.J. Hand. Drawings by Richard Meyer.*

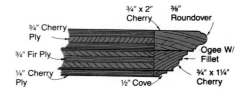

Section of Built-Up Mantel

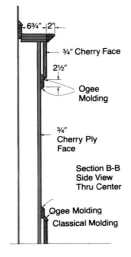

Fireplace Layout

Fireplace Layout labels: Crown Detail Same As In Basic Layout; ¾″ x 2½″ Cherry Stile; Panel ¼″ Cherry Ply Grain Horizontal; 3½″ Rail 2½″ Exposed Above Mantel; Custom Molding; B; ¾″ Cherry Block 2″ Wide 4″ High; ¼″ Cherry Ply 10½ x Length To Suit; 10″; Cherry Face; Capital; Tiles; 2″ Cherry Rails; ¾″ Cherry Ply Face; Frame; Paneling Stile; Wall; Column Side; Column Side ¾″ Cherry Ply 6″ Wide; 9″; Section A-A Thru Right Column Left Column Reversed; ¾″ Cherry Ply 5¼″ Wide; 6½″; 9¼″; Base; A; B

Section B-B labels: 6¾″; 2″; ¾″ Cherry Face; 2½″; Ogee Molding; ¾″ Cherry Ply Face; Section B-B Side View Thru Center; Ogee Molding; Classical Molding

8

chippendale dining room set

Nothing adds a touch of elegance to your meals like well-crafted, matched table and chairs. And there are few designs for a dining set more elegant than Chippendale.

This Chippendale ensemble was designed and built by Thomas Stender of Boston, New York. Tom has been building custom furniture since 1975, specializing in fine furniture in the tradition of eighteenth and early nineteenth century craftsmen. He doesn't do "reproductions," however. Like all of Tom's furniture, this dining set is his original design, crafted along traditional lines.

Wood selection and joinery

The preferred wood of the period was mahogany, though many American craftsmen worked in native hardwoods, particularly walnut and cherry. Tom used cherry for the dining room set featured here.

Perhaps more important than the type of hardwood you use is its grain pattern and cut. Like most Chippendale designs, the table and chairs incorporate cabriole legs. These legs are notoriously weak at the ankles. Tom's cabriole patterns are stronger than many because he resisted the temptation to exaggerate the curve. But you will realize the full advantages of his design only if you use leg stock with perfectly straight grain. Any figuring will weaken the legs.

When choosing stock for the table top, consider the cut. The two drop leaves are unsupported, and therefore prone to cupping with changes in temperature and humidity. Quarter- or rift-sawn lumber will reduce that tendency. Such wood is sawn so that the face of the boards are perpendicular to the annual rings. Curve of the rings through the wood is considerably reduced, and so is the tendency to cup.

Like many classic designs, both the table and the chairs depend on mortise-and-tenon joints for their structural strength. Some of these joints—particularly those that join the chair legs to the seat rails—require a good deal of skill and patience. You could substitute simpler joints, such as dowels to join the chair parts. But these joints would require bracing and reinforcement. The finished project would be heavier than Tom's original design, and not quite as strong. If you are hesitant about attempting any joint, make it in scrap wood first. Work out any problems that you may encounter before you commit good hardwood.

While you're working, remember to cut the joinery in the legs and other shaped parts while the stock is still square, *before* you shape them. It's almost impossible to cut accurate joints once you've removed the flat faces from the wood.

Cabriole legs

If you've made cabriole legs for any other projects, you understand how to make a compound cut with your bandsaw. Cut the design in one face, tape the waste back to the wood, turn the stock 90 degrees, and cut the design in the second face. Tom's cabriole legs, however, are not quite that simple. They have turned pad feet, ears, and other fine touches that require additional work.

The extra work starts with preparing the stock. The legs for the table are cut from true 3-by-3-inch stock—all four sides are square to each other. The stock for the front chair legs is trapezoid-shaped. The front faces and the inside side faces are 2¾ inches wide and square to each other. The back faces are square to the front and the inside side faces, but somewhat less than 2¾ inches wide. The *outside side* faces of the legs are angled in, front to back, at 6 degrees.

Once you've prepared the leg stock, trace the pattern on the two inside faces of each leg. Be sure the back edge of the leg pattern is flush with the inside corner, and mark the line where the knee breaks from the post. This will give you a constant reference every time you reposition the pattern.

Mount the stock on a lathe. Turn the pad and heel of each foot, being careful *not* to turn up past the heel. Remove the stock from the lathe and cut the mortises. Then cut the faces of the corner posts down to the knee. Do *not* cut the waste from the posts yet.

Glue the ear stock to the legs, carefully lining up the tops of the ears with the reference line. Remember that the gate legs on the table only have one ear. Also, remember that the ear blocks for the side ears of the chair legs must have one side angled at 6 degrees to match the posts. Trace the leg pattern onto the ends of each ear, and the ear pattern onto each ear back. Adjust the upper blade guide of your bandsaw so that it just clears the ear stock, and cut the knee, saving the scrap. Lower the blade guide to clear the leg stock only, and cut the foot, ankle, and leg taper. Again, save the scrap.

Rough out cabriole leg shapes on your bandsaw. Use a compound cut—cut one profile, tape waste back to the leg stock, and cut a second profile. Adjust upper blade guide as needed to clear the ears.

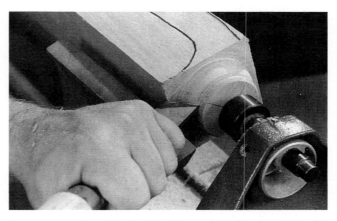

Turn the pad and heel of both front chair legs and all table legs. Do not turn up past the heel.

Saw out knuckles and fingers of the knuckle joint on your bandsaw, then scoop out excess stock between each finger with hand chisels.

Tape the scrap back to the workpiece and turn the stock 90 degrees (or 84 degrees if you're making the chair legs). Repeat the cuts, raising and lowering the blade guide as needed. When you remove all the scrap, you'll have rough cabriole legs. To finish them, smooth the sawn surfaces and round the corners with a spokeshave.

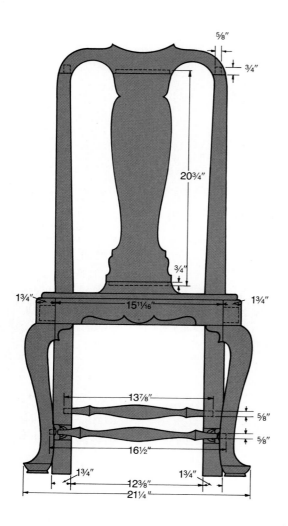

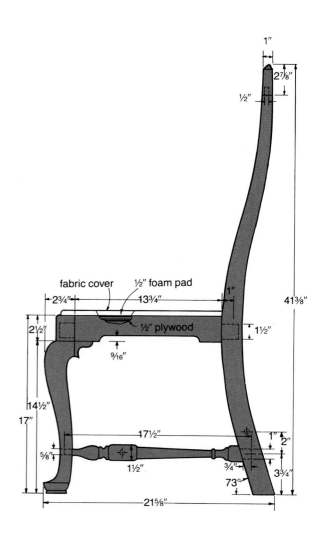

Assembling the side chairs

Backs and back legs of the chairs also require some compound cutting on the bandsaw. To make the backs, first resaw thick stock to make the curves of the side profile, as shown in the patterns. The *finished* backs should be ³⁄₈ inch thick, so resaw the stock about ¹⁄₁₆ inch thicker to leave room for scraping and sanding. Tape the scrap back to the resawn backs, and cut the front profiles.

Cut the back legs in the same manner, only reverse the sequence. Cut the front profiles first, tape the scrap back to the stock, and cut the side profiles.

To add a bit of decoration to the back legs, round over the edges except those in the immediate vicinity of the seat rail mortises and the side stretcher mortises. Leave these areas square. The transition from round to square and back again will create a pleasant visual effect.

Once chair parts are assembled, they require quite a bit of handwork. The crest rails must be carved and shaped, then blended into the back legs so that the pieces look continuous. This is also the time to upholster the chair seats. To do this, mount a pad to a sheet of ¹⁄₂-inch plywood, then cover it with the fabric of your choice. Your local library probably has many books on upholstering that cover the fine details. Or you can take the plywood seats to a professional and have him do it for you.

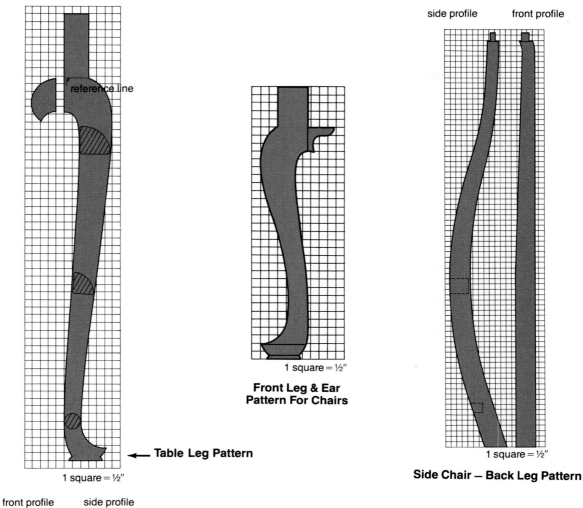

reference line

← **Table Leg Pattern**

1 square = ½"

1 square = ½"

**Front Leg & Ear
Pattern For Chairs**

side profile   front profile

1 square = ½"

Side Chair — Back Leg Pattern

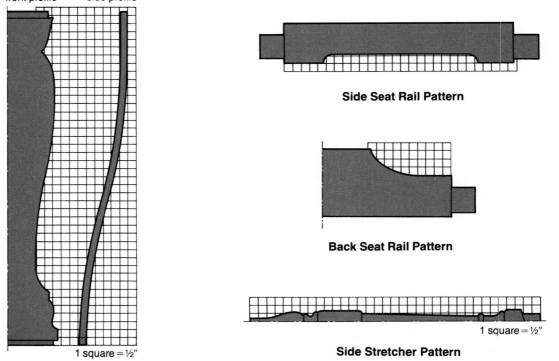

front profile   side profile

Side Seat Rail Pattern

Back Seat Rail Pattern

1 square = ½"

Side Stretcher Pattern

1 square = ½"

Back Pattern

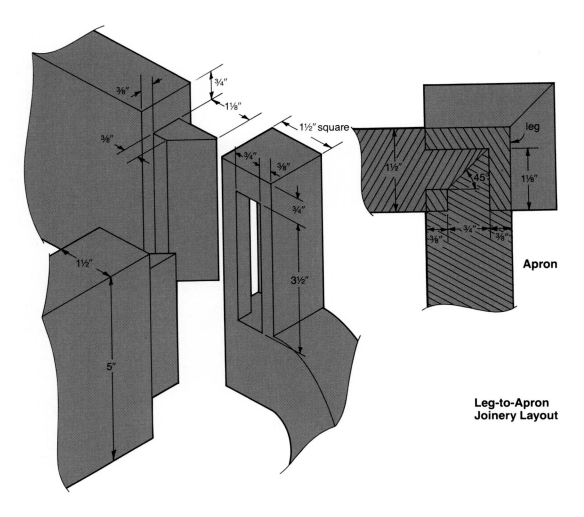

Apron

**Leg-to-Apron
Joinery Layout**

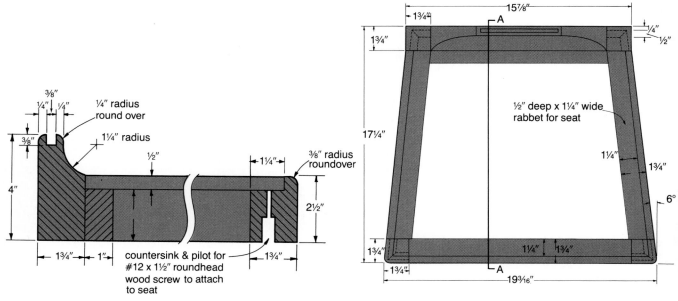

Side Chair — Section A

¼" radius
round over

1¼" radius

½"

⅜" radius
roundover

countersink & pilot for
#12 x 1½" roundhead
wood screw to attach
to seat

**Side Chair
Seat Layout**

½" deep x 1¼" wide
rabbet for seat

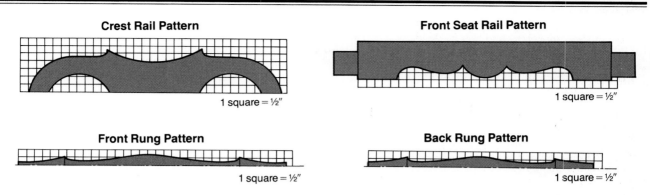

Crest Rail Pattern

1 square = ½"

Front Seat Rail Pattern

1 square = ½"

Front Rung Pattern

1 square = ½"

Back Rung Pattern

1 square = ½"

Gateleg Table

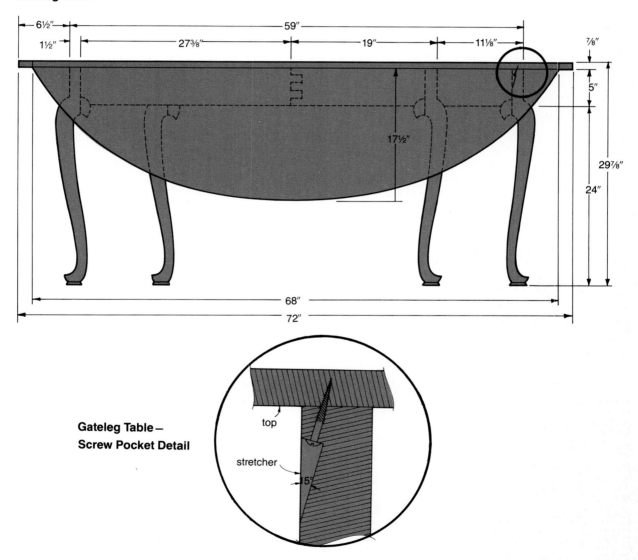

6½"

1½"

59"

27⅜"

19"

11⅛"

⅞"

5"

17½"

29⅞"

24"

68"

72"

**Gateleg Table —
Screw Pocket Detail**

top

stretcher

15°

Assembling the table

To complete the table, you'll need to make two joints in addition to the mortises and tenons that join the table legs to the aprons. These are "knuckle" joints so that the gate legs can swing out, and rule joints where the drop leaves join the table top.

Knuckle Joints. These are wooden hinges that pivot from 180 to 90 degrees. Lay out the top profiles of the joint first, on both the gates and the long side aprons. Cut this profile on the bandsaw, creating a knuckle in the ends of the parts. Turn the stock 90 degrees so that it rests on the wide faces, then cut the fingers, stopping where the narrow diagonal face meets the curve of the knuckle. Cut three fingers in the gate pieces and two in the side aprons—five mating fingers per joint, each 1$\frac{9}{32}$ inches long and 1 inch tall.

With a hand chisel, scoop out the excess material between each finger, where indicated on the drawings. Be careful not to carve into the diagonal faces, which serve as a stop for the gate when it pivots to 90 degrees. When the fingers fit properly, clamp them together in the "open" position (180 degrees) and drill a $\frac{1}{4}$-inch stopped hole for the pivot pin.

Rule Joints. Make the rule joints before you cut the oval shape of the top. This joint consists of a matching thumbnail and cove. Use a router or shaper to cut the thumbnail in the table top and the cove in the drop leaves. Join the top and the leaves with special drop-leaf hinges. Locate hinge pins at the center of the arc of the rule joints.

Assemble the parts of the table, then raise the leaves. Mark an oval on the top 72 inches long and 52$\frac{1}{2}$ inches wide. To draw this oval, first put two small nails along the long axis, 11$\frac{1}{4}$ inches in from the edge of the table (centers x and y, on the drawings). Make a loop of string 121$\frac{1}{2}$ inches long and put it over the nails. Stretch it taut, and use it as a string compass to draw the oval. Cut the oval shape with a saber saw, then sand away the millmarks from the edge.

Finishing

Be especially careful to apply as many coats of finish to the underside of the top and leaves as you do to the top surface. This will help keep the parts from warping or cupping—*by Nick Engler.*

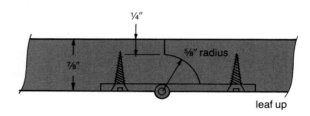

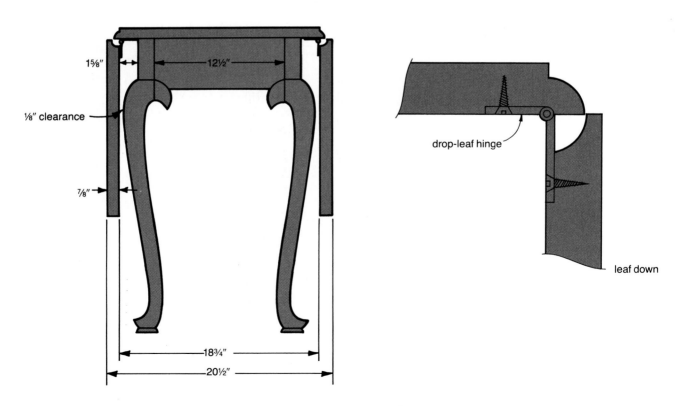

Gateleg Table

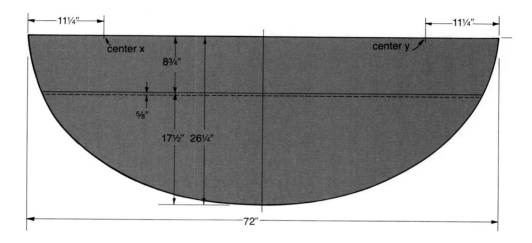

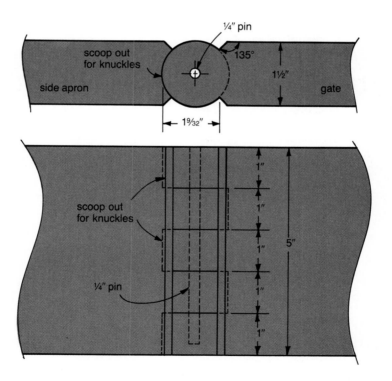

Gateleg Table — Knuckle Joint Layout

super shelving unit

Round front edges of the shelves and inside edges of the door frames as shown for a pleasing visual effect.

Doors to the middle portion of the A/V cabinet unit are mounted on flipper door slides, so that they can be pushed back into the cabinet.

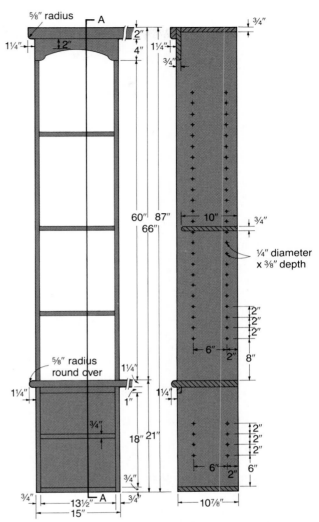

**Display Shelves Unit
Front View**

**Display Shelves Unit
Section A**

I t was a tough design problem. Ethan Perry, a furnituremaker from Frenchtown, New York, was asked to design and build a wall system for a Philadelphia home. His clients, however, used baseboard heat. That meant the system could not rest on the floor or interfere with the flow of air around the heaters.

After some thought, Ethan came up with the design you see here. His system is mounted to the walls, where it floats several inches above the floor. Not only does this solve the heating problem, it creates a unique visual effect. Suspended in air, the shelves and cabinets seem less obtrusive than normal sit-on-the-floor units. Although Ethan's system is every bit as massive as others, it seems wonderfully light and graceful.

Adapting the design

Like most wall systems, Ethan's overall design is composed of several units, each unit offering a particular type of storage and/or display space. As shown in the drawings, there are four major units in this system. There is a narrow display shelving unit with open, adjustable shelves for showing off collectibles. The bookcase unit is somewhat wider, and has a cabinet base. The audio/visual cabinet unit consists of three small storage cabinets, stacked one atop the other, in which you can store records, tapes, a stereo, a small television, and a VCR. Finally, the corner cabinet unit provides both display and storage space, while making use of wasted corner space.

Ethan's clients wanted an open area in the midst of the wall system to sit and read. Ethan decided to flank this open area with two display units. He then filled in the space to the right of the reading area with a bookcase and an A/V cabinet, and to the left with a corner unit. Your own arrangement of these units will depend on your needs, your tastes, and the space available. Use your imagination; parts of this system might prove useful wherever you need storage and display space.

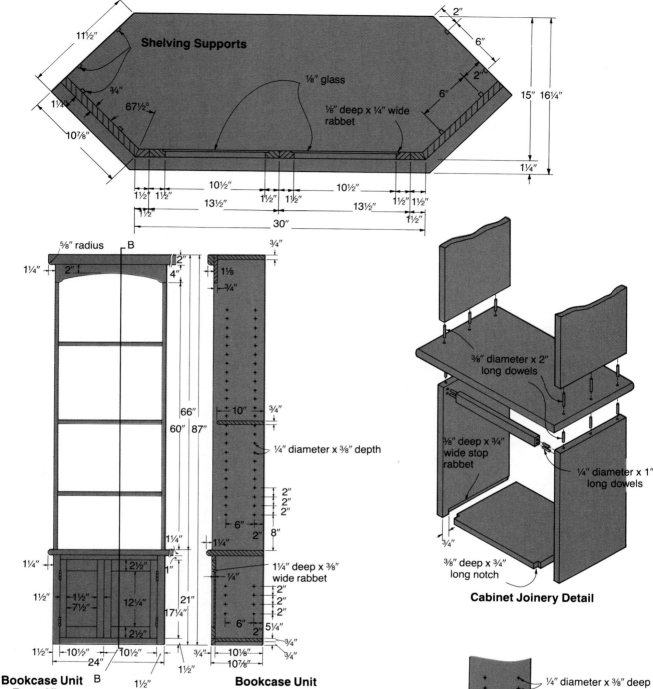

Shelving Supports

⅛" glass

⅛" deep x ¼" wide rabbet

⅝" radius

B

**Bookcase Unit
Front View**

**Bookcase Unit
Section B**

¼" diameter x ⅜" depth

1¼" deep x ⅜" wide rabbet

⅜" diameter x 2" long dowels

⅜" deep x ¾" wide stop rabbet

¼" diameter x 1" long dowels

⅜" deep x ¾" long notch

Cabinet Joinery Detail

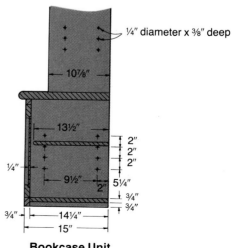

¼" diameter x ⅜" deep

**Bookcase Unit
Section B – Alternative Cabinet Base**

Remember that when you place two units next to each other, they *share* a single side panel. For example, in Ethan's arrangement, the right side of the corner cabinet unit is also the left side of a display shelving unit. Don't make units with independent side panels and try to butt them together. Once you've drawn up the arrangement you want, the entire wall system will have to be built and installed as a single piece of cabinetry.

Also remember that although the units don't touch the floor, they do butt up against the ceiling. As drawn here, they will butt up against an 8-foot ceiling and float 9 inches off the floor. Depending on the height of your ceiling, you may want to adjust the vertical dimensions. You may also want to adjust the distance from the floor to the base of the units, depending on what has to sit under the wall system.

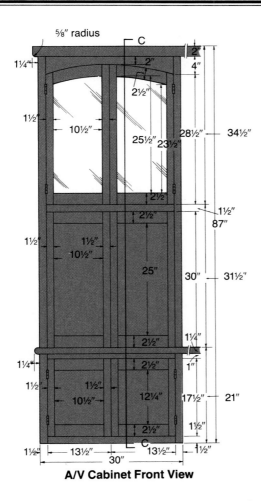

A/V Cabinet Front View

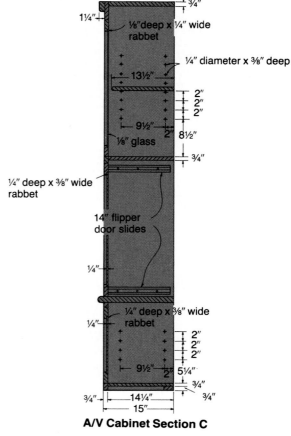

A/V Cabinet Section C

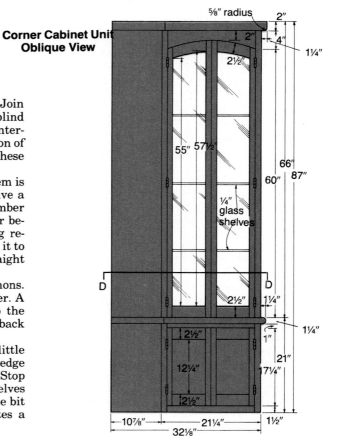

Corner Cabinet Unit Oblique View

Building the units

Construction of the various units is relatively simple. Join tops and bottoms of the cabinets to the sides with blind rabbets, and dowel upper and lower sides to the counter-top. The A/V cabinet, corner cabinet, and lower portion of the bookcase are fitted with front frames. Dowel these frames together, and fit them with flush doors.

Perhaps the trickiest part of making the wall system is in building and fitting the doors. Flush doors can give a craftsman fits unless you use *absolutely* straight lumber for the rails and stiles. Carefully inspect this lumber before *and* after you machine it. Sawing and jointing relieves internal pressures in a board, which may cause it to bow after it's cut, even though it was perfectly straight beforehand.

Join the rails and stiles with slot mortises and tenons. Make this joint on your table saw, using a dado cutter. A simple tenoning jig helps keep the work square to the cutter. Glue rails and stiles together, then rabbet the back of the door frames to accept a panel or glass.

Lines of all the units are elegantly simple; there is little decoration. If you wish, however, round over the front edge of the shelves and the inside edge of the door frames. Stop the cutter 1 inch before you reach the ends of the shelves or the corners of the door frames; leave this last little bit square. The transition from round to square creates a

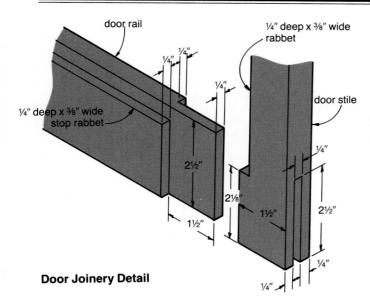

Door Joinery Detail

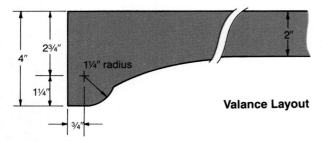

Valance Layout

Locate all structural studs and ceiling joists where the wall system is to be mounted. Screw or bolt the lower cleat to the studs in the wall, as shown in the drawings. Screw the upper cleat to the wall system. Rest the wall system on the lower cleat, and bolt the upper cleat to the wall, then screw the wall system to the lower cleat. Finish installing the system by screwing the top of the units to the ceiling joints. The ceiling screws don't support any weight, but they do keep the upper portions of the units from tipping forward—*by Nick Engler.*

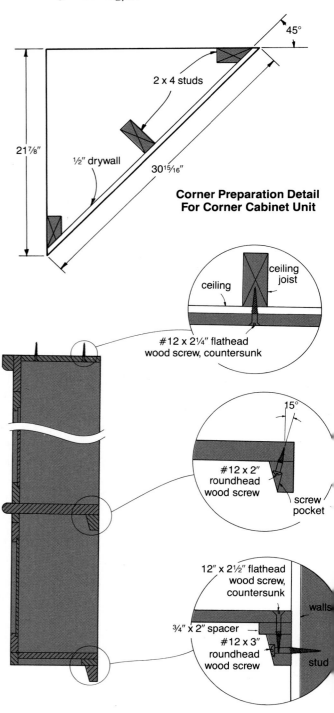

**Corner Preparation Detail
For Corner Cabinet Unit**

Mounting Details

pleasant visual effect, especially when repeated in all the doors and shelves.

Assemble and finish the entire wall system in your workshop. However, *do not* glue the upper sides to the countertop. If the upper portions are detachable from the lower portions, it will be much easier to transport and mount the finished units. To make sure that everything fits, mount the panels and the glass in the doors, then mount the doors to the cabinet frames. Most of these doors are mounted with 2½-inch brass butt hinges and held closed with magnetic "Tutch" latches. The exception is the doors to the middle portion of the A/V cabinet unit. Ethan was afraid that these doors would get in the way if they swung free. So he mounted them on "flipper door" slides. The doors open, then slide back into the cabinet. All the hardware used to build this project is available from The Woodworker's Store, 21801 Industrial Blvd., Rogers, MN 55374.

Mounting the wall system

All four units in the wall system are supported on the wall by cleats. The lower cleat, which supports most of the weight, is one long strip. The upper cleat is cut into segments. Each segment is as long as the width of the unit it supports, so that the cleat will fit between the side panels.

If your wall system includes a corner cabinet unit, you'll need to do drywall work to the corner before you mount the system. Build a simple frame and install a false wall that cuts the corner at 45 degrees, as shown in the drawings. This false wall need only extend from the ceiling to the countertop—it's only purpose is to look good behind the glass doors in the upper portion of the unit.

frame-and-panel oak cabinet

Cabinet borrows styling from an old-fashioned oak icebox, while bookmatched door panels add a strong design interest.

It is finished in varnish without stain, letting the oak quickly take on a natural warm patina.

The warm natural color of oak, sturdy frame-and-panel design, and old-fashioned brass "ice box" hardware combine to give this cabinet an honest, timeless look. I designed it with flexibility in mind. Right now, it stands behind a sofa, holding my son's toys. When he gets older, I can evict his toys, then rearrange the adjustable shelving inside and convert it to a hi-fi or china cabinet.

The cabinet's dimensions can be modified to suit your needs. That's one of the beauties of building your own furniture: You can custom-tailor your work.

Construction

Although this cabinet may seem complicated at first glance, it is really quite simple to build. Start by cutting

out parts for the front and back frames from solid ¾-inch oak. Use lap joints throughout. You can cut them with a router, or with a dado blade on a table or radial arm saw. Note that the stiles, or vertical members, lap in front of the rails (horizontal members), and that they extend down past the bottom rail to create feet. These will later be covered by decorative false feet and connected by a skirt. Cut the rabbets in all four end stiles before assembling the frame. Cut the dadoes for the panels in the rear frame parts with a ¼-inch straight bit in your router.

Once the frame parts are cut, glue and clamp the front frame together. Make sure all parts are square as you snug up on the clamps (Fig. 1).

While the front frame is drying, cut out the panels for the rear frame. If your cabinet will stand against a wall or

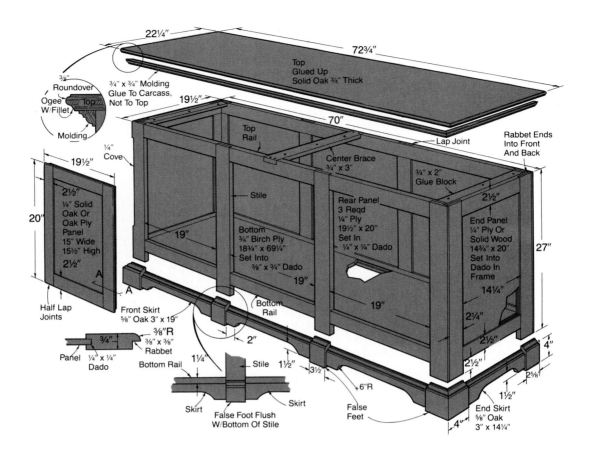

a sofa, you can save time and money and use ¼-inch lauan plywood for the panels. But if the back will be visible, you might want to use oak plywood or even fancy bookmatched panels of solid oak, which I'll cover in a moment.

After your panels are cut, dry-fit the back frame together with its panels to make sure everything fits. Then glue the frame together with the panels free to float in their frames as humidity levels rise and fall.

Make your end frames and panels next. I used bookmatched panels of solid oak for these. To make a matched panel, select a piece of nicely figured ¾-inch oak half as wide as your finished panel width. Very carefully slice it in half edgewise right down the center (Fig. 2). I used a bandsaw for this, but you can also use a table saw and handsaw. Raise the blade as far as it will go, and rip the board down the center of one edge. Flip the board and rip the other edge, too. Depending upon the width of your panels, these two kerfs will probably not be deep enough to meet. So, finish off your cut with a handsaw.

Once the board is cut, flip it open like a book and glue the two pieces together edge to edge (Fig. 3). Let the glue dry, then plane the entire panel down to ¼-inch thickness. *Important:* Take as little wood as possible off the front face of the panel. If the panel is still too thick, plane the rest off the rear face. The more stock you take off the face, the more the grain pattern will change. And as it changes, you'll start to lose the symmetry of grain you want in a bookmatched panel.

Once panels are ready, glue up end frames with panels floating in place as you did with the cabinet back.

Assembling the carcase

Simply glue the ends into the rabbets cut in the front and back frames. I used a rabbet joint at this point for three reasons: It helps align the parts, adds a bit more strength

than a plain butt joint, and, most important, it hides the end grain in the stiles.

False feet, skirt, and top

Cut these out of oak, rout as shown in the plans, and glue in place (Fig. 4). These parts give the cabinet a solid-looking base, with feet thicker than skirt for stability. Since my cabinet back is concealed, I didn't carry them all the way around the back of the cabinet.

I glued my top up from solid oak and then routed the edge. You can also use ¾-inch oak veneer plywood instead, but if you do, band the plywood with 1 × 2 oak mitered at the corners. This will hide the plies and give you solid wood that you can edge-rout for a finished look.

Undertop molding

The molding is fastened to the cabinet carcase just beneath the top. Take an oak board a few inches longer than your cabinet. Put a classical edge-forming bit in your router and use it to rout one edge of your board. Set your table saw to rip at ¾ of an inch, and rip off the edge you

just routed. This will give you a perfect ¾-by-¾-inch classical molding. Rout the edge of the board again, and rip off another molding. Repeat one more time and you'll have enough for the whole job.

Miter your finished moldings and glue them in place on the cabinet carcase, their top edges dead flush with the top edge of the cabinet frame (Fig. 5).

Shelf supports

With the top still off, drill all front and rear stiles with a ¼-inch bit to accept spade-type shelf support brackets. Use a piece of scrap wood as a hole layout pattern. Drill it with a straight row of holes spaced evenly one inch apart. Stand the pattern inside the cabinet with its row of holes centered on a stile, then clamp in place and drill your shelf support holes right through the holes drilled in the pattern (Fig. 6). Repeat this for the other seven front and rear stiles. *Note:* Put a stop on your bit so you won't drill all the way through the stiles. I made my own stop by drilling through a length of ¾-inch dowel, then cutting the dowel off so only ¼ inch of the bit stuck through it.

Mounting the top

The top is fastened to the carcase with screws driven up through a ¾-by-3-inch center brace, which is glued and screwed inside the cabinet (Fig. 7), and ¾-by-2-inch blocks, glued one at either end. If your top is solid wood it must be free to swell and contract with changes in humidity, or splitting will result. Therefore, the screw at the center of each support block is a snug fit, while the screws at the ends pass through slots in the blocks and have washers under their heads. As the top moves with the weather, these screws can slide in their slots. They'll still hold the top down flat and prevent warping, but will allow it to swell and shrink as needed.

No such precautions are necessary for a plywood top, which is dimensionally stable.

Doors

These are made pretty much like the cabinet ends, with bookmatched panels (Fig. 8). If you have a plate joinery machine, you can use it for the door and speed things along. I used lap joints just like those in the cabinet frames. Doors are the ⅜-inch overlay type, and the edges

have ⅜-inch-square rabbets and overlap the door openings. This makes the edges of the doors look slimmer, and also makes end grain in the door frames invisible.

For hardware, I used solid bass ice box fittings. You can get these from Renovator's Supply, Millers Falls, MA 01349. Do not install your hardware yet, however. Finishing comes first.

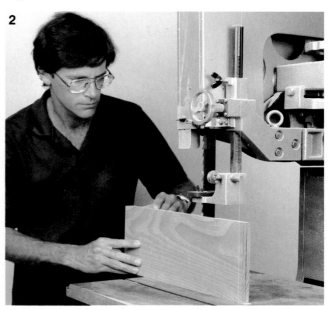

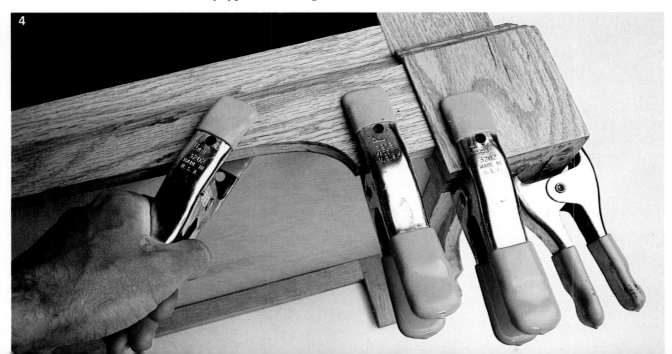

5

8

6

7

Finishing

If you have access to a good spray gun, lacquer is the fastest and easiest route to a good finish. But varnish provides a richer, more durable finish. Avoid the temptation to stain. Your oak may look a bit pale and characterless at first, but in a matter of months your cabinet will mellow to a deep warm glow you could never get with a stain. The secret is a minimum of three coats, with careful sanding in between.

Start by sanding everything with 120 grit paper. Next, brush on a coat of McCloskey Tungseal. Let this set up until it is good and dry, then sand the whole project with 220 grit paper.

Now switch to a good alkyd varnish, which is easier to apply, easier to sand, and easier to repair than polyurethane varnish. I like McCloskey's Heirloom semi-gloss for all but the last coat, for which I use the same varnish in a slightly flatter eggshell finish.

Brush on a coat of varnish and let dry for at least a day. Lay your doors down flat, face up. This will eliminate any possibility of drips and sags. When this first coat of varnish has dried, sand lightly with 220 grit and brush on a second coat. Let dry and evaluate the finish. Is it almost perfectly smooth? If so, your next coat should be the last. If not, sand again and apply a third coat of semi-gloss.

How does your finish look now? If it looks good, your final coat should look fantastic. If you like the sheen of the semi-gloss varnish, stick with it for the final coat. For a slightly flatter sheen, switch over to the eggshell.

But before you apply that final coat, sand well with 320 waterproof paper, used wet. Pay special attention to the top, since this is the most prominent part of the cabinet.

Brush on your final coat in a dust-free room and let dry. Mount your hardware and you are just about home. All that remains is your shelving, which should be sized and spaced as needed. I made mine from ¾-inch birch plywood. Oak plywood would be even better—by A.J. Hand. *Drawings by Richard Meyer.*

through-the-wall cabinetry

My dining room seemed spacious when my children were young. The 12-foot-square room held a table and chairs with plenty of elbow room left over.

But the kids have grown up and moved away, and my wife and I have begun to entertain guests at dinner. So I decided to fix up the dining room by adding two display cabinets—17 and 32 inches wide—that hold attractive serving pieces, glassware, and liquor bottles. But the 18-inch-deep cabinets ate up floor space, making the room tight and cluttered. Even

"Before" shot at left graphically illustrates the space you can reclaim with the simple technique of pushing cumbersome cabinets through the wall. Cabinet backs at right protrude through storage wall of the adjacent garage. Because garage is unheated, 1-inch rigid insulation (not shown) was fastened to the cabinets to maintain energy-efficiency.

getting around the 40-by-72-inch dining table was difficult—one cabinet was protruding almost to the back of a chair.

There was only one fast, inexpensive way to increase the floor space without getting rid of the cabinets: Push them through the wall.

Sound crazy? It isn't—it's actually a simple operation. In my house, the wall in back of the cabinets doubled as a storage wall of the adjacent garage. I cut two holes in the wallboard, removed the studs blocking the way, installed framing, rerouted the electrical wiring, and bumped the cabinets through the wall, leaving the cabinet faces flush with the dining-room wall. The cabinets remain accessible, but now they're taking up floor space in the garage instead of in the dining room.

What if your cabinets can't protrude into a garage or utility space? It doesn't matter. You can bump cabinets through any interior partition and even through exterior walls.

The basic steps in bumping a cabinet into another room are the same as those for a garage. The only difference is how you finish the bumped-into area. In an unheated space you'll need to insulate the cabinets. If you push a cabinet into another room, you'll have to disguise the protrusion and even off the wall. For an exterior bump-out you'll need something for the cabinet to be pushed into—in this case, an easy-to-build insulated box that tucks under the eaves.

Begin any of the three bump-outs by cutting a hole through the wall the size of the cabinet, plus a ¼-inch clearance on the top and side jambs to make installation easier. Don't cut away the sole plate, which contributes to the lateral rigidity of the house frame—you may weaken the wall. I recommend keeping the plate for two other reasons: I think raising a cabinet 2 inches off the floor enhances the look of a bump-out. And it lets you replace wall-to-wall carpeting without fuss.

For interior bump-outs, frame the opening for the cabinet with 2 × 4s (see drawing) nailed to the sole plate

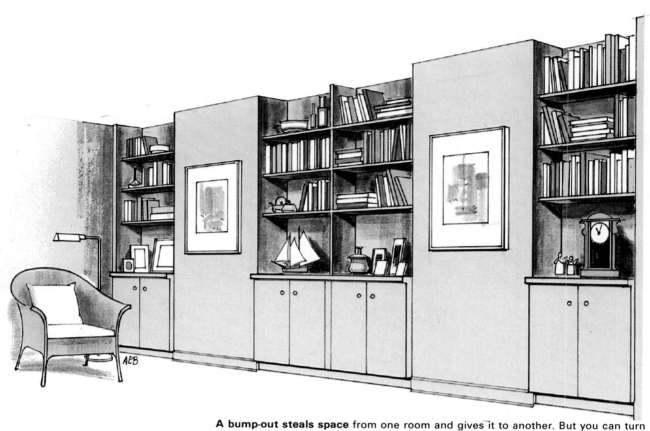

A bump-out steals space from one room and gives it to another. But you can turn that loss to advantage and disguise the protrusions at the same time, as shown above. Install display shelves between cabinets, then cover cabinet backs with paneling or full-length mirrors. Below: No space to bump a cabinet into? Then shove it outside! By tucking the bump-out into existing eaves, you can anchor the frame of the insulated box to the roof rafters.

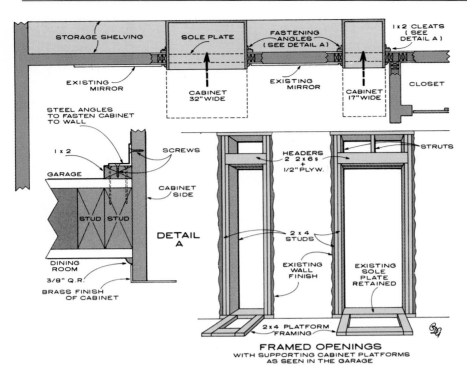

FRAMED OPENINGS
WITH SUPPORTING CABINET PLATFORMS
AS SEEN IN THE GARAGE

For dining room, framing is nailed to the top and sole plates. Be sure to use additional struts for wider bump-outs. Slide the cabinet onto the platform, then fasten 1 × 2 cleats to the top and sides. To anchor the cabinet, screw angles to the cleats and studs.

and bridged by a 2 × 6 header. In the room the cabinet will be bumped into, build a platform from 2 × 4s that's equal to the height of the sole plate. This will ensure that the cabinet is level and that its weight is evenly distributed. A platform serves a second purpose: In an unfinished, unheated garage or utility space, it keeps the cabinet off the floor, partially shielding it from dampness and cold. Finally, slide the cabinet in place, and secure it to the frame with steel angles.

You'll need a sturdier frame to support an exterior bump-out. The frame must bear the weight of the cabinet by attaching to the roof rafters and sole plate. This design means that the depth of the box can't exceed the length of the eave overhang. Use 2 × 4s doubled with 2 × 6s to augment the house frame. In most cases a 2 × 6 header is sufficient, but a wide cabinet and rafters at least 2 feet on center may require a 2 × 8—*by Carl De Groote. Photos by Greg Sharko. Drawings by Adolph Brotman.*

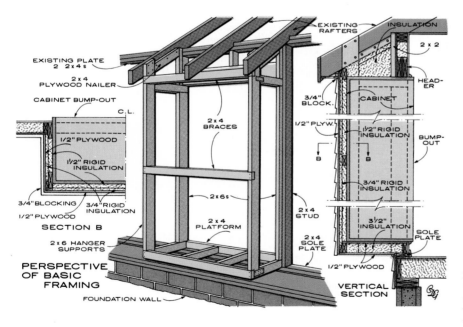

PERSPECTIVE OF BASIC FRAMING

SECTION B

VERTICAL SECTION

For exterior wall, to frame an insulated box for an exterior bump-out, nail horizontal 2 × 4s and ½-inch plywood to the sole plate. Then toenail 2 × 6 hangers. Be sure to add insulation between and over the frame members, then nail on plywood cladding and siding.

For interior partition in an interior bump-out, stagger cabinets' placement so that display shelves fit between protruding backs. You should then use framing studs installed for cabinets to anchor shelves. The space can also be used for enclosed storage closets.

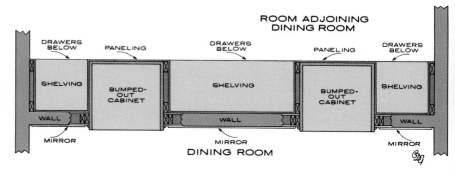

DINING ROOM

knockdown custom storage wall

My needs were urgent and multiple: a variety of drawers and cabinets to organize my storage plus generous shelves to hold toppling stacks of books, with lighted display niches for artifacts brought back from China. I also needed to create a work alcove by means of an L-shaped partition.

My sketches resulted in a structure that looks like a custom built-in for which a cabinetmaker would charge several thousand dollars. Actually, it was quickly assembled for several *hundred* dollars. I used Louisiana-Pacific's Waferwood panels for the vertical partitions to which the whole assembly anchors; standard knockdown kitchen cabinets from Sears; and an L-shaped counter top and shelving of particleboard, faced with Solicor laminate and supported along the front edges by 3/4-inch chrome tubing available at modular-furniture shops. (Unfaced back edges and ends are fastened to the Waferwood with two No. 10 flathead screws driven through its back face.) Both ends of the shelf unit are closed—on the left with a Waferwood panel that flanks a passageway; on the right with a tall two-compartment closet that is framed by 2 × 4s. Exposed Waferwood edges are capped with wooden strips enameled before installation to match the counter-top laminate.

My first inspiration was to scale the unit to available ready-made cabinets. Standard 24-inch-deep base cabinets were ideal along the front, but the other leg of the L ran down a narrow hall, so I couldn't use base cabinets there. Instead, I thought, why not press 1-foot-deep wall cabinets into service? The Sears Tempocraft knockdowns shown range from $65 for the single-door, 2-foot-wide wall cabinet to about $100 for the four-drawer base cabinet.

One problem: The base cabinets stand 34½ inches high, the wall cabinets only 30 inches. But since the latter come with no toe-kick, I'd have to provide a base for them, anyway. So the solution was to set a 2 × 6 on edge, trimmed to bring the top edges of the wall cabinets to the same height as that of the base cabinets. (Cleats screwed along the bottom of the partition panel at the same height lift the backs of these cabinets off the floor.)

Ready-made kitchen cabinets put me ahead in another sense. Even my unfinished knockdowns had prefinished interiors: Side panels, shelves—even the insides of each drawer—had a factory-applied simulated wood-grain facing. And there was another bonus. Wall cabinets usually come with top panels recessed an inch or two. Because my storage wall was erected near my front door, this provided a ready-made cache for storing keys, wallet, and sunglasses. So I hinged the counter-top sections over these two cavities. Note that these

lids have the same thickened front edge as the rest of the counter top. This is created by gluing a ¼-by-¼-inch wood strip along the underside of the ¾-inch substrate before a 1-inch-wide edge laminate is applied.

For help in fabricating the laminate-faced counter top and shelves while I assembled and finished the cabinets (with a single coat of low-luster polyurethane varnish), I called on cabinetmaker and author of several *Popular Science* workshop books, Rosario Capotosto. Ro took the accompanying step-by-step photos showing the making of these panels. The captions tell that story. The best substrate is ¾-inch high-density particleboard, but to avoid any warping it's best to laminate both faces even when only one will show. The exception is the counter top. This is so because the underside will be firmly anchored to the cabinets.

Note that in photo 6 an auxiliary wood fence has been clamped to the saw's fence so the thin laminate won't slip under the gap between the saw fence and the table. In photo 7 the slipsheet method positions the lami-

nate after both it and the particleboard substrate have been coated with special non-pigmented contact cement. The slipsheet is pulled gradually free as contact is made; then the laminate is pressed down firmly with a laminate roller or a wood block struck with a mallet. After the excess is routed flush, the edges are dressed with a fine sanding block (photo 8).

Because the laminating was such an important part of this project, I chose Solicor—one of the new color-clear-through laminates featured in the chapter, "Eight Elegant Edges with Layered Laminates," in this Yearbook. Solicor is a Wilsonart laminate made and sold nationally by Ralph Wilson Plastics Co. (600 General Bruce Dr., Temple, TX 76501-5199). The custom colors shown are Camel and Mandarin Red, the latter chosen because of its association with the Orient.

In assembling the shelves to the supporting partition panels, I had to work up from the counter top because chrome tubes support the outer edges. To create sockets for seating both ends of each tube, I drilled carefully

All five cabinets in counter were brought home in flat cartons from Sears store. Each comes with assembly sheet

author studies. Three front units with drawers are base cabinets, complete except for counter top.

Two shallower units around corner are wall cabinets with hinged lids, raised on baseboard to match counter height.

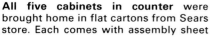

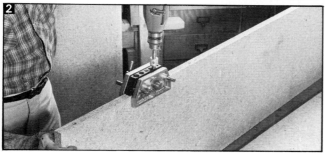

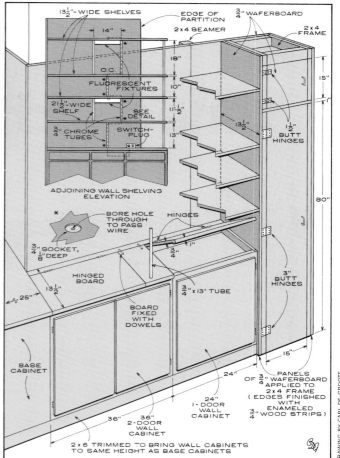

Adjoining wall shelving diagram labels:
13½"-WIDE SHELVES · EDGE OF PARTITION · ¾" WAFERBOARD · 2x4 SEAMER · 2x4 FRAME · 14" · 18" O.C. · FLUORESCENT FIXTURES · 10" · SEE DETAIL · 15" · 1" · 21½"-WIDE SHELF · 11½" · 13½" · 1½" BUTT HINGES · ¾" CHROME TUBES · SWITCH-PLUG · 13" · ADJOINING WALL SHELVING ELEVATION · 80" · BORE HOLE THROUGH TO PASS WIRE · HINGES · ¾" SOCKET, ⅛" DEEP · ¾" · 1" · HINGED BOARD · 13½" · 25" · BOARD FIXED WITH DOWELS · ¾" x 13" TUBE · 3" BUTT HINGES · BASE CABINET · 36" 2-DOOR WALL CABINET · 36" · 24" 1-DOOR WALL CABINET · 24" WALL CABINET · 15" · PANELS OF ¾" WAFERBOARD APPLIED TO 2x4 FRAME (EDGES FINISHED WITH ENAMELED ¾" WOOD STRIPS) · 2 x 6 TRIMMED TO BRING WALL CABINETS TO SAME HEIGHT AS BASE CABINETS

DRAWING BY CARL DE GROOTE

Once cabinets are assembled and finished, they're bolted to each other and lag-screwed to partition panels (1). Note metal corner braces to which counter top will be secured. Doweling jig (2) is essential for drilling matched holes in edges of front shelves and butting ends of side shelves. Dowels are also used to join fixed panel of side counter top to wooden strip along back (3); strip is for hinging particleboard valet-tray lids, also edged with wood at back for better screw-holding. Several passes with carbide-tipped cutter (4) make it easy to snap Solicor panel to size (5) along clamped straightedge. Narrow edging strips must be sawn (6). For tips on slip sheet (7) and corner dressing (8), see text.

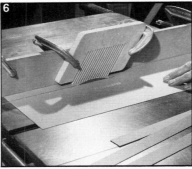

through the attached laminate with a ¾-inch spade bit. Only where indicated in the sketch by asterisks did I drill a smaller hole through the shelf to pass the lamp cord for display lights. Concealing the wires by running them up through the tubes complicates the assembly but is much neater. (Two tubes must be drilled to pass the wire out through the sidewall.)

Each L-shaped shelf is installed as two panels. In my case, each narrow side panel went up first, then dowel pegs were tapped into the holes in its exposed end before the mating front panel was tapped in place over those dowels. I had previously marked the lowest shelf position on the partition panels and drilled through from the back and end panels, countersinking for the No. 10 flathead screws that are driven into the edges. The vertical dimensions shown are for a ceiling just over 8 feet high—*by Al Lees. Color photos by Greg Sharko. Black-and-white Photos by Rosario Capotosto. Drawing by Carl De Groote.*

zoned kitchen built-ins

What room do homeowners upgrade first, once they decide to hang on to their current homes in light of new-housing costs and scarcity? A half-dozen American polls all say "the kitchen." So *Popular Science* went in search of a professional design specialist in this area (the coveted industry accreditation is CKD after your name, for Certified Kitchen Designer).

I knew I'd found the right pro when I heard Ellen Cheever lecture on kitchen trends, pointing out that in today's double-career households the notion of the kitchen as the Woman's Place is absurdly outdated. Though in most homes the woman remains in charge here, she's increasingly helped out by her spouse—particularly when guests are to be entertained. In some cases this is little more than the barbecue chef moving indoors, once the patio-party season is over. But most men, the surveys confirm, want a place in the kitchen where they can function without colliding with the principal cook.

So I asked Ellen Cheever, CKD (who operates her own renovation firm out of Sacramento but doubles as design director of Maytag's Kitchen Idea Center in Newton, Iowa), to research the typical homeowner, choose a typical outdated kitchen layout, and design a kitchen that could be built out of any home workshop.

After months of consultation and some help from designers at Armstrong World Industries, we came up with the floor plan and cabinet/appliance layout shown on these pages. You can build several of the key units in your own shop.

Our plan opens up the kitchen (within the same basic floor space) to provide side-by-side work areas that don't overlap. The man's domain, especially the work island—as well as the drink-mixing bar, covered in the following chapter—is scaled to his greater average height to avoid uncomfortable stooping. All major work areas—food-preparation sinks, cooking appliances, and refrigeration

Guests for dinner—so this home's two cooks collaborate in a spacious kitchen that offers them duplicate work areas, without overlap. In the photo below she's at the main range—Maytag's downdraft, which is vented down through the floor, so needs no hood for its surface cooker, grill, or oven. He's popping vegetables into his own microwave. In the photo at right she's placing dessert in the main freezer while he digs into his own ice maker. On the next page she's at her double sink while he's busy at a work island (with a higher counter surface to compensate for his height); the island has a separate sink.

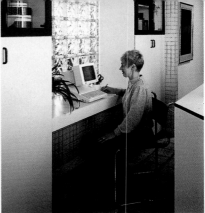

Zoned built-ins include, above-right, a broad work space for an Apple home computer, cookbooks, and household records. Typical of the convenience built into the cabinets: The folding ironing board stows behind a false drawer front. Also included is a NuTone Food Center in the surface of the work island. Recessed power head drives the sharpener.

units—are duplicated, in reduced versions, for the secondary cook. To see how this arrangement avoids traffic jams, check the before-and-after floor plans at far left.

Even if you're not ready to tackle a complete remodeling of your kitchen, you'll find many ideas tucked into this one that can be put to work in your home. To highlight a few of them that aren't covered in captions:

● Traffic flow through the kitchen shouldn't cross a work triangle. We improved the flow through the original floor plan by moving the back door to the left. The redundant dining table was discarded because, in reorganizing the home's space, an adjacent dining area was created. Part of

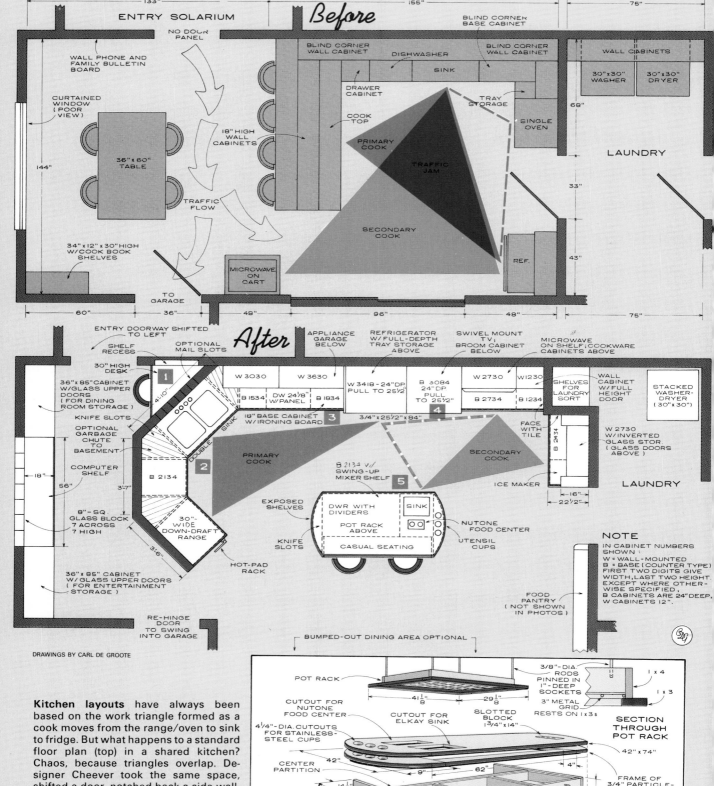

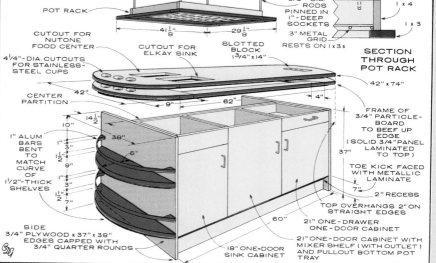

Kitchen layouts have always been based on the work triangle formed as a cook moves from the range/oven to sink to fridge. But what happens to a standard floor plan (top) in a shared kitchen? Chaos, because triangles overlap. Designer Cheever took the same space, shifted a door, notched back a side wall, and rearranged counters and appliances to provide separate work triangles for both cooks. Not only is there no overlap —look at the steps saved between appliances! The adjacent laundry can be smaller because a stacked unit takes half the floor space of a separate washer and dryer. The work island sketched at right can be built around three purchased base cabinets, or build your own. Pots hang from overhead rack on S-hooks.

78

1. For the location of the features in the photos, see key numbers on the "after" floor plan. The phone niche's unit has a built-in message cassette.

2. The shelves and wastebasket in the sink all slide out for easy access. In usually wasted space in front of the basins, a tip-out bin stows cleaning items.

3. On back of the wall-cabinet door is a spice rack with adjustable shelves; below it is an appliance garage.

4. Next to the fridge is a cabinet for bulky cleaning items. It supports a swivel-mount TV. Over the fridge is a full-depth cabinet with a rack for trays.

5. Cabinets in the island have a pull-up mixer shelf and divided drawer.

the original door frame was utilized as a shelf access above the triangular phone desk.

● Counter space was expanded into the area gained, and a wraparound effect was achieved to cut the distance between the range and sink. The backsplash panels around and between the sink cabinet and range were framed with 2 × 4s and ¾-inch plywood.

● We chose Wood-Mode custom cabinets because they offer so many convenience options, but you can salvage existing cabinets or build your own—equipping them with many of the built-in features shown here. The hardware and slides are available by mail (see list of participating manufacturers included).

● All cabinet doors and exposed sides were faced with the same almond-tone plastic laminate applied to the counter tops. The edges were trimmed in a dark-blue laminate to match the ceramic tile. Wood strips ¾ inch wide were enameled a matching color and tacked along the tops of all the cabinets to tie the assembly together.

● A dropped acoustical ceiling mutes kitchen clatter. Before it's installed, support rods for the pot rack are firmly secured up through the grid system; tiles above the work island are pierced to fit around these rods—*by Al Lees. Photos by Carl Vernlund. Drawings by Carl De Groote.*

PARTICIPATING MANUFACTURERS

The following manufacturers were chosen by Popular Science for participation in this project: **Amana Refrigeration,** Amana, IA 52204 (TC-20G refrigerator-freezer); **Apple Computer,** 20525 Mariani Ave., Cupertino, CA 95014 (Apple IIc system); **Armstrong World Industries,** Lancaster, PA 17604 (Floor tile: Glazecraft Center Square in cream with blue-gray accents; Ceiling tile: Chandelier Pebblewood, installed with an Easy Up kit); **Dal-Tile Corp.,** 7834 Haway Freeway, Dallas, TX 75217 (4½-inch-square tile for backsplash and corner column); **Elkay Mfg. Co.,** 2222 Camden Ct., Oak Brook, IL 60521 (stainless-steel sinks and faucets); **GE Consumer Electronics,** Syracuse, NY 13221 (Space-maker undercabinet radio/cassette player/clock timer); **Maytag Co.,** 403 W. Fourth St. N., Newton, IA 50208 (30 inch slide-in downdraft grill-range, touch-control dishwasher, CME-700 microwave); **NuTone,** Madison & Red Bank, Cincinnati, OH 45227 (Food Center with counter-top power head, knife sharpener, blender); **Scotsman,** Albert Lea, MN 56007 (15-inch Auto Ice Maker); **Uniden Corp.,** 6345 Castleway Ct., Indianapolis, IN 46250 (Extend-A-Phone 1035 with message cassette); **Wood-Mode Cabinetry,** Kreamer, PA 17833 (Vanguard custom cabinets).

The latest feature in most redesigned kitchens is an "appliance garage"—closable counter-top storage for portables like toasters, blenders, and irons. The one in photo 3 can be easily built (sketch at right), cutting the groove with a router. The tambour door could be one of the new laminates or traditional wood. The box has no bottom so appliances can slide in and out.

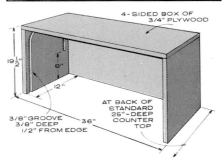

4-SIDED BOX OF ¾" PLYWOOD

19½"

8"

12"

36"

AT BACK OF STANDARD 25"-DEEP COUNTER TOP

⅜" GROOVE ⅜" DEEP ½" FROM EDGE

build in a service bar

Unit above is at one end of the open kitchen featured in the previous chapter.

A host needs elbow room to keep guests supplied with refreshments—and to select the wine and glasses for the dinner table. This unit organizes everything in one self-sufficient serving center. It even sports its own ice maker—a 15-inch undercounter model from Scotsman (Albert Lea, MN 56007). There's a base cabinet with a drawer and two doors, plus a glass-doored wall cabinet to display glassware and trays.

The floating upper cabinet is doubly anchored—to the back wall and to the compartmented wine towers that flank it. Beneath this cabinet are racks that take the wide bases of stemware. (Storing glasses upside down is not only attractive, it protects them from dust and breakage.)

The service bar in the photo and sketch was built around two ready-made Vanguard units from Wood-Mode Cabinetry (Kreamer, PA 17833), but you can build your own, rabbeting the door frames of the upper cabinet to take either glass or acrylic panes. If you don't want the ice maker, replace it with another storage cabinet.

The counter top is bulked up with two ¾-inch layers to present a 1½-inch edge. The easiest way to achieve this is to attach a solid panel of particleboard to a frame of 6-inch-wide pieces of lumber or plywood. This assembly is then anchored in the usual way to the top of the base cabinet (with screws up through the corner braces), but it must be supported at its right end by a ¾-inch plywood panel. You'll probably also want to support its back edge with a wall cleat or metal angles.

The two wine towers are identical: They're four-sided boxes with no front or back, but with seven equally spaced inner shelves. Assemble with glue and finishing nails, fastening each bottle cradle in place before adding the shelf above it. Set all nailheads slightly below the surface, and cap with wood dough, sanding it flush for painting.

Finishing? You'll want to match your unit to its setting. It will look as

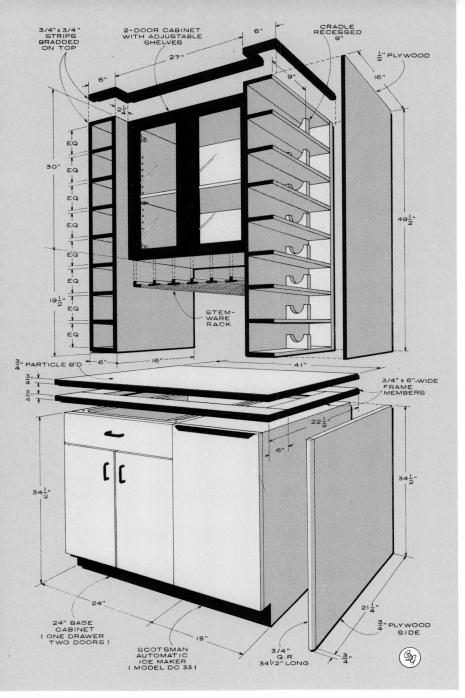

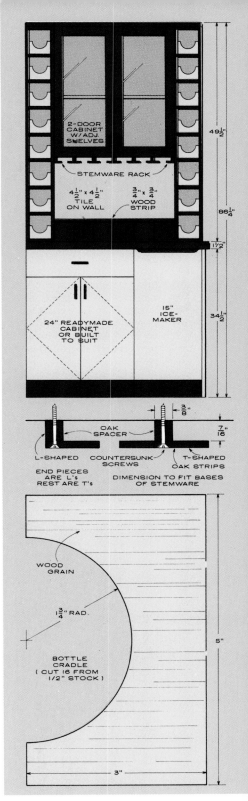

much at home in the corner of a dining room or den as it does in this open kitchen. For the prototype, we applied an almond-colored plastic laminate to the counter top, then capped the edges with dark-blue laminate strips. The counter-top laminate should lap the edge laminate, not vice versa. You cut it oversize, snug the edge strips against its underside, then trim the projection flush with a router.

It's easier to laminate the counter top before the wine towers are in place. They simply rest on top of it and are fastened to the wall behind with L-brackets or cleats. The edges of the wine bins and the door frames of the cabinet that's hung between the bins are painted to match the counter-

top-edge laminate. When assembly is complete, 3/4-inch-square wood strips are mitered as shown, painted to match, and bradded on top to tie the components together visually.

Because we were matching the unit to its kitchen setting, we used a tile backsplash at the rear of the counter, cementing a row of ceramic tile to the wall between the wine towers. We capped the row with a wood strip painted to match, but this could be replaced with a shallow shelf for such packaged bar foods as olives, maraschino cherries, and nuts. Other bar supplies—jiggers, strainers, ice tongs—are kept in the drawer—*by Al Lees. Photo by Carl Vernlund. Drawings by Carl De Groote.*

Above: tipped template for the cradle that's glued and bradded across each of the 16 compartments, 9 inches from the front edge. This slants the bottles forward so wine stays against the cork to prevent drying. Blow the template up to full size in a photo enlarger, or redraw it on cardboard to the dimensions shown. Top sketch shows how to glue and screw hardwood strips and spacers on the underside of the glass-doored cabinet to form stemware racks.

butcher-block carving table

Some craftsmen are often dismayed that a piece of store-bought furniture costs less than raw materials to duplicate it. But the value of a homemade butcher-block table can greatly exceed the cost of materials—and the quality will surpass that of anything you can get in a furniture store.

Traditional end-grain butcher-block tables instantly convey the impression that the builder has excep-tional expertise. Yet, if a few simple procedures are followed, the job is quick. It's also wise to save the templates you make. I started out by building one for my daughter-in-law —but this one is number nine.

Handsome butcher-block carving table, in maple, combines traditional design elements with modern conveniences such as handy slots for knives, a shelf, and casters for easy moving.

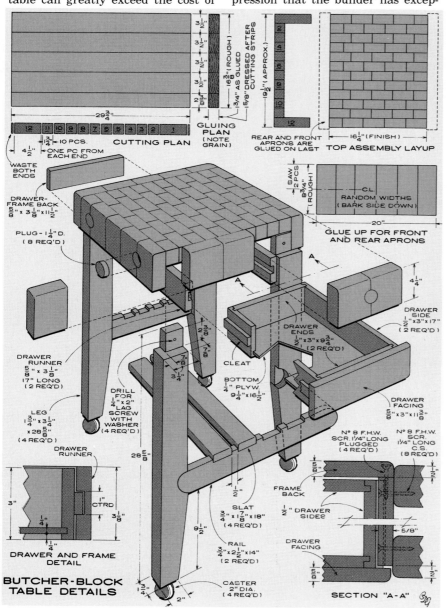

Try to buy your wood from a hard-wood-lumber specialist. You'll pay less and have a better selection than you would at a lumberyard. Hard maple is the traditional material for end-grain butcher blocks. Avoid the "ring porous" woods such as oak because it's hard to seal the end grain. Select clear planks that are free from brownish streaks. Tell the clerk that you want eight-quarter material (minimum 1¾ inches thick) in 60-inch lengths.

Maple machines well, but more slowly than many other woods, so sharpen your tools and tune your machines. It's especially important that your jointer knives are sharp because you'll be dressing across the side grain and you want to avoid "crack out" at the end of the cuts without having to turn the stock.

The next step is to rip and dress the edges of the top wood. Be careful here because this is the point at which you determine the ultimate beauty of the top. Lay the pieces on a bench and examine the end grain. Shuffle the pieces around to get the most pleasing grain pattern. You should aim for a sinuous pattern that flows, as nearly as possible, from edge to edge without interruption.

Have everything ready for gluing before you start. A dry run to adjust the clamps is a smart idea. Use a yellow aliphatic glue such as Elmer's Professional or Titebond. Apply the glue to both surfaces, and flatten the bead with a thin paddle. Plenty of clamps and only moderate pressure should squeeze out glue along every line.

Detach the clamps after an hour or so—before the squeezed-out glue has completely dried. Remove most of the excess glue with a scraper. Now draw a diagonal pencil line across the top of the panel. This will make it easy to maintain the orientation of the segments after they're cut off.

Cut off a 4½-inch apron piece from one end, and reset the saw's fence for cutting the center segments. The last piece to come off is the 4½-inch blank for the opposite apron. You'll have to reset the fence twice, but you'll be maintaining the grain pattern and getting a smooth color gradation.

As the pieces come off the saw, lay them on the bench in their original order. The diagonal line will tell you whether you have mixed up the pieces. Number one end of each piece, and underline each number. Then rotate the pieces clockwise so each underline is on your left. Next, flip alternate segments 180 degrees so their

marked ends face the opposite direction. You'll now have the underline on the left on both sides of your assembly, with all numbers in sequence—odd on one side, even on the other (see drawing). This procedure gives an interesting, repetitive pattern.

Dress the sides of the segments and aprons in the jointer to clean off the glue and form a good surface for adhesion. Small variations in individual segment thickness won't matter.

Now glue the top. It's best to glue the center pieces first and add the aprons later. Make sure the wood is protected from clamping marks. You'll save aggravation and sanding belts if you again take the assembled panel out of the clamps and scrape off the squeezed-out glue before it's set.

The procedure for building the front and rear aprons is similar to that employed for the rest of the top (see drawing). With the end aprons in place, do your first rough sanding on the top. Knock down the remaining glue, and partially level the top. This will give you a flat surface to ride against the fence as you joint the edges smooth and flush. Now glue on the front and rear aprons.

Set the completed butcher-block assembly up on its side to let the glue dry. Then joint the sides, and trim the bottom on the table saw. Drill 1¼-inch-diameter holes in the apron sides, and insert tapered circular maple plugs.

Sanding the top

With this large a panel you can make the end grain as smooth as glass. Level the top, working down from coarse to fine sanding belts. A high-speed (4,000 rpm) disc sander with a sponge-backed wheel from an auto-paint store does a fast, smooth job on end grain. Eighty-grit paper on the wheel quickly removes any scratches left by the belt sander. However, some work with the orbital sander is still required to remove the glazed effect of unidirectional sanding.

Legs

That semi-circular pocket for the shelf support makes a strong and good-looking joint. It's easy to make, too. First you'll need a simple plywood template. Using a fly cutter on the drill press, cut a round hole, sized to produce a 2½-inch circle when used with a template follower on your router; this is the pocket template. Then, using this template, cut a hole in a piece of hardboard; this becomes the template you'll use to mark the ends of the shelf supports.

Clamp two leg blanks together, edge to edge, and mark them out for the bottom taper and the pocket position. Now clamp the plywood template down, centered over the pocket position. A couple of small finishing nails driven through the template and about ¼ inch into the wedge-shaped waste will make sure the template doesn't move as you make successive cuts with the router to bring the pocket depth to ¾ inch.

When you cut the tops of the legs, be careful! They are rights and lefts. It would be simple to cut the wrong way and wind up with three lefts instead of two.

Turn the top upside-down on the workbench and clamp a pair of legs in place. Leave about ⅛ inch clearance on each side. With the legs carefully squared to the top, measure for the shelf support length. When you make the supports, it's best to cut the dadoes in a double thickness piece and then split it. This way you'll be sure your slots will be perfectly in line.

Now put that hardboard circle to work in marking for the pocketed ends. If you saw and sand to the *outside* of your pencil line you are assured of a perfect fit. It helps, too, to set the table of the sander at a one-degree angle so the support ends have a slight taper.

Not only must the legs be perfectly parallel, their ends must be square with each other. Apply glue to the pockets, insert the support, and clamp the ends lightly. Bar clamps across the legs, above and below the supports, will permit you to adjust parallelism as you pull the supports tightly into their pockets. Check end squareness before you tighten the gluing clamps. Masking tape under the pockets will save you a messy cleanup as glue runs down over the wood.

When the glue dries, clamp the leg assemblies into the top and install the slats. Cut them just a little long, round the corners and glue them in place. Again, a couple of strips of masking tape under the dadoes will save cleanup.

Drawer frame

The drawer frame is a simple "U" with the sides grooved to take a cleat that is glued onto the drawer sides. Measure over the legs on the outside and cut the frame sides an inch shorter. The side and rear frames are fastened in place with screws; cut maple plugs for the screw heads in the rear frame piece.

The drawer has softwood sides and a ⅝-inch-thick applied maple front. The structure shown on the drawing is sound, and very simple to make. Then you can make a handy and protective rack for your carving knives by cutting single saw grooves 1¼ inches apart as shown in the illustration.

Finishing

Lightly sand the entire job, and you're ready for finishing. The exposed end grain in this piece will cause the top to shift if the bottom is not sealed against humidity, so the very first finishing job is to *thoroughly* seal the underside. Use commercial sealers, shellac, or thinned varnish. Then permanently install the leg assembly.

Because the top surface will drink a tremendous amount of finishing oil, partially seal it with a light coat of vinyl penetrating sealer (I ordered mine from Craftsman Wood Service), then apply a coat of sanding sealer to the aprons and legs. Follow the sanding sealer with a couple of coats of varnish, and you're ready to put the top finish on and *into* the wood.

You may be tempted to use salad or vegetable oils on the top: Don't—they never dry. Don't use salad-bowl finishes, varnish, or other surface finishes either, because they will chip and show knife marks. Carefully sand the top to bare wood (the penetrating sealer will be far down in the pores), and apply a clear finishing oil, like Watco Danish oil. Let your first coat cure a couple of days, then apply a coat each day until the surface won't absorb any more. These finishes contain toxic solvents, so wait at least a week before allowing food to contact the top. Install the casters.

Your butcher-block table top is now ready to withstand years of slicing without showing knife marks. It will be used and treasured by your children, too—assuming they haven't already prevailed on you to make duplicates for their own kitchens—*by Cy Wedlake. Photos by Jim Wedlake. Drawing by Carl De Groote.*

dual-sink vanity and lighting valance

Side-by-side sinks facing twin oak-framed mirrors make a handsome solution to early-morning bathroom skirmishes. Suspended between two walls, the vanity slab can support 400 pounds, if constructed to technical artist Carl De Groote's specs. The matching valance, which De Groote rates at 220 pounds, is sturdy enough for heavy plants and storage of little-used items.

Papering the front of both vanity and valance to match the wall gives the units a custom-designed look. And you can use standard lumber for the aprons. Cabinet-grade birch plywood is used for the vanity top and valance bottom, however.

Construction is straightforward. First build the two plywood slabs, then cut holes in the valance slab to match the recessed ceiling light fixtures you've bought. Cut holes in the vanity slab for the lavatory and the plumbing lines, then rough-in the plumbing. Divert the supply and drain lines through the wall, as shown in the drawing.

Now start papering. Wallpapering the back and side walls before installing the vanity and valance will save fussy fitting, but this is true only if you're sure you can mount the units without damaging the paper. Two prepasted scrubbable and strippable coordinating wall coverings from the

Benchmark Naturally Collection (National Gypsum Co., 128 Corporate Pl., Wakefield, MA 01880) were used here.

Next, mount the valance back and sides, securing the 1 × 6s and 1 × 8s to the studs with 2½-inch No. 8 roundhead screws. Join them at the corners with vertical cleats fastened by 1½-inch No. 7 flathead screws. Use the same screws for the rest of the valance, to secure the center cleats that support a 1 × 8 brace and to fasten horizontal cleats around the frame for attaching the apron and bottom.

Construct the vanity the same way, then make the oak mirror frames. Finish all exposed wood, including the

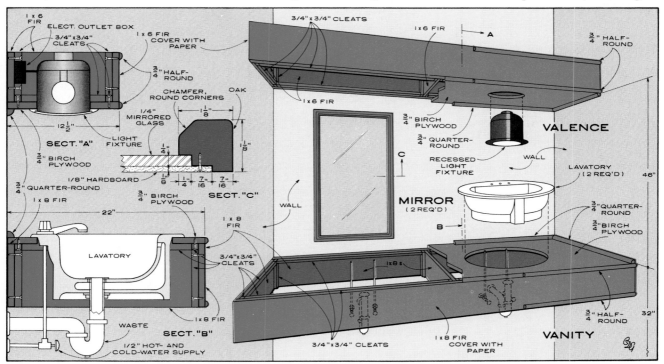

pine molding stained to match the birch plywood, with a low-luster polyurethane sealer.

Now paint or prime the aprons to smooth them before applying wallpaper. Apply wallpaper strips to the front of both units, then fasten the stained pine trim strips as shown.

Finally, insert the light fixtures into the valence, drop the sinks into the vanity, make electrical and plumbing hookups, mount the mirrors—and enjoy elbow-room grooming in the morning—*by Susan Renner-Smith. Drawings by Carl De Groote.*

storage for split-level sleeping

Terry Penn faced a familiar problem—how to cram beds, toys, clothes, and play space for two active children into one small room. "My objective was to design and build something compact with plenty of storage space—and still have room for play," he says. His solution: use a number of familiar tricks to create a unique set of built-ins.

Each of the room's components—the corner cabinet, loft bed, captain's bed with drawers, and understairs bins—are common space-stretching ploys. Unified in a harmonious design, they create a multi-use area with ample storage. What's more, the built-ins both liberate existing space and create more for play.

The multilevel platform provides extra play space, and its two hidden hatches stow toys and games. The stepped platform also separates the two beds so each child has a small private space.

Angling a captain's bed out from under a loft bed saves almost as much space as bunk beds would—without producing the cramped, airless feeling of a lower bunk. And the deep drawers in the lower bed add more needed storage for clothes and bed linens, as well.

"I used particleboard, plywood, and common moldings for the construction," Penn says. "The room has held together very well after more than a year of use—and abuse." His major expense was the professionally installed carpeting—*by Susan Renner-Smith. Illustrations by Eugene Thompson.*

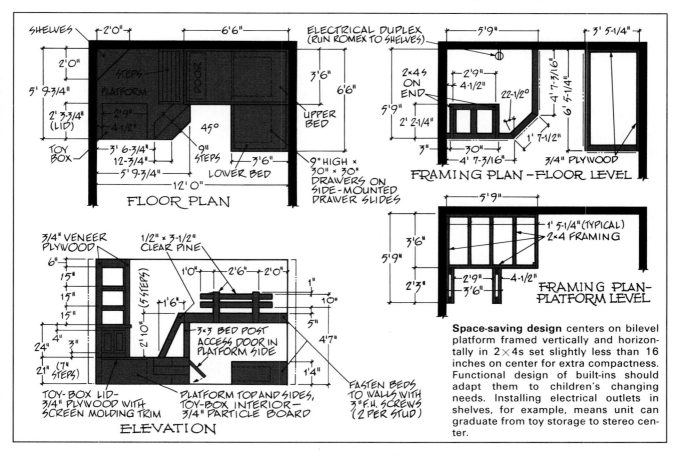

Space-saving design centers on bilevel platform framed vertically and horizontally in 2×4s set slightly less than 16 inches on center for extra compactness. Functional design of built-ins should adapt them to children's changing needs. Installing electrical outlets in shelves, for example, means unit can graduate from toy storage to stereo center.

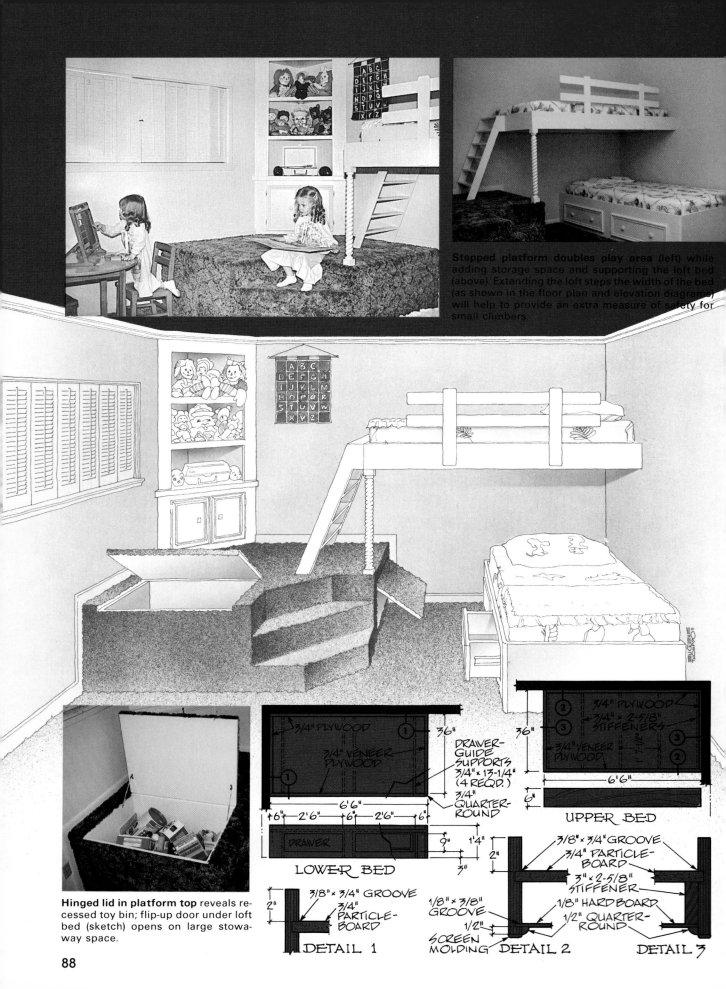

Stepped platform doubles play area (left) while adding storage space and supporting the loft bed (above). Extending the loft steps the width of the bed (as shown in the floor plan and elevation diagrams) will help to provide an extra measure of safety for small climbers.

Hinged lid in platform top reveals recessed toy bin; flip-up door under loft bed (sketch) opens on large stowaway space.

LOWER BED

3/4" PLYWOOD
36"
3/4" VENEER PLYWOOD
DRAWER-GUIDE SUPPORTS 3/4" × 13-1/4" (4 REQD.)
3/4" QUARTER-ROUND
6'6"
6" 2'6" 6" 2'6" 6"
DRAWER
9" 1'4"
3"

UPPER BED

3/4" PLYWOOD
2
3/4" × 2-5/8" STIFFENERS
36"
3
3/4" VENEER PLYWOOD
6'6"
6"

DETAIL 1

3/8" × 3/4" GROOVE
3/4" PARTICLE-BOARD
2"

DETAIL 2

1/8" × 3/8" GROOVE
1/2"
SCREEN MOLDING

DETAIL 3

3/8" × 3/4" GROOVE
3/4" PARTICLE-BOARD
3" × 2-5/8" STIFFENER
2"
1/8" HARDBOARD
1/2" QUARTER-ROUND

cleated storage wall

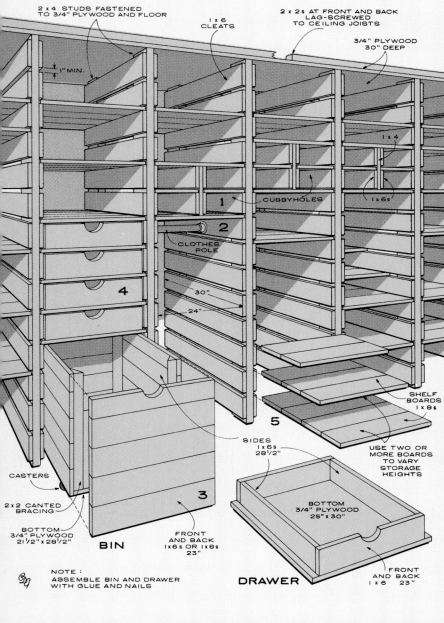

2 x 4 STUDS FASTENED
TO 3/4" PLYWOOD AND FLOOR

1 x 6
CLEATS

2 x 2s AT FRONT AND BACK
LAG-SCREWED
TO CEILING JOISTS

3/4" PLYWOOD
30" DEEP

1" MIN.

1 x 4

CUBBYHOLES

1 x 6s

1 CLOTHES POLE

2

30"

24"

4

5

SHELF
BOARDS
1 x 8s

USE TWO OR
MORE BOARDS
TO VARY
STORAGE
HEIGHTS

SIDES
1 x 6s
28 1/2"

BOTTOM
3/4" PLYWOOD
25" x 30"

CASTERS

2 x 2 CANTED
BRACING

BOTTOM
3/4" PLYWOOD
21 1/2" x 28 1/2"

3

FRONT
AND BACK
1 x 6s OR 1 x 8s
23"

FRONT
AND BACK
1 x 6   23"

BIN

DRAWER

NOTE :
ASSEMBLE BIN AND DRAWER
WITH GLUE AND NAILS

Storage options include vertical dividers for family files (1), out-of-season clothes space (2), a pull-out bin on casters (3), and smaller drawers (4). The unit can be deeper than the 30 inches shown, but you risk losing items behind others on deep shelves. Using 1 × 8s instead of plywood (5) lets you step shelves to store items of various heights (four boards make a shelf).

Remember when you first moved into your house? How empty the garage was—and the attic, and even the basement? In my house, all of those spaces soon filled up with miscellaneous objects that seem to resist orderly arrangement. But the modular wall-hugging shelves shown here can organize the most diverse storage-room clutter.

Basically a series of ceiling-high 2 × 4s sandwiched between 1 × 6 cleats, the modular unit requires no hardware. Grooves formed by the cleats support shelves and drawers, making the system simple to assemble—and flexible enough to take care of changing storage needs. Because all dressed lumber is milled to standard widths, it's ideal for the cleats. For this project, Western Wood Products Association used blue-stain ponderosa pine 1 × 6s (2½ feet long) for the cleats, fir 2 × 4s for the verticals, and a mix of 1 × 8s and ¾-inch plywood for shelving. Drawer and bin fronts are assembled from 1 × 6s or 1 × 8s. The handsome grain pattern of the lumber makes for a unified look without the wild grain of fir plywood.

Because the cleats allow you to vary shelf heights and insert bins, drawers, and even clothes poles (see drawings) as needed, the only dimension that can't change after installation is the width of the modules. For the garage wall unit shown, WWPA's designer, Terry Ferguson, worked with 2-foot modules, halving them to create ski storage and small cubbies on the left. He doubled the module for the luggage shelves on the right. (But don't let shelves bridge two modules except for storage of light items.)

When deciding how many cleats you need to fill the space between floor and ceiling, plan for a 1-inch space between cleats, and remember that the actual width of a 1 × 6 is 5½ inches. This dimension also sets the minimum depth of shelves and drawers at a little more than 5 inches.

Note that although drawer fronts

Clutter-clearing storage shelves slide between cleated supports for easy rearrangement. Shelves may be plywood, as shown here, or lumber (see drawing). The sturdy pull-out drawers and bin (inset) provide roomy storage.

and backs set flush with the uprights, the sides are recessed, and the drawers have no glides. Both long edges of the drawer bottom project into the spaces between the cleats to function as runners (see detail). If greatly overloaded, the drawers will require some tugging to open—so plan enough drawers to avoid overstuffing. (Waxing the drawer grooves will help, too.)

To begin construction, lag-screw two 1 × 2s to ceiling joists to serve as top plates. Nail the plywood top to this frame, and toenail 2 × 4 vertical supports to the plywood. Rip shelves from ¾-inch plywood, and crosscut 2 × 6s to identical 2½-foot lengths for cleats. You'll find that a stack of boards all ripped to size go up quickly using common nails.

Make the drawers and bins, and, if you like, add doors to some open-shelf modules for lockup security. Your options don't stop there, either. To protect the storage unit from dirt, you can brush or spray on a coat or two of semigloss sealer. Or you can paint the shelves to contrast with or match the walls—*by Susan Renner-Smith. Drawing by Carl De Groote.*

work station for portable sanders

With this easy-to-build work station, your portable power tools will do double duty. The bench-top mountings hold your pad sander, belt sander, and drill so that you can use them as stationary sanding tools. But detaching the tools is easy, so you can quickly put them back into service as portables.

Both sanders are on pivoting platforms and thus can be used in a vertical or horizontal position. The drill provides rotary-sanding capability. It takes a variety of sanding drums or a disc you can make or buy. The saber saw was an afterthought on my part and is optional. (If you include it, be careful of the protruding blade.)

I designed the prototype sanding station around good-size tools: a Sears Craftsman 4-inch belt sander and 4½-by-9⅛-inch pad sander. Thus the mounting plates should be large enough for any brand tool.

The heart of my mounting system is a yoke into which you slip the tool's handgrip, and a pipe strap bent to fit over the grip's projecting top. I lined all straps and yokes with weatherstripping, but I didn't allow for its thickness in forming and sizing them. That ensured a snug mounting for the tools and minimum vibration. Tool levelers—blocks of wood sized for the job and weatherstripped—complete the mounting system.

Constructing the shop

Saw the legs (1 in the lead drawing) to size, then form the 2¼-by-10¾-inch notch in the top rear of each leg. Be sure the legs are perfect triplets, then begin the assembly by adding the two frame pieces (2, 3) and the back brace (4). Cut the tool supports (5, 6) and the short leg (7) to size, and glue and screw them in place. Also, nail through the back brace into the front edges of the tool supports.

Glue and nail the drawer guides (8) to the legs, then construct the drawers (9-12). Bore 1½-inch-diameter finger holes instead of adding knobs, which can grab clothing.

Cut the top piece (13) to overall size,

Belt and pad sanders can be used vertically or horizontally. Drill takes sanding disc or drums. Drawers store abrasives, accessories. (Saw's an option.)

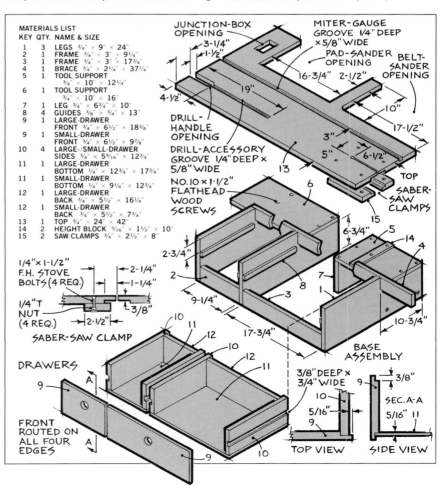

MATERIALS LIST

KEY	QTY.	NAME & SIZE
1	3	LEGS ¾" × 9" × 24"
2	1	FRAME ¾" × 3" × 9¼"
3	1	FRAME ¾" × 3" × 17¾"
4	1	BRACE ¾" × 2¼" × 37¼"
5	1	TOOL SUPPORT ¾" × 10" × 12¼"
6	1	TOOL SUPPORT ¾" × 10" × 16"
7	1	LEG ¾" × 6¾" × 10"
8	4	GUIDES ⅜" × ¾" × 13"
9	1	LARGE-DRAWER FRONT ¾" × 6½" × 18⅜"
9	1	SMALL-DRAWER FRONT ¾" × 6½" × 9⅞"
10	4	LARGE-/SMALL-DRAWER SIDES ¾" × 5⁹⁄₁₆" × 12¾"
11	1	LARGE-DRAWER BOTTOM ¼" × 12¾" × 17¾"
11	1	SMALL-DRAWER BOTTOM ¼" × 9¼" × 12¾"
12	1	LARGE-DRAWER BACK ¾" × 5½" × 16¼"
12	1	SMALL-DRAWER BACK ¾" × 5½" × 7¾"
13	1	TOP ¾" × 24" × 42"
14	2	HEIGHT BLOCK ⁵⁄₁₆" × 1½" × 10"
15	2	SAW CLAMPS ¾" × 2½" × 8"

JUNCTION-BOX OPENING

MITER-GAUGE GROOVE ¼" DEEP × ⅝" WIDE

3-¼"
1-½"

PAD-SANDER OPENING
BELT-SANDER OPENING

19"
16-¾" 2-½"
4-½"
10"
17-½"

DRILL-HANDLE OPENING

DRILL-ACCESSORY GROOVE ¼" DEEP × ⅝" WIDE

NO.10 × 1-½" FLATHEAD WOOD SCREWS

3"
5"
6-½"
13

TOP SABER-SAW CLAMPS

6
15
6-¾"
5
14
4

¼" × 1-½" F.H. STOVE BOLTS (4 REQ.)

2-¼"
1-¼"

¼" T NUT (4 REQ.)
2-½"
3/8"

SABER-SAW CLAMP

2-¾"
2
9-¼"
3
8
7
1

10-¾"

DRAWERS

9
A
10
11
10
12
11
12
11

17-¾"

9
10
5/16
9

BASE ASSEMBLY

⅜" DEEP × ¾" WIDE
3/8"

FRONT ROUTED ON ALL FOUR EDGES
A

9
10

TOP VIEW

SEC. A-A
5/16" 11

SIDE VIEW

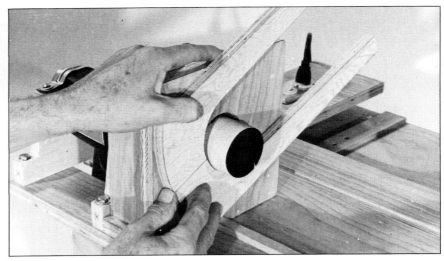

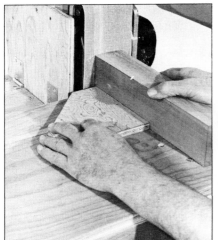

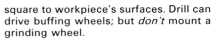

Sanding drums chucked into a mounted drill have many uses. Accessory support shown ensures that sanded edges will be square to workpiece's surfaces. Drill can drive buffing wheels; but *don't* mount a grinding wheel.

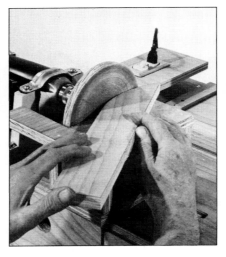

Custom-made 6-inch-diameter sanding disc (made of wood covered with aluminum) works well with variable-speed reversing drill and accessory sanding table.

Sanding table can also be used with drum sanders. (This is one of 3M's new drums.) Table surface should be at or just above center line of drill chuck.

Belt sander's open end (top) can be used to smooth inside curves. Tilted and locked in its vertical position (center), belt sander can handle end sanding of good-size pieces. For edge sanding, lock belt sander in horizontal position, and move work against belt's direction of rotation. (Keep a firm grip, and don't stand behind work.) Miter gauge ensures accurate miters (above). Keep gauge to right side of tool, and be sure to hold or clamp it securely.

Stationary pad sander is especially useful when you want a supersmooth finish on stock that is too small to hold safely. Move the work slowly across the abrasive. Note combination switch-outlet that's used for all tools.

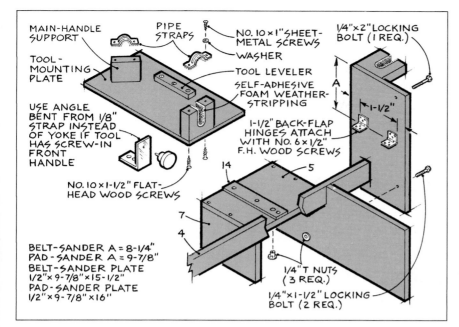

MAIN-HANDLE SUPPORT

PIPE STRAPS

NO. 10 × 1" SHEET-METAL SCREWS

WASHER

1/4" × 2" LOCKING BOLT (1 REQ.)

TOOL-MOUNTING PLATE

TOOL LEVELER

SELF-ADHESIVE FOAM WEATHER-STRIPPING

USE ANGLE BENT FROM 1/8" STRAP INSTEAD OF YOKE IF TOOL HAS SCREW-IN FRONT HANDLE

1-1/2" BACK-FLAP HINGES ATTACH WITH NO. 6 × 1/2" F.H. WOOD SCREWS

1-1/2"

A

NO. 10 × 1-1/2" FLAT-HEAD WOOD SCREWS

14

5

7

4

BELT-SANDER A = 8-1/4"
PAD-SANDER A = 9-7/8"
BELT-SANDER PLATE 1/2" × 9-7/8" × 15-1/2"
PAD-SANDER PLATE 1/2" × 9-7/8" × 16"

1/4" T NUTS (3 REQ.)

1/4" × 1-1/2" LOCKING BOLT (2 REQ.)

Mounting plates for belt and pad sanders are hinged to edge of tool supports on workbench. Cut plates to sizes noted; mark hinge positions; and attach hinges to each plate then to corresponding tool support. (Numbers are keyed to cross reference.) Add height blocks, which should just compensate for hinge thickness. With each plate vertical, drill two holes for locking bolts and mating T nuts (drill 1/8-inch pilot holes, then enlarge to 1/4 inch; enlarge holes

for T nuts to 5/16 inch). Drill holes for bolts that hold plates horizontally *after* sanders are mounted. Tool levelers, handle supports, pipe straps, and yokes are sized to fit. First form yokes, cutting overlong then sawing from bottom for final fit. Cut tool-handle supports and levelers, and place to suit. Line supports, yokes, and straps with weatherstripping. For sanders with screw-in front handle, be sure to use angled metal strap instead of mounting yoke.

and use a table saw or router to shape the miter-gauge groove and the drill-accessory groove. Use a saber saw to form the openings for the drill handle, junction box, and sanders.

If you decide to include a saber saw, use a router to form the recess for it in the underside of the bench top. Drill a 1/4-or 5/16-inch hole for the saw blade, then use the saw to form the blade's access slot.

Glue the top to the base assembly, and drive in 6d finishing nails, spaced 3 to 4 inches apart. Set the nailheads, and fill the cavities with wood dough.

Tilting mounts for sander

Cut the sander-mounting plates, and assemble them as shown in the drawing. The sanders must be level, and most of the abrasive surface must be above the bench top and perpendicular to it. Secure each sander in its yoke, and size the levelers and handle supports. Be sure the tools' vent holes won't be covered.

The simplest way to add the drill is to buy and bold on a commercial accessory to hold it. I prefer the yoke mounting because it holds the drill more securely.

The accessories are mostly for use with the drill. There's a sanding disc, a table you can use with it and with drum sanders (see photos), and a vertical support for drum sanding. Also, I made a miter gauge to use with the belt and pad sanders.

Be sure to work carefully through all phases of construction. Taking ten minutes to do a five-minute job will pay off. Use cabinet-grade birch or maple plywood, and sand all parts before assembly. Sand once more after assembly, then finish with a couple of coats of sealer (sanding between coats and after the final one). Polish all work surfaces with paste wax.

I used a combination switch-outlet and suggest that you stick with a single outlet. You don't want to start one tool accidentally while another's running. A safety must: for sanding jobs, wear goggles and dust mask—*by R.J. DeCristoforo. Drawings by Gerhard Richter.*

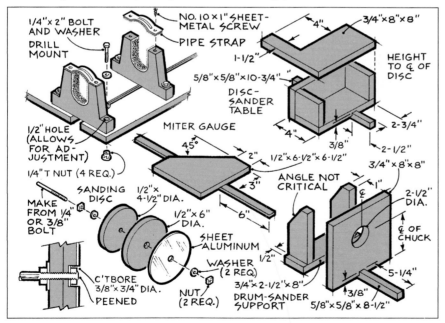

1/4" × 2" BOLT AND WASHER

DRILL MOUNT

NO. 10 × 1" SHEET-METAL SCREW

PIPE STRAP

4"

3/4" × 8" × 8"

1-1/2"

HEIGHT TO ℄ OF DISC

5/8" × 5/8" × 10-3/4"

DISC-SANDER TABLE

2-3/4"

1/2" HOLE (ALLOWS FOR ADJUSTMENT)

MITER GAUGE

45°

4"

3/8"

2-1/2"

1/4" T NUT (4 REQ.)

2"

1/2" × 6-1/2" × 6-1/2"

3/4" × 8" × 8"

SANDING DISC

1/2" × 4-1/2" DIA.

ANGLE NOT CRITICAL

1"

℄

2-1/2" DIA.

MAKE FROM 1/4" OR 3/8" BOLT

3"

1/2" × 6" DIA.

6"

℄ OF CHUCK

SHEET ALUMINUM

1/2"

WASHER (2 REQ.)

5-1/4"

C'TBORE 3/8" × 3/4" DIA.

PEENED

NUT (2 REQ.)

3/4" × 2-1/2" × 8"

DRUM-SANDER SUPPORT

3/8"

5/8" × 5/8" × 8-1/2"

Drill is cradled in two yokes and secured with pipe straps; handle slips through slot in bench top. Make pattern for yoke arcs with a contour gauge, or fold a sheet of paper and cut out shapes. Horizontal center line of chuck must be parallel to work surface. Oversize holes for yoke locking bolts allow lateral adjustment. Disc-sander table's surface must be at or just above center line of

disc. Center of hole in drum-sander support must match drill chuck's center line. For sanding disc, use 1/4- or 3/8-inch bolt as an arbor. Threaded portion must be exact length for items to be mounted. Peen free end heavily to lock on disc so it can safely rotate in either direction (with reversible drill). Then attach aluminum sheet-metal cover with a suitable contact cement.

dual-storage garden center

There comes the day when your usual glance out the kitchen window stops you short with the realization that your backyard storage shack has become a blight on the landscape. When this happened to me, I researched commercial sheds and soon saw that I'd be replacing my eyesore with something nearly as bad.

I wanted a shelter with the elegance of the lawn and garden it would serve, so I sought out a landscape architect. As we discussed what the structure could provide, the project grew into the split-shed design you see above. This automatically separates the lawn gear from the garden equipment and—by providing two relatively shallow, facing "closets"—avoids the jumble of a large one-room catchall. The breezeway between the sheds lightens the bulk and cuts off less of my kitchen-window view.

As a bonus, the structure gives focus to the outdoor play of our small children. The elevated deck gets them off the damp grass (and provides a

great jump-off platform). We even built a big sandbox into one corner, with a hinged lid to keep out rain and debris. I've come to appreciate the veranda effect of the deck, and often rest here after outdoor chores (in a lawn chair that stores in one of the sheds) while overseeing the activities of my heirs. When they outgrow the sandbox, it will be converted into a large planter by replacing the sand with

soil. The lid can then be removed or left permanently hooked up against the wall as a decorative framed panel.

We built the box by framing it right through the platform so that its frame rests on grade. (Following the advice of the Western Wood Products Assn., which worked with the designer, we

Tucked into the two sheds are shelves for storing lawn and garden equipment. There's floor space for a mower and tiller, which roll down the ramp.

Deck joists bridge beams supported by nine posts. Cedar 2×4s are nailed across the joists (left). The ragged forward edge will be trimmed with a circular saw to leave a square pit for the sandbox. Framing for the sheds is erected on sill plates spiked to the deck, then covered with cedar siding.

Siding is trimmed flush with the door openings, then run up the gables.

Sandbox/planter is a frame within a frame. You can add a sturdy cedar plat-

form at a level that gives you the proper depth of sand or soil (see text).

used cedar or pressure-treated lumber throughout so ground contact would be no problem.) When we noted the depth of this pit, however, we decided it would take a wasteful volume of sand to fill it, so we installed a platform of cedar planks that would give us the proper depth of sand. The cracks between the planks allow for drainage, should the cover ever be left up during a rain. If we later want to plant an ornamental tree or large shrub here, I'll remove the platform and fill the pit with soil down to grade.

The two rectangular sheds measure about 5½ by 7½ feet, and the interior walls can be lined with tempered perforated hardboard to take a variety of tool hangers. We finished the exterior with a handsome silver-gray

stain. My youngsters promptly claimed both sheds as playhouses and had to be evicted so we could plan our lawn and garden storage.

Construction procedures are shown in the dimensioned drawings and the photos above. The first step is to lay out and dig for the nine concrete piers. In areas subject to frost heave, it's best to drop these piers just below the front line and pour some gravel into each hole to rest the tubular forms on before filling them with ready-mix concrete. Embed a post anchor at the top of each pier to take the 4 × 6 posts once the concrete sets. You don't even have to strip the forms before backfilling; if you apply a skirt as shown, the piers won't be visible, and they protrude only a few inches

above grade anyway.

Using a string level, trim all nine posts to identical heights, then bridge them with three 4 × 10 beams as shown in the construction drawing. Check each beam with a carpenter's level as it is installed. This method ensures a level deck even if there's a compound slope to your yard. The height of the posts also determines the final height of the deck itself. The dimensions shown in the drawing are for a deck that's three easy steps up from grade; this can vary to suit the demands of your site.

Joist hangers are the easiest way to install the 2 × 8s between the beams. Since this support framing is also hidden (once the 2 × 4 cedar decking is nailed on), you can use pressure-

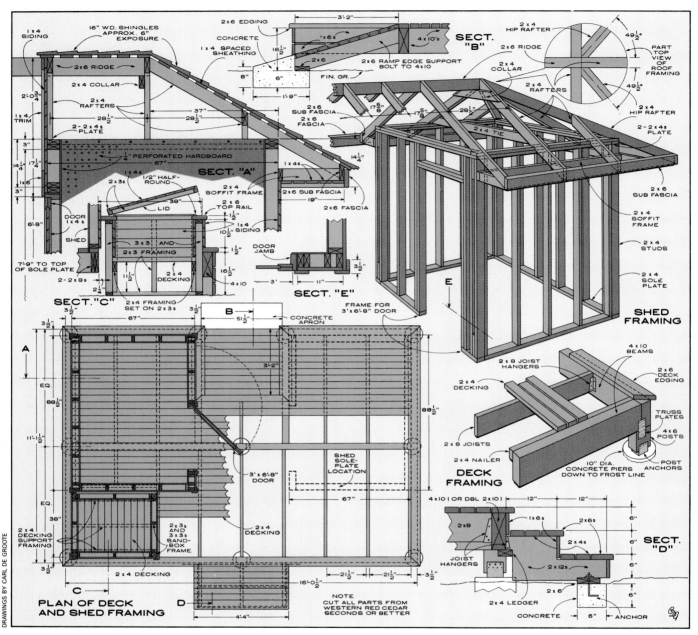

PLAN OF DECK
AND SHED FRAMING

DRAWINGS BY CARL DE GROOTE

treated lumber here without any finish.

Outline the periphery of the deck with a ribbon of 2 × 6 cedar, mitered at the four corners. (The only break in this ribbon is to allow for the descent of the ramp.) Next, surface the area within this frame by nailing down cedar 2 × 4s. If you're including the sandbox/planter of our design, don't, of course, deck this corner. In nailing on the 2 × 4s, center any end joints on a joist, and stagger such joints so that they don't align. Be sure to place all deck boards "bark side" up so that any cupping as they weather will tend to shed water toward the cracks. A good rule of thumb is to use 16-penny nails as spacers between the last

board nailed down and the next one to be applied.

Drive one nail into each joist the deck board crosses, in a zigzag pattern about an inch from each edge. When nailing near ends, it's best to predrill to avoid split-out. Use only aluminum or hot-dipped galvanized nails to avoid rust stains later. This also applies to nailing on your siding planks.

Once the deck is complete, you have a work platform on which to erect the shed framing. Frame all four walls of both sheds, then tie the two frames together with the framing for the hip roof. Lay out the ridge, cut 12 identical common rafters, and nail this assembly in place. Measure for the hip rafters and install as shown above.

Various siding patterns are available, including beveled lap, if you want more surface texture.

It took nine bundles of cedar shingles to do this roof (plus two bundles of hip and ridge shingles). Note that we skipped a roof deck, instead nailing on properly spaced lath to which the shingles were nailed. For an airy design, we left the space between the sheds unroofed, staining the two exposed rafters on each side of the continuous ridge to match the siding. If you prefer more shelter over the shed doors, you can always extend the shingling—but consider a central skylight or two—*by Cathy Howard. Design by Julia Lundy, A.S.L.A. Drawings by Carl De Groote.*

inside-out sun deck

From the curb, the house seemed to match its real-estate listing: "3 BR ranch, att dbl gar, patio." But when I hopped around back, that "patio" proved to be the typical bad joke of most developments. The only access to it was the garage's back door ("before" photo within). Inside, the home's major drawback was a cramped, dark dining room. Before putting down earnest money, the prospective home buyer asked me to propose an addition that would make the home attractive for entertaining.

Tacking a room onto the kitchen/dining wall and adding an open deck would go far in that direction—but it would also block two foundation windows that brought light and air to the basement. The solution? Float the addition above them, leaving access through the crawl space beneath.

The other problem was financing, so we designed the addition to be completed in two stages, as shown in the table at lower left. This spreads costs over two summers while providing instant amenities with Phase I. By carefully framing the enclosed porch to take standard window sizes, you can wrap it in screening for this coming summer, then add the glazing next year, or whenever possible.

If you match the siding and roofing to the existing house, the add-on will look like part of the original design. The open deck was easy to erect, thanks to Wickes Lumber's new 5/4 radius-edged, pressure-treated Deck Plank lumber, with precut components and plans. We also used the component railing system offered by Wickes Lumber.

INTERIOR

Two-phase cost spread

First Year:	Second Year:
Basic addition	Windows all around
Patio-door access	Pass-through casement
Deck	Finished ceiling
Screening	Paneling
Floor tile	Lattice skirting

PHASE I

For this project's first summer, we built the enclosed porch and open deck, and replaced the existing slider with Peachtree's hinged-panel patio door for direct access from the dining room. We covered the porch floor with a frost-free ceramic tile.

The following year, the first step was to replace the screening with storm-screen window units. We then added light-colored paneling and ceiling tile and replaced the double-hung kitchen window with a casement that becomes a pass-through for serving refreshments. Since this porch is still the only source of daylight for both kitchen and dining room, we kept its furnishings bright. The owners might even add a skylight some time in the not-too-distant future. If your new sun porch happens to face south, you'll benefit from solar gain as a welcome bonus—*by Phil McCafferty. Drawings by Carl De Groote.*

BEFORE

All-too-typical back stoop from the attached garage (above) meets a totally useless patio slab—this one even lacks access to the kitchen and dining room (windows at right in photo). First-phase addition, shown on preceding page, adds a screened porch and open deck. Phase II (left) provides a comfortable sun room. Shown here is the completed project, with final details in place.

PHASE II

1. **Floor joists** span 2×12 bolted to the house and a beam supported by posts.
2. **Posts and 4×12 headers** on a plywood platform support the roof framing.
3. **New room** is now under shelter, so the window is replaced with a patio door.
4. **Three support posts** are added, and the open deck is framed; header is nailed across trimmed joists.
5. **For Phase II,** windows replace screening.

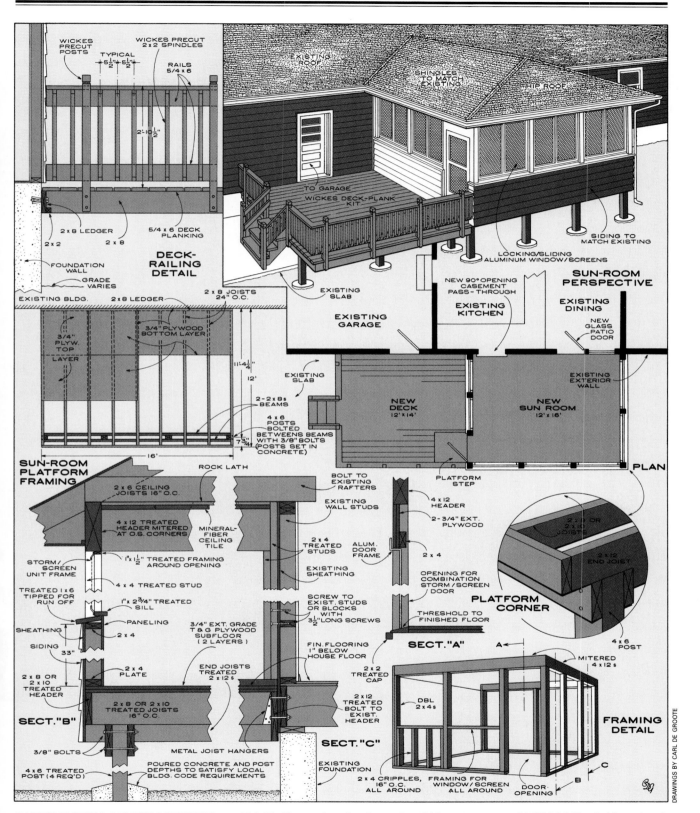

DECK-RAILING DETAIL

WICKES PRECUT POSTS
WICKES PRECUT 2 x 2 SPINDLES
TYPICAL
RAILS 5/4 x 6
2'-10½"
2 x 8 LEDGER
5/4 x 6 DECK PLANKING
2 x 2
2 x 8
FOUNDATION WALL
GRADE VARIES
EXISTING BLDG.
2 x 8 LEDGER

EXISTING ROOF
SHINGLES TO MATCH EXISTING
HIP ROOF
TO GARAGE
WICKES DECK-PLANK KIT
SIDING TO MATCH EXISTING
LOCKING/SLIDING ALUMINUM WINDOW/SCREENS

SUN-ROOM PERSPECTIVE

2 x 8 JOISTS 24" O.C.
EXISTING SLAB
EXISTING GARAGE
NEW 90° OPENING CASEMENT PASS-THROUGH
EXISTING KITCHEN
EXISTING DINING
NEW GLASS PATIO DOOR
EXISTING EXTERIOR WALL

3/4" PLYW. TOP LAYER
3/4" PLYWOOD BOTTOM LAYER
11'-4½"
12'
EXISTING SLAB
2-2x8s BEAMS
4 x 6 POSTS BOLTED BETWEENS BEAMS WITH 3/8" BOLTS (POSTS SET IN CONCRETE)
7¾"
16'

NEW DECK 12' x 14'
NEW SUN ROOM 12' x 16'

PLAN

SUN-ROOM PLATFORM FRAMING

ROCK LATH
2 x 6 CEILING JOISTS 16" O.C.
4 x 12 TREATED HEADER MITERED AT O.S. CORNERS
MINERAL-FIBER CEILING TILE
STORM/SCREEN UNIT FRAME
1"x 1½" TREATED FRAMING AROUND OPENING
TREATED 1 x 6 TIPPED FOR RUN OFF
4 x 4 TREATED STUD
1" x 2¾" TREATED SILL
SHEATHING
PANELING
SIDING
2 x 4
33"
2 x 4 PLATE
2 x 8 OR 2 x 10 TREATED HEADER
2 x 8 OR 2 x 10 TREATED JOISTS 16" O.C.
3/4" EXT. GRADE T & G PLYWOOD SUBFLOOR (2 LAYERS)
END JOISTS TREATED 2 x 12s
FIN. FLOORING 1" BELOW HOUSE FLOOR

SECT. "B"

3/8" BOLTS
METAL JOIST HANGERS
POURED CONCRETE AND POST DEPTHS TO SATISFY LOCAL BLDG. CODE REQUIREMENTS
4 x 6 TREATED POST (4 REQ'D)

BOLT TO EXISTING RAFTERS
EXISTING WALL STUDS
2 x 4 TREATED STUDS
EXISTING SHEATHING
SCREW TO EXIST. STUDS OR BLOCKS WITH 3½" LONG SCREWS
4 x 12 HEADER
2-3/4" EXT. PLYWOOD
2 x 4
ALUM. DOOR FRAME
OPENING FOR COMBINATION STORM/SCREEN DOOR
THRESHOLD TO FINISHED FLOOR

PLATFORM STEP
2 x 8 OR 2 x 10 JOISTS
2 x 12 END JOIST

PLATFORM CORNER

4 x 6 POST
MITERED 4 x 12 s

SECT. "A"

A

SECT. "C"

2 x 2 TREATED CAP
2 x 12 TREATED BOLT TO EXIST. HEADER
EXISTING FOUNDATION
2 x 4 CRIPPLES, 16" O.C. ALL AROUND
FRAMING FOR WINDOW/SCREEN ALL AROUND

DBL 2 x 4s
DOOR OPENING

FRAMING DETAIL

C
B

DRAWINGS BY CARL DE GROOTE

PARTICIPATING MANUFACTURERS
The following products were chosen by *Popular Science* for this project: **Armstrong World Industries,** Box 3001, Lancaster, PA 17604 (fissured ceiling tile); **Brite Aluminum Products Inc.,** 2155 West Wabansia, Chicago, IL 60647; **Charmglow Products,** Box 310, Bristol, WI 53104-0310 (barbecue grill); **Color Tile,** Box 2475, Fort Worth, TX 76113 (frost-proof ceramic tile); **Masonite Corp.,** Box 311, Towanda, PA 18848 (Royalcote Woodfield chestnut paneling); **Peachtree Doors,** Box 5700, Norcross, GA 30091 (Prado hinged patio door, casement window); **Samsonite Furniture,** Box 189, Murfreesboro, TN 37130 (Body Glove in Buttercream 'n' Blue fabric); **Wickes Lumber,** Box 2030, Vernon Hills, IL 60061 (Deck Plank).

bolt-plate shelters

It floats above the forest like a temple in a Chinese scroll. The Victorians would have labeled it a "folly"—their term for any fanciful structure (usually decorating a lawn or garden) that was built for other than a sound practical purpose. Yet this folly can provide you with both outdoor shelter and out-of-season storage. And it's assembled with special steel connectors, called Starplates, that you can find at most home centers.

I hung my folly off a mountain to show that similar structures can be built anywhere, and I used the new plates, which let you bolt 2 × 4s into a sturdy web like a full-scale Erector set. How you cover your frame depends on the use the structure will serve. For a true folly, you could lattice the roof framing to provide patterned shade; other possibilities are shown.

Because I wanted winter closure, I chose to nail lap siding on the lower half of the walls, wrapping the upper half in a special new black-coated aluminum screening. Shutters close the interior space from weather, and a large hinged panel at the front winches down for the spectacular view. In a backyard setting this panel could serve as a ramp for wheeling-in lawn mowers, carts, and bikes.

Was construction as easy as manufacturers of the assembly plates claim? Initially, yes. One promotion brochure promised a "two-hour frame-up." What this neglects to mention is that it may take several days to trim, drill, and sand the struts for assembly, and many days of tedious angle-cutting if you plan to apply plank siding or roof shingles. (I did both, and it took an entire summer's weekends.) Of course, I complicated the roofing even further by building where I had limited access and by piercing the roof with skylights (see list of Manufacturers).

Construction plans for the basic frame are shown, along with step-by-step assembly photos. I had to erect a floating deck before I could start my gazebo (explained in the caption for photos 1 through 7). If you erect your structure on a flat yard, you're way ahead.

Prepare the 21 struts as shown in the sketch (pressure-treated lumber is best, especially for struts in ground contact). Assemble the five base struts, then erect eight wall struts and tie them together with the five eaves struts. To duplicate my square door frame, you'll have removed the two full-length base struts at the front corner to use elsewhere, replacing them with struts only long enough to butt against two vertical jambs that frame the opening. Unless you can bolt these jambs into a deck frame, as I did, you'll want to sink them into concrete footings.

You're now ready to proceed with the roof. In photo 8, the five-rafter frame is complicated with extra 2 × 4s to provide nailers for sheathing seams and framing for skylights; note the use of miter plates recently added to the Starplate system to avoid compound-angle cuts. In photo 9, I'm lifting half of a ½-inch CDX plywood sheet through the framing to nail in place (you can get two such right-angle triangles out of each 4-by-8-foot sheet).

Photo 10 shows the tricky, wasteful angle-trimming required to apply lap siding. Planks are anchored to the frame with a pair of nails at each end; there's a 2 × 4 crosspiece behind the top edge of each top plank.

Popular Science-built gazebo (turn page for plans) is seen on facing page floating off mountain with its front view panel winched down. Two inset photos show it from opposite side: At left, triangular access panel is propped up for entry; at lower right, panel and interior shutters are locked for winter.

Adjusting size and skin to sheltering need

Three other Starplate shelters show system's versatility. Staple polyethylene film over frame (top) for a free-standing greenhouse that can be disassembled and stored during winter. Keep a sandbox dry by erecting a scaled-down shelter (middle). An ideal shed for lawn-and-garden-equipment storage is yours (bottom) if you cover all walls and hinge triangular plywood panels as lockable access doors.

The interior shutters in photo 11 were made from ½-inch plywood and waferboard. The larger ones are hinged to eaves struts so they swing up against the ceiling when open. Smaller ones bolt in place; when removed, they store under the deck. The last photo shows the double-hinged view panel being winched down over the deck's edge—*by Al Lees. Drawings by Carl De Groote.*

PARTICIPATING MANUFACTURERS

Source	Item	Source	Items
Kant-Sag/ United Steel Products Box 80 Montgomery, MN 56069	Starplate bolt plates, miter plates, roof cap	**Leslie-Locke** Box 723727 Atlanta, GA 30339	Horison flush-mount Skylight
Keystone-Seneca Wire Cloth Co. Box 386 Brookhaven, MS 39601	Senaclad coated aluminum screening	**Sears** (retail stores only)	Weatherbeater water-repellent oil stain (brown for shutters, door panels)
Koppers Co. Forest Product Group Pittsburgh, PA 15219	Wolman wood stain (semitrans-parent Glade for siding, struts)	**Teco** 5530 Wisconsin Ave. Chevy Chase MD 20815	4 × 4 post bases, joint hangers

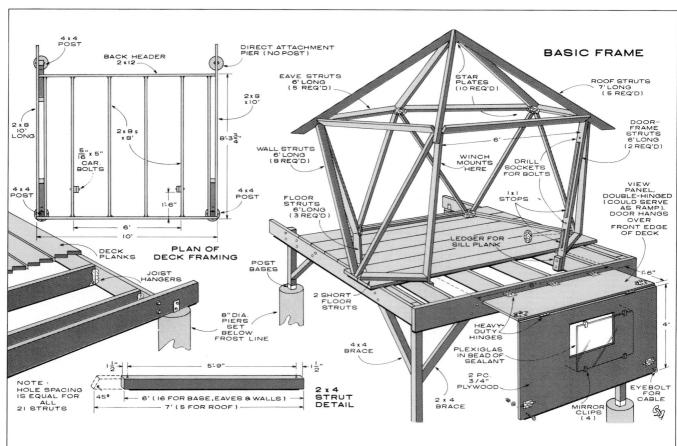

Steps in erecting deck: To create metal anchor for corner that rests directly on pier (1), cut tubular form to exact height, wedge in position atop concrete footing, bolt scrap 2×4 between metal plates (with extra bolts through lower holes), lay across form, and fill to rim with concrete. Wait two days, remove 2×4, and save to use as template for drilling joist. Doubled outer joists flank 4×4 posts (2); to prevent racking, bolt 4×4 knee braces between. Drilling at remote site was possible with Skil's battery-powered Boar Gun and a long bit. Placement of inner joists (3) was eased with Teco hangers nailed to inner faces of front and back beams prior to erection. Redwood deck planks were nailed across joists (4) so trial base frame, bolted to Starplates, could be centered on deck. Two side corners jutted beyond frame, so longer planks were installed there. Planking completed up to threshold, full-length struts at front are trimmed back to butt door jambs (5). Jambs pass through deck and bolt through framing (6); note that face block is needed to support threshold at each end. Four remaining Starplates are now anchored to deck. Top of each jamb bolts to inside of its plate (7). For comment on photos 8 through 12, see text.

103

permanent picnic table

During spring, summer, and fall at our Montana cabin, we spend most of our time outside. After a few seasons trying to resurrect and maintain a picnic table built of cedar planks, we decided to apply our experience in cold-molded boatbuilding toward a table for our purposes. The result is a table for the great outdoors. It will last almost indefinitely with minimal maintainance, look good, and never suffer the rot, warpage, splitting, and water absorption that deteriorate unprotected outdoor wood furniture.

As we detailed in the 1986 *Do-it-Yourself Yearbook*, laminating up thin stock with epoxy offers multiple advantages. Thin stock is cheaper than thick pieces, more readily available, and comes in a wider selection. The epoxy glue line also acts as a moisture barrier, and the drier wood can be kept the stronger and more durable it will be. Lamination lets you use less-than-select grades of wood and compensate for uneven grain, knots, and weak spots. And, epoxy laminations will be stiffer than a single grown piece and suffer far less warpage.

All parts of the picnic table, except for the plywood top, molding, and bracing beneath, are laminated from standard ¾-inch-thick mahogany. You can expand the design to build a larger table using the same wood-epoxy techniques. Virtually all tools and materials listed are available locally. For epoxy, fillers, and related accessories, contact Gougeon Brothers, Inc.—distributors of the WEST System materials on which the following techniques are based—PO Box X908, Bay City, MI 48707.

Laminating

Always spread epoxy evenly on both surfaces to be glued using a roller, acid brush, or plastic squeegee. We thicken catalyzed epoxy slightly with red microballoons (a filler) for a mix that's still thin enough to spread easily yet thick enough to fill small gaps and defects.

Extreme clamping pressure isn't needed for epoxy (Fig. 1). Use small plywood pads under clamps if heads are dirty or if high pressure is used, however. Three-quarter-inch mahogany requires clamping every 6 to 9 inches. Use closer spacing or plywood pads to spread pressure on thinner stock. Screws aren't needed, either. But if you use them, countersink with a tapered drill and Fuller countersink, then seal holes with mahogany plugs glued in place with epoxy. We rough-cut pieces to be laminated about ⅟16 inch oversize. After curing—which takes from about one hour to four hours depending on temperature—we clean up excess and drips with a plane or bandsaw. This means positioning of pieces as you glue isn't as critical.

Prefinishing

Do as much prefinishing as possible before final assembly. This saves time and allows better detailing, coating, and sealing when using epoxy. Pay particular attention to end grain such as bottoms of diagonal legs, seat ends, and wheel perimeters. We lay all disassembled pieces on cleats, roll a coating of epoxy on all accessible areas and let it dry, then reposition the pieces and do the balance. When sealing with epoxy, be sure to remove bubbles and dust craters with a flat cabinet scraper between coatings and use sandpaper only when preparing to paint or varnish.

Table top, edge molding, and blocking

Half-inch mahogany plywood is used for the top; with the edge molding and framing beneath, it is very strong and stiff. For a larger 4 × 8 table top, ¾-inch plywood would be a good choice. Try to choose an attractive piece of ply for the top, one with grain that matches your molding and legs. Coat both top and bottom sides of the ply with three coats of epoxy before construction.

The mahogany edge molding for the table top is 3 by ¾ inches wide. The rabbet or notch for the ½-inch plywood top can be cut most easily with a standard ⅜-inch rabbeting bit in a router (Fig. 2). The rabbet can also be cut freehand by clamping the moldings onto a workbench, table saw, or shaper. We cut the rabbet for the table shown at ⁹⁄16 inches deep, which left a ⅟16-inch excess for a slight edge that protrudes above the surface of the plywood top; it will be trimmed later.

After rabbeting the notch on top of all four pieces, make the 45-degree mitered cuts on each end of each piece. Once the first cut is made, clamp the molding in position on the table top and mark for the other end cut. We cut the two long sides first and glued and clamped them in place (Fig. 3). After the epoxy set, we removed the clamps and attached the two remaining molding pieces the same way. You could also hold the molding in place with small wood screws until the epoxy sets, then remove the screws and plug the holes.

Once all four pieces of molding are glued in place, lay

Tools and Materials Needed

- Drill with tapered, straight, and countersink bits
- Circular saw
- Jack plane
- Back saw
- Router with ⅜" rabbeting and ⅜" bullnose bits
- Sandpaper: 60, 80, and 100 grit plus sanding block
- Pipe clamps
- Block plane
- Scraper and file (for sharpening scraper)
- 14 C-clamps—3½" capacity
- T-square
- Framing square
- Jig saw
- ¾" parting chisel
- Organic fumes mask for indoor work
- Epoxy tools: mixing pots and sticks; foam rollers and

- handle; plastic squeegee; acid brushes; surgical gloves; clean-up soap
- Foam or bristle brush
- 1 sheet ½" luan mahogany plywood
- 50 board feet ¾ × 7½" luan mahogany
- 1 gallon WEST System epoxy resin with catalyst
- Small amount red microballoons
- 1 quart sunscreen varnish
- 2 bronze ⅜ × 3½" carriage bolts with washers and nuts
- 2 teflon washers
- 14 running feet 2 × 4 clear fir
- 1 dozen No. 16 2½" flathead wood screws (optional)

the table top on a flat surface and carefully trim the hardened epoxy drips and extra 1/16 inch of wood from the top. Use a sharp block plane for initial trimming, then finish with a cabinet scraper to bring the surfaces flush without gouging the plywood table top. Lightly sand with 100 grit

paper (start with 60 or 80 for rougher wood), then round edge gently and roll on three epoxy seal coats. Sand with the wood grain only, especially with plywood, which shows cross-sanding scratches.

After sealing, lay the top down and fit appropriate blocking in place. The blocking not only supports the plywood top but provides added attachment for the legs. We used clear fir for the blocking, an inexpensive wood that takes epoxy well and gives good support. We cut and fitted each piece individually in place on the marks, then glued them down using large C-clamps and small pads over the blocking and around the table top (Fig. 4). Clean drips and excess with a sharp plane or chisel and you're ready to build the legs.

Diagonal legs

See the working drawings for the lengths and angles to cut. After the diagonal legs are laminated, sealed, and cleaned up, they are then half-lapped. This produces a very strong joint and also makes a leg that is on the same plane all the way across instead of staggered.

Before cutting the half lap, temporarily clamp the legs in place to ensure proper fit all around and get the exact angle for the half-lap cuts (Fig. 5). Mark the half-lap joint on the two pieces to be cut, then make square cuts exactly halfway through each piece with a back or dovetail saw. Don't try for a tight fit. There should be slight clearance so that the epoxy can seal the grain.

Make two or three cuts halfway through with the back saw before using a ¾-inch parting chisel to take out half the wood. The epoxy glue line at the middle is the depth

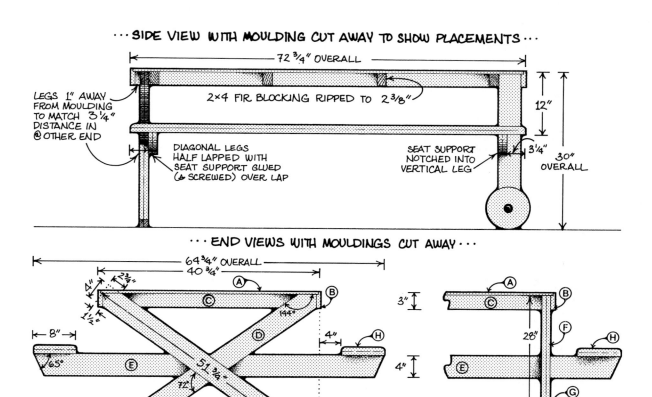

··· SIDE VIEW WITH MOULDING CUT AWAY TO SHOW PLACEMENTS ···

72 ¾" OVERALL

LEGS 1" AWAY FROM MOULDING TO MATCH 3 ¼" DISTANCE IN @ OTHER END

2×4 FIR BLOCKING RIPPED TO 2⅜"

12"

DIAGONAL LEGS HALF LAPPED WITH SEAT SUPPORT GLUED (& SCREWED) OVER LAP

SEAT SUPPORT NOTCHED INTO VERTICAL LEG

3 ¼"

30" OVERALL

··· END VIEWS WITH MOULDINGS CUT AWAY ···

64 ¾" OVERALL
40 ¾"

144°

8"

65°

51 ¾"

72°

45°

4"

1 ½"
4 ¾"

2"
1"

3"

28"

4"

2 ½"

1 ½"

8"

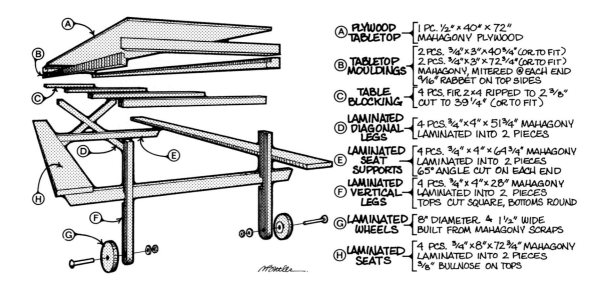

guide; when you get to it you know you're halfway through. Do this on both pieces, run a trial fit, then apply epoxy to both pieces and clamp. Lay this piece on a flat workbench and clamp with a piece of wax paper underneath to ensure perfect alignment. Legs should stand square and plumb when placed in position. If not, correct by bracing or clamping until the epoxy sets (Fig. 6). When glueing end grain, first coat all surfaces with catalyzed unthickened epoxy resin, then go over once again while still wet with microballoon-thickened epoxy.

Vertical legs and wheels

After prefinishing both vertical legs, cutting to length, and drilling for wheel bolts, be sure they stand square off the underside of the table top by checking with a framing square. Attaching the vertical legs is similar to glueing in the diagonal legs.

Wheels are 8 inches in diameter, cut from scrap end pieces of the same mahogany stock used for the rest of the table (Fig. 7). They are made of two glued-up pieces, the grain staggered at a 90-degree angle for strength and durability. Laminating two pieces of 3/4-inch stock makes a 1 1/2-inch-thick wheel wide enough for use on grass, gravel, or packed dirt. A wheel three or more laminations wide gives more support for use in deep loose sand. Rubber or carpet strips tacked around the perimeters allow smooth rolling on cement.

Bolt holes through wheel centers should be drilled over-

size, rounded slightly with a countersink, and sealed with three coats of epoxy. When epoxy sets, redrill to bolt size. This seals the edge grain from moisture and the salts that leach out from the metal bolt. We used bronze carriage bolts because bronze looks good with mahogany and acquires a rich antique patina. Stainless steel also works well, but avoid the rustprone plated bolts. Use a teflon washer to provide clearance between wheel and leg and to ensure easy rolling. Tighten moderately. To prevent one of the nuts working off its bolt while rolling, place a dab of silicone seal on the bolt end and be sure to let it set before moving the table.

Seats and seat supports

Laminated seat supports are simple to build. When prefinished, they are attached to the inside edge of the vertical legs at one end of the table and the diagonal legs at the other. The only tricky part is achieving perfect alignment and exact distance down from the table top on both sides. Mark the distances, then clamp the supports in place using plywood pads under the clamps (Fig. 8). Sight across to ensure alignment. With supports in place and properly aligned, drill screw holes to help in relocating after epoxy has been applied.

We notched the seat support flush into the vertical legs for extra support. Mark the position when alignment is correct and cut the notch with a back saw and chisel. Again, avoid a tight fit so the epoxy can seal all the grain.

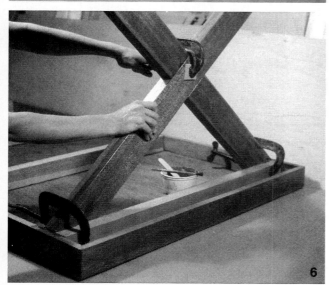

Seats are simply laid on the supports, positioned, and glued down. If fastenings are desired, they can be placed from below, through the seat support and into the seat bottom, to avoid collecting water.

Finishing techniques

If an epoxy-sealed table is painted, it will last for years without any maintenance at all. But a clear or natural finish requires a sunscreen ingredient to protect the epoxy resin from the long-term harmful effects of sunlight radiation. All epoxied surfaces should have a final light scraping before sanding and varnish. After scraping and before sanding, wash all surfaces with soap and warm water and rinse well to remove the waxy residue that tends to clog sandpaper. Lightly sand all surfaces to be varnished with 100 grit paper. Don't sand too hard on the edges or remove too much of the protective epoxy. Wash the table again after sanding, wipe, and let dry thoroughly.

Spar varnish is probably the best choice for a clear finish. Spar is inexpensive and easy to apply. It also remains softer and more flexible than other clear finishes. Apply full-strength from a newly opened can, using thinner only if the varnish will not spread evenly. Use a foam roller followed with a small disposable foam brush or better quality China bristle brush—*by Paul and Marya Butler. Drawing by Marya Butler.*

floating ground-level deck

Like many homeowners, I have a back door—two in fact—set just inches above ground level. I wanted to hide the existing concrete pads by each door under a deck, but a conventional add-on would rise above my low thresholds, so I might have settled for an ugly slab patio instead.

The solution: Raise a 14-by-28-foot deck just a fraction of an inch above grade on concrete footings, and float it over the pads. The beam and joist design would keep the deck low enough to fit under the doors. To dress up the deck and create maximum seating, I shaped both outside corners. The built-in bench rail is topped with double 2 × 6 planks for a broad seat. Another built-in bench doubles as a table. You can adapt my design to float over any size patio slab by adjusting the placement of the footer piers.

Start construction by sinking the footers—except the four that will support the angled corners—below the frost line. Remember to extend the footers only a hair's breadth above grade, just enough to lift the pressure-treated lumber off the ground. You can position the four remaining footers, two on each side, after you've framed the rest of the deck.

Next, attach a ledger to the house. Then set the inside beam (I used triple 2 × 6 beams for my 28-foot run) in place on the footers. I didn't tie together the beams and footers; the ledger and the deck's weight will hold the structure in place. (If you live in an area that's often hit by high winds, secure the beams to the footers with anchor plates.) Nail on joist hangers to attach joists to the ledger and beam. Lay the two remaining beams in place, and spike the three together.

Install the double 2 × 6 band joists, or headers, at the deck's front. Again,

use hangers to secure joists to the header and beam. With the deck partially framed, you're ready to install the angled corners.

First, set the locations for the piers 30 and 60 degrees from the center beam (see drawing). Now, cut the beveled-end band joists to butt over these piers, as shown, and nail the 2 × 6 members together with the beveled 4 × 4 posts backing up the joints. The beveling is best done on a 10-inch radial-arm saw. If you haven't got one, you can either ask your local lumberyard to do the angle cutting or plane the bevels by hand.

To fit the posts into the beam-header or joist-header joints, set your saw for a 15-degree cut, then rip the post's face. For the header-to-header intersections, you need to double-bevel one face. Keep the saw set at 15 degrees, and rip to a center line down the post's face. Then turn the board end-for-end, and bevel the other half.

Next, install the joists that fan out from the center beam. Where they meet the band joist at a 90-degree angle, use joist hangers. When the angle was less than 90 degrees, I simply nailed the joist's outer end to the side of the post. This leaves these two joists offset, but won't show when the decking is applied. Then gang-nail the inner ends of these joists over the inside pier—there's no need to bevel them for a snugger fit.

Now you're ready to install the decking. I installed the planks at a 45-degree angle in the corners to create a pattern. To prevent the ends of the boards from lifting, I doubled up on the three center joists so that both sides of every butt joint were fully supported—*by Mike McNally. Photos by Greg Sharko and Coachman Studios. Drawings by Carl De Groote.*

Start construction by laying out stakes for footings for the rectangular deck (upper photo). Position the beams on the footers so there's room to gang-nail joists from the angled corners. Drill before nailing the headers to the posts in angled corners to prevent splitting. Four predrilled posts secured to the joists

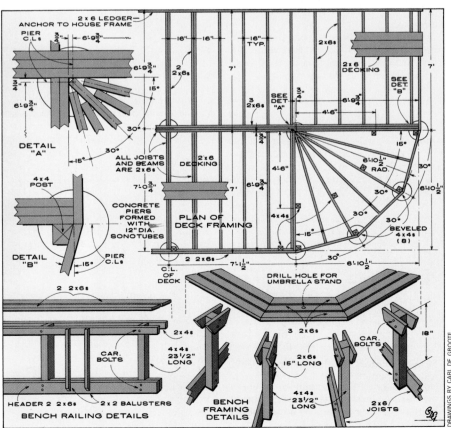

with carriage bolts support the inner bench. The bench top rests on oversize cleats cut from 2×6s. Install posts for the seat-rail every 5 feet. To support 2×6 planks, attach 2×4s to the sides of each post, flush with the top. Insert blocking between the rails for more nailing surfaces.

DRAWINGS BY CARL DE GROOTE

drop-in-place parquet patio

It's almost like laying tiles over an inside floor: Grab a panel, drop it in place, and move on to the next. However, Deck Squares are larger, and the covered area is usually outside your house.

You can create a new patio with the squares, or use them to cover an existing slab that's cracked or pitted. "Install a new walkway," says Ken Woodfill, sales manager for Ajax YardWorks, maker of Deck Squares (3325 Ferguson Rd., Fort Wayne, IN 46809). "Make a planter, or refinish the concrete floor in your basement." If that sounds like there's a lot left to your imagination, you're right. That's one of the main advantages of Deck Squares.

The slatted squares come preassembled in two sizes—2 or 3 feet square—and are pressure treated for a 20-year lifetime with no additional finishing.

To cover an old slab, you merely lay the squares on top of the concrete surface. If there's an overlap at the slab edges, trim the Deck Squares to fit. To hold the squares in place, simply nail a 1 × 2 finishing strip around the perimeter.

If you wish to extend the squares past the slab, add support joists as shown in the drawing. Place 2 × 6s

(for an average-height slab) around the slab's perimeter, and use these boards as the anchor points for the extension joists. The joists are placed in a 24- or 36-inch on-center grid pattern (depending on the size of the squares you choose); Deck Squares are placed on top and held with 2½-inch galvanized nails.

Similarly, a grid pattern of joists is

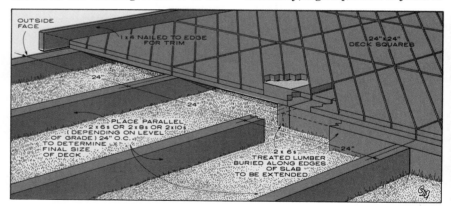

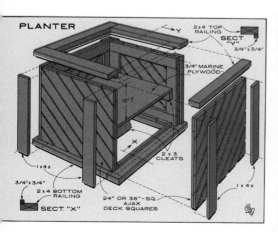

Flower planter is easily assembled using four Deck Squares and 1 × 4 trim pieces. Use exterior ply for the shelf; its height in the box depends on the size of the shrub. Multiple planters can be grouped as shown at right.

used to create a new patio. (Ajax supplies a grid planning sheet.) Once the joists are installed, the first square is nailed in place at one corner. The edge of the square should cover only half the width of the next joist, allowing room to mount the adjacent square. All squares are butted up tightly against each other; when complete, a 1 × 4 finishing strip is added around the perimeter.

For walkways, a simpler grid pattern is used. However, as shown in the photo at left, steps or different levels can be added by changing the joist height in certain areas.

Although Ajax originally designed the squares for decking, there are lots of other uses. For instance, four Deck Squares nailed together as a box made the planter shown. Four squares mounted on a base of tiered risers make a patio coffee table. The table can be surrounded with benches made of Deck Squares that are supported by a frame of 2 × 6s with 2 × 4 legs. Squares can even serve as a cover for a sandbox, as shown below. The box is made of 2 × 10s with an exterior-plywood base. (Be sure to drill a few drain holes for water in the base.)

Raised decks can be enclosed with squares mounted along the sides. With the addition of hinges and locking hardware, some squares (or groups of squares) become access doors: Now the clutter of yard gear you stow under the patio won't be seen.

Deck Squares are available through local home-improvement stores. A 2-foot square is $10; 3-foot, $17—*by William J. Hawkins. Drawings by Carl De Groote.*

Before and after: Slab patio above was covered and extended with Deck Squares for the result at right. Added touches: Deck Squares table and sandbox with cover. Patio designs can have different levels or steps and need not be rectangular. At top, a step is added to the walkway by increasing the joist height. A cut and recleated square creates the angle above the step.

build a lap pool

A swimming pool that you build yourself needn't dominate your entire yard. We've found that our new 8-by-32-foot pool allows full-lap swimming by two persons, yet its practical size simplifies construction, heating, and cleaning.

Other popular sizes (see drawing) can easily be adapted to your yard. Concrete-block walls, lined with insulating foam and a plastic cover, go up quickly. We've also designed a modular pool deck that eliminates problems with long lengths of bent and knotted lumber. Pool materials, including pump, filter, and plumbing, cost about $1,500; the deck is about $750.

After excavation is completed, set the first course of concrete blocks on a poured footing. Stagger the remaining blocks for "rebar" reinforcement as shown in the sketch. Next, pour concrete grout into the holes. Then slip wooden cap rails over the top bolts, and level them. That's about 2 ½ days of assembly so far.

Nail a plastic track for the pool cover to the wooden sides. This cover rolls out from a spool below the deck and latches at one end for child safety.

Next, tack-glue insulating foam to the walls. Tamp a 2-inch sand bottom into place. (With a contoured bottom, water depth is 44 to 45 inches.) Snap the interlocking edge of the tailored vinyl pool liner into the track. Fill the pool with water to the outlet or skimmer level, then attach the remaining track fittings, which serve to sandwich the liner material.

We're convinced that vinyl pools make more sense than concrete pools. Cleanup is easier, fewer pool chemicals are necessary, and a replacement liner isn't very expensive.

The parquet-style deck construction is the easiest we've ever worked with, although the amount of cutting involved requires a good saw; you might want to rent one. When cut into smaller lengths, bent redwood boards are no problem. Even major flaws and knots can be trimmed away.

To order detailed construction plans for this project, send $10 to Stevenson Projects, Dept. LP200, Box 584, Del Mar, CA 92014—*by Suzanne and Peter Stevenson. Drawings by Carl De Groote.*

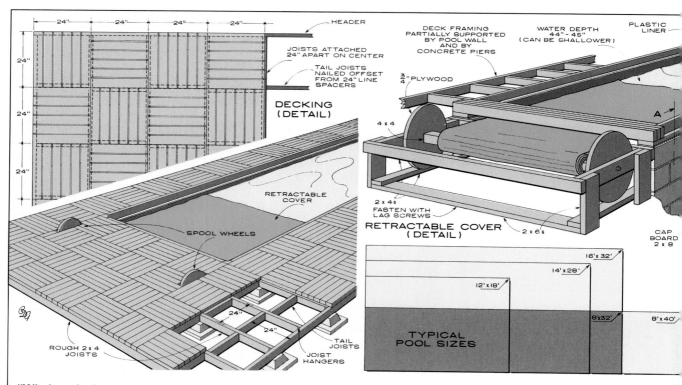

"Window-shade" pool cover is reeled out from concealed spool. Cover is stored out of direct sunlight to minimize deterioration. Two-foot-square deck modules simplify layout for pool sizes with even-numbered dimensions (shown).

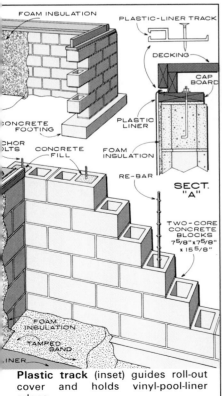

Plastic track (inset) guides roll-out cover and holds vinyl-pool-liner edges.

Labels in diagram:
FOAM INSULATION
PLASTIC-LINER TRACK
DECKING
CAP BOARD
CONCRETE FOOTING
PLASTIC LINER
ANCHOR BOLTS
CONCRETE FILL
FOAM INSULATION
RE-BAR
SECT. "A"
TWO-CORE CONCRETE BLOCKS 7 5/8" x 7 5/8" x 15 5/8"
FOAM INSULATION
TAMPED SAND
LINER

Covering pool with its retractable liner aids solar warming and helps retain heat.

Cover takes about one minute to rewind on spool, less time to unwind.

three affordable retaining walls

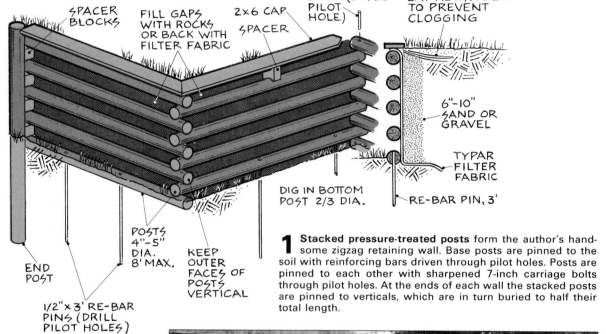

SPACER BLOCKS

FILL GAPS WITH ROCKS OR BACK WITH FILTER FABRIC

2×6 CAP SPACER

7" PIN (DRILL PILOT HOLE)

LAY NEWSPAPER TO PREVENT CLOGGING

6"-10" SAND OR GRAVEL

TYPAR FILTER FABRIC

DIG IN BOTTOM POST 2/3 DIA.

RE-BAR PIN, 3'

END POST

POSTS 4"-5" DIA. 8' MAX.

KEEP OUTER FACES OF POSTS VERTICAL

1/2" × 3' RE-BAR PINS (DRILL PILOT HOLES)

1 **Stacked pressure-treated posts** form the author's handsome zigzag retaining wall. Base posts are pinned to the soil with reinforcing bars driven through pilot holes. Posts are pinned to each other with sharpened 7-inch carriage bolts through pilot holes. At the ends of each wall the stacked posts are pinned to verticals, which are in turn buried to half their total length.

I had a problem: My backyard rose one foot in every two, looming some 15 feet overall. That meant my young children had no safe place to play and were frequently found crying and dirty at the bottom of the bank. The obvious solution: a series of retaining walls with flat terraces between. But I knew that masonry retaining walls would be costly; my neighbor's 5-foot wall had cost more than $4,000. And I needed at least 12 feet of height in all.

Thus I went to wood. My research turned up several designs made of pressure-treated posts and timbers, as you see on these pages. I decided to use pine posts, stacked zigzag fashion, to form my walls. They were less expensive than timbers: Eight-foot-long

posts cost less than $5 each. And the stacked zigzag design required no foundations or deadmen (horizontal anchors).

To provide structural strength, I planned the angles where the points project (see photo) to be 30 degrees or more (from the horizontal if the line were extended across the base of the point). This design does require that the wall be built on firm soil; the hardpan in my yard was just fine.

I selected the largest posts for the base course, buried them about two-thirds into the soil, and spiked them to the ground after making sure that the tops were level. The posts generally have a slight taper, so I laid them with the larger butts all at the same end in one course, and in the next placed the butts at the opposite end. I leaned the wall inward slightly to offset any shifting during backfilling. Where posts had to be cut, I saturated the cut ends with a wood preservative at least three times.

With this construction method, you have to fill as you build, and that quickly raised another question: what to do about those alternating gaps between posts? First I tried wedging in large rocks salvaged during my digging. That was time—and rock—consuming. So I decided to use a polypro-

2 **A vertical post wall** (above) can be built up to 4 feet high with 4- to 5-inch-diameter posts (which must be 50 percent below grade). Each post is nailed to its neighbor (drawing above left) as it is placed. An alternative design (left) uses 5-inch-diameter vertical posts up to 4 feet apart with smaller horizontals laid between. Verticals should be set in cement at least 50 percent below grade.

SPIKE AS YOU GO

TOPS CAN BE EVEN, UNEVEN, OR CAPPED

SET POSTS 50% BELOW GRADE, TAMP WITH FIRM SOIL, GRAVEL OR CEMENT

RAILS 2½" MIN. DIA.

3'-4'

MAIN POSTS 5" MIN. DIA.

RAIL JOINTS BEHIND POSTS. IF LONGER RAILS USED, STAGGER JOINTS

SET POSTS 50% BELOW GRADE IF CEMENT USED. IF NOT, INCREASE DEPTH

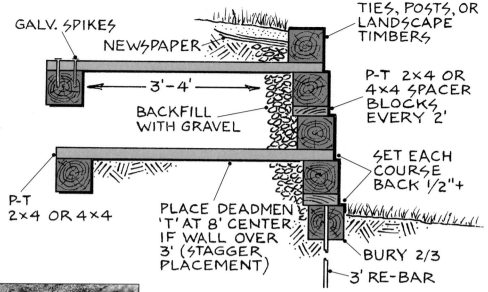

GALV. SPIKES

NEWSPAPER

TIES, POSTS, OR LANDSCAPE TIMBERS

3'–4'

BACKFILL WITH GRAVEL

P-T 2×4 OR 4×4 SPACER BLOCKS EVERY 2'

SET EACH COURSE BACK 1/2"+

P-T 2×4 OR 4×4

PLACE DEADMEN 'T' AT 8' CENTER IF WALL OVER 3' (STAGGER PLACEMENT)

BURY 2/3

3' RE-BAR

3 **Spaced timber wall** at far left uses railroad ties separated by 2×4 pressure-treated blocks, with each course set back from that below. Deadman Ts (above) are required to stabilize the wall if it is more than 3 feet high. Spaced timber wall at left combines stacked 4×4s and rock-covered terraces.

pylene fabric from Du Pont called Typar. It has impressive puncture strength, won't rot, lets water pass easily, and can be stapled in place. I paid 16 cents a square foot for it. To cap the tops of the walls, I used cedar 1 × 6s braced with wood blocks as needed, though 2 × 6s would be better.

I built three walls, each about 4 feet high; each was stepped at least 4 feet back from the next lower wall. In less stable soil, the setback would have to be increased. (Local building codes should give you some guidance on this.) With fine-grained backfill like mine, it's necessary to put 6 to 10 inches of drainage rock or compacted sand behind the Typar to stop soil particles from plugging the fabric.

I built 180 feet of 4-foot-high wall for about $800 (Canadian) worth of materials. It's been a couple of years since I laid down my tools, and the walls are still looking good—*by Bruce Shepherd. Drawings by Gerhard Richter.*

four unique fences

Sing a song of the American fence, and you'll find that the harmony is there but you're short on melodic variations.

The harmonic line comes from the standard picket, board, or post-and-rail fences, which can supply privacy, act as a windbreak, or cordon off an area, clearly delineating mine from yours. They're all functional, but hardly architecturally arresting. There's not a rhapsodic melody among them.

That's where this sampling of unique yet functional fences comes in. These four easy-to-build fences can be erected on level or sloped ground. And each features an intriguing design that also influences its surroundings.

The slat-shaded arbor built into fence No. 2 sculpts sun and shade to create a light-defined cozy area. And the curbside portion of the planter-box fence (3) holds greenery and flowers to integrate the yard and structure. A low fence, it invites a cheery greeting from passers-by.

Which fence is right for you? If you only want to outline an area, consider the planter-box fence. The other fences can all ensure privacy—your choice depends on your needs.

Building a privacy fence means making a trade-off between ventilation and seclusion. Erect too heavy a structure, and you risk creating an airless outdoor room. But you'll need a sturdy windbreak for a wind-swept

site. The more a fence cuts off wind, the stronger it must be.

Fence No. 1, for example, is an impressive windbreak. On the other hand, wind filters through the reed fence (4), so the fence will temper a strong breeze but won't cut it off. This fence's delicate texture and structure help it blend in with a well-kept yard. If you want to create a shaded outdoor room, consider fence No. 2, with its lattice canopy.

To erect any fence on a slope, think in terms of building a staircase. First determine the structure's length. Then figure out how far the fence has to drop by calculating the distance between the slope and the horizontal plane. Average that distance over the

1 **Four-foot-long** slat-topped sections balance the rugged 8-foot-long "rooftop" segments and admit light and air. A concrete collar around the sunken posts adds stability to the heavy fence. Note the alternating 1×2s and 1×6s.

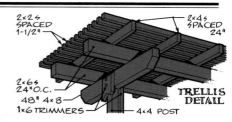

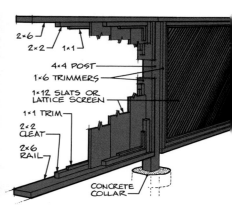

2 **Oriental-like overhang's** carefully laid slats help mold sun and shadow to create a restful poolside hideaway. The gridded superstructure is anchored to a lattice fence, which wraps around to create a light and airy outdoor room.

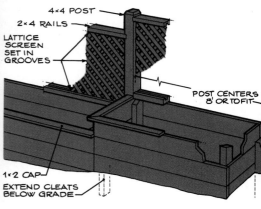

3 **Sturdy planter boxes** anchor the low part of the fence. Note the mitered cleat top, which helps hide the nailers. The higher portion of the fence, with solid-board bottom, ensures privacy while continuing the lattice pattern.

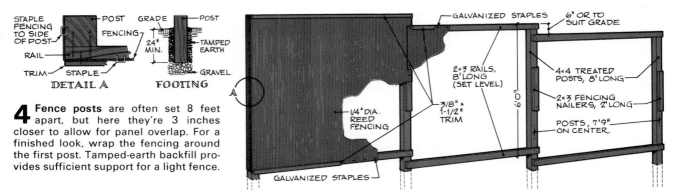

STAPLE FENCING TO SIDE OF POST — **POST** — **GRADE** — **POST**

FENCING — **24" MIN.** — **TAMPED EARTH**

RAIL — **POST**

TRIM — **STAPLE** — **GRAVEL**

DETAIL A   **FOOTING**

GALVANIZED STAPLES — **6" OR TO SUIT GRADE**

2×3 RAILS, 8' LONG (SET LEVEL)

3/8" × 1-1/2" TRIM

1/4" DIA. REED FENCING

GALVANIZED STAPLES

4×4 TREATED POSTS, 8' LONG

2×3 FENCING NAILERS, 2' LONG

POSTS, 7'9" ON CENTER

6'0"

A

4 Fence posts are often set 8 feet apart, but here they're 3 inches closer to allow for panel overlap. For a finished look, wrap the fencing around the first post. Tamped-earth backfill provides sufficient support for a light fence.

number of proposed panels to make each step down of equal height. There is no prescribed step height—it must be matched to the grade.

Panel fences are usually built in 6- or 8-foot-long segments. This aesthetically pleasing dimension coincides with precut lumber sizes, so you can save time and avoid waste by using pieces that require little cutting.

The reed fence's panels should also be a conventional length. In this case, though, it's more a matter of looks than saving money. The fence panel here is ¼-inch-diameter reed woven together with vinyl-covered steel wire

and stapled to the frame. The designer purchased the 6-foot-high fencing in 15-foot-long rolls from Montgomery Ward; it's also available in many lawn-and-garden supply stores. The 24-foot-long fence shown here cost $70 to erect.

A word on wood care: Left untreated, redwood weathers to a driftwood gray. You can assist Mother Nature by coating the boards with a bleaching oil or stain, which brings on a uniformly weathered look. If you prefer your redwood pristine, coat the boards with a clear sealer. This will arrest the natural color at a buckskin

tan and allow the grain to show through. If your fence is to be in a moist, shaded area, buy a sealer or stain with a mildewcide. A reed fence, incidentally, weathers to an eye-soothing silver-gray.

If you're interested in building a redwood fence, you might find helpful two booklets from the California Redwood Association (591 Redwood Highway, Suite 3100, Mill Valley, CA 94941): "Fences," 50¢, and "Tips for Garden Projects," 35¢—by *Richard Layne. Drawings by Eugene Thompson.*

20 knockdown fasteners

N o, it's not time to throw away your dowels, nails, nuts and bolts, or screws—yet. But if you're planning to build projects that are easy to take apart, store in a tight spot, and reassemble, then a variety of knockdown fasteners will come in handy.

These clever devices offer a fast, sturdy method of forming secure joints that fit together and come apart in ingenious ways—without wearing out the hardware or the holes. But that isn't the fasteners' only asset.

Building with knockdown devices may be faster than using screws and glue for some projects. Knockdown furniture is typically built with easy-to-make butt or overlapping joints rather than complicated and time-consuming mitered and dadoed joints. That also makes figuring part dimensions easier because you don't have to consider the depth of complicated joints. Also, you can sand and finish the parts before assembly: It's easier and faster to sand a flat board than one with joints cut in.

Second, with a knockdown joint the wood is free to swell or contract without being damaged. In conventional furniture, a joint locked up with glue can't give and can crack from excessive swings in temperature and humidity.

You don't have to sacrifice looks to use knockdown fasteners, either. You can hide some fasteners in blind holes. Others, such as the joint connectors shown in photo 1, fit inside the project. Often those that can be seen are unobtrusive, or can be hidden with decorative caps. You are, however, limited in your design options. A basic rule: Simple is better. I recommend using knockdown fasteners for straightforward projects like chairs with flat sides, shelves, bed and sofa frames, rectangular cabinets, flush cabinet doors, simple legs, and flat panels.

1. Here are two shortcuts in assembling cabinets. To secure the plastic connector from Constantine (right), push the two slotted mating pieces together, then insert a steel wedge bar into the slot. Remove the bar, and the joint comes apart. In a like device (left) from The Woodworkers' Store, a metal locking clip slides over plastic blocks to hold them fast.

2. Hanger bolts (top) from Constantine can be dressed up with crown-head nuts (bottom) for indoor furniture. The threaded nut (middle) takes a machine screw and is mounted $1/16$ to $1/8$ inch below the surface. To hide the screw head, use a cover plug. The nut is available from Armor, Craftsman, DRI, Trend-Lines, Woodcraft, and The Woodworkers' Store.

3. To install Jawbolt (from Jaw Mfg.), drill the mating pieces and tap in the assembled bolt. A few turns with an allen wrench flares out the anchor.

4. Knockdown sawhorses cut workshop clutter. A 2-inch-high plastic model from Sears, Trend-Lines, and Woodcraft holds a 2×4 flat. The two-piece sawhorse is bolted together; to disassemble, unscrew the wing nut. A stamped-steel version from Constantine holds a 2×4 on edge.

Keep in mind that not every joint in a knockdown piece must use a knockdown device. For example, narrow stock can be glued up into panels for drawers that won't be taken apart, even though they'll be in a knockdown cabinet.

There are a few dos and don'ts for knockdown hardware. You must be exact when lining up the mating components of a fastener. There are several ways to accomplish this. For bolt-type fasteners (see photos 2 and 5), align and clamp the wood pieces together, then drill through both parts. If the hole in one piece needs to be enlarged to accept the hardware, as it does for threaded nuts (see photo 2), unclamp the pieces and redrill. If you're sinking blind holes, drill one member first. Then use dowel centers to transfer thelayout to the mating part. If you're working with hanging devices like shelf brackets (see photo 11),

5. Connector bolts with cap nuts from The Woodworkers' Store are ideal for connecting the sides of adjoining cabinets and for fastening cabinet sides to interior vertical supports. The flathead bolts come in two lengths for connections from 1 3/16 to 2 1/4 inches thick.

6. To install this rugged bed-rail fastener from The Woodworkers' Store, inlay one piece on the bed rail, the other on the bed post. For bed frames, there are also knockdown surface-mount corner fasteners from Armor, Craftsman, and Woodworker's Supply. Bed-rail fasteners can also be used on chair and sofa frames.

7. For hidden hardware, use the invisible plug and socket connectors from The Woodworkers' Store—they fit into blind holes. To connect them, push the joints together. In the Elite fitting from The Woodworkers' Store, the shaft is threaded into a hole that's pushed into a hole. The other end fits into a cammed disc that turns to lock.

8. Tite Joint fasteners from Craftsman and The Woodworkers' Store apply even pressure for assembly of counter tops, wood panels, and furniture. To tighten or loosen the fasteners, insert a small supplied rod in the ball nut and turn. There's also a special drill bit and drill guide.

fasten one of the mating components to the wood. Then hold it to the mating surface and carefully mark the location of the hardware's side and end. Finally, drill the holes and fasten the remaining hardware piece.

The don'ts are simple but crucial. Don't be stingy with the number of devices you use. On a wide-railed, heavy water-bed frame, for example, use two bed-rail fasteners on each corner. And don't skimp on the screws that fasten the devices in place. Use the longest screws appropriate, and be sure they are driven into sound material. Finally, don't subject the piece to excessive loads. Knockdown fasteners may not be as strong as conventional fasteners, so it's good practice to protect them from stress when possible. If a cabinet top will carry a load, for example, make the top overlap and rest on the sides rather than have the sides overlap the top. Another option is to use cleats and aligning blocks for support—*by Phil McCafferty. Photos by Greg Sharko.*

SOME SOURCES OF KNOCKDOWN FASTENERS
Armor Products, Box 445, East Northport, NY 11731; **Constantine,** 2050 Eastchester Rd., Bronx, NY 10461; **Craftsman Wood Service Co.,** 1735 W. Cortland Ct., Addison, IL 60101; **DRI Industries,** 11100 Hampshire Ave. S., Bloomington, MN 55438; **Jaw Manufacturing Co.,** Box 213, Reading, PA 19603; **Sears, Roebuck and Co.,** Sears Tower, Chicago, IL 60684; **Theatrical Warehouse,** 1108 Quaker St., Dallas, TX 75207; **Trend-Lines,** 375 Beacham St., Chelsea, MA 02150; **Woodcraft Supply Corp.,** Box 4000, Woburn, MA 01888; **The Woodworkers' Store,** 21801 Industrial Blvd., Rogers, MN 55374; **Woodworker's Supply of New Mexico,** 5604 Alameda N.E., Albuquerque, NM 87113.

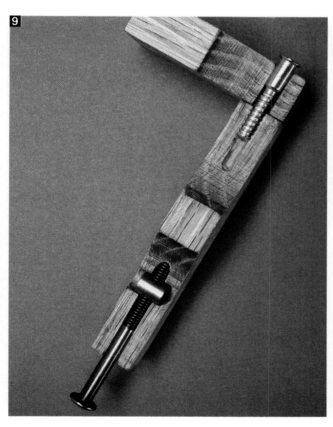

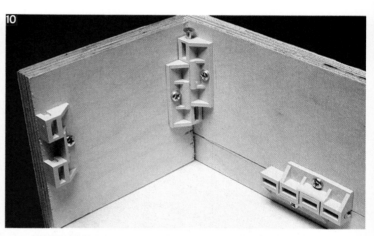

9. Lag screw (top) is available in 1 1/2- and 2-inch lengths. The flat head can accept a decorative brown cap. To install the cross-dowel bolts (bottom), use a screwdriver to turn the slotted threaded dowel so it can accept the bolt. Both fasteners are from The Woodworkers' Store.

10. Knockdown fasteners are a boon to the theater, where bulky scenery is used repeatedly and storage space is tight. One stage-struck device is the Brooks Fastener System, from Theatrical Warehouse. To install it, drill four holes for the two identical plastic pieces. Secure them and slide the pin in, and you've formed a tough right-angle joint.

11. Here are three ways to hang wall units, cabinets, or shelving with knockdown fasteners from Constantine and The Woodworkers' Store. The taper connector (left) comes in 4- to 6-inch lengths. The two parts of the hanger (center) interlock with the help of a slightly raised tongue. The fastener is only 1/8 inch thick when mounted. The hardware at right uses protruding screws to hook into a mating surface.

12. For knockdown furniture legs, use nut plates available from Craftsman and The Woodworkers' Store. Ready-to-use commercial legs have mating fasteners installed. If you make your own legs, use 5/16-inch hanger bolts for fasteners.

router tips from a pro

The router deserves a better reputation. You probably know that it's the best tool for cutting rabbets, rounding off edges, or creating decorative flourishes. But that brief list doesn't come close to exhausting its capabilities.

Choose the right bit and add one of the easy-to-make jigs featured here or a commercial accessory (see table at end of chapter), and in minutes you can cut precise dovetail, dado, mortise-and-tenon, or tongue-and-groove joints. Or you can form rounds for table tops, hollow out a block (for trays or bowls), or cut openings in wall panels. You can even turn your router into a stationary shaper by buying or building a special table. There's no other tool that matches this versatility.

And you can do all this without dipping deeply into your coffers. For less than $80 you can get a 1- to 1½-horsepower router. That's all the power you need. All routers operate at high speeds (up to 25,000 rpm), which is one of the reasons the tools cut so smoothly.

Bits are usually extra and come in three varieties: all steel, high-speed steel with tungsten-carbide cutting edges, and solid tungsten carbide. The tungsten-carbide bits can cost three times as much as their steel cousins, but their smoother cuts and longer life make them worth the price, especially for workhorse bits. For some jobs, like trimming abrasive laminate, a tungsten-carbide bit is mandatory. But there's nothing wrong with buying a steel bit if you plan to have only occasional use for it.

Bits come in an array of shapes and sizes, each with a specific job. Which ones do you need? That depends on the kind of woodworking you do. You'll find straight and dovetail bits handy for precision joinery. (A purist may object to using a router for dovetailing, but the results would make

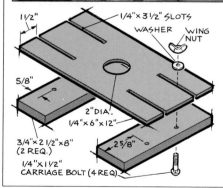

1½"   1/4" x 3½" SLOTS
WASHER   WING NUT
5/8"
2" DIA.
1/4" x 6" x 12"
3/4" x 2 1/2" x 8" (2 REQ.)
2 5/8"
1/4" x 1 1/2" CARRIAGE BOLT (4 REQ.)

Here's an easy way to increase a router's uses: Replace the original base with this special base (left). Use the router's original base as a template to locate attachment holes. The base features adjustable guides secured with wing nuts that help center the router while it straddles the work. These come in handy when you're cutting mortises (above), for example. Secure the workpiece in a vise clamp—an excellent way to hold narrow pieces steady while you cut a groove.

any craftsman proud.) And if you like to add finishing touches to your handiwork, there are scores of decorative bits, including cove, corner-round, and Roman ogee.

To guide your router you'll need a pilot, an edge guide, or one of the jigs featured here. A pilot is a smooth steel shank that's either an integral part of a bit or a separate component that can be screwed onto a bit's end. The pilot rides against the work edge, guiding the router and controlling the width of the cut.

There are two kinds of pilots: fixed or ball bearing. The former work OK, but they can heat up from friction and leave burn marks on the wood. That's

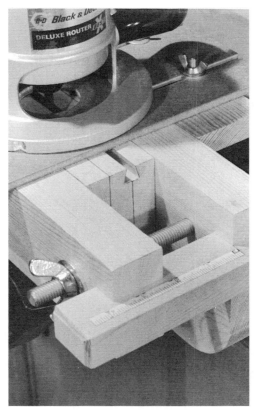

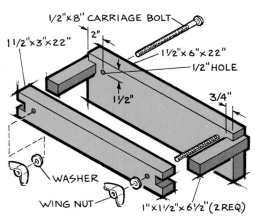

To cut a dovetail slot (above), remove one of the base's guides; adjust the remaining one to let the bit cut into one edge of the workpiece. To protect the work and help level the router, sandwich the workpiece between scrap pieces in the vise clamp (above). A self-adhesive ruler on the clamp helps line up cuts. To cut a second slot, turn the router around so the guide is against the clamp's opposite edge, and make a second pass. Use the same technique to cut a tongue for tongue-and-groove joints.

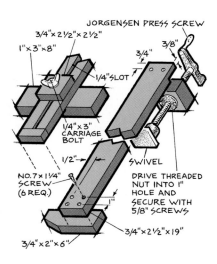

You can form tenons fast when you use a router. First, select a block of stock that's wide enough to supply the number of rails you need. Then slip a wide, straight bit into the router, and make as many passes as it takes to reach the tenon's length (above left). After you rip your pieces from the wood block, flip them over and assemble them in the clamp guide as shown (right). Then use the router to finish trimming the tenons (center). You can either dress the tenons to fit a round-end mortise or use a narrow chisel to make the mortise ends square.

why I recommend a ball-bearing pilot, which turns freely, rotating only as you move the tool. Whichever you use, keep the pilot pressed firmly against the work edge and make sure that the edge is straight and smooth. The pilot will faithfully follow any bump or crevice—and guide the cutter to duplicate it.

An edge guide is a basic commercial accessory that's used to cut a straight groove parallel to the stock's edge.

The width of the cut depends on the bit. The guide is easy to use. Just keep it snug against the wood, and make sure the router is level during the cut.

There are probably more commercial accessories and custom-designed jigs available for a router than for any other shop tool. Some accessories can be costly, but you can make some out of scrap wood to perform a variety of chores that let you take full advantage of your router.

You can use the clamp guide, for example, for help in forming tenons, rabbeting, and cutting a variety of grooves. The vise clamp and special router-base guide make a fine combination for cutting mortises, slotlike dovetails, and tongue-and-groove joints. The vise clamp is especially adept at gripping narrow pieces whose edges must be shaped. And the circle guide helps make fast work of cutting table tops, for example.

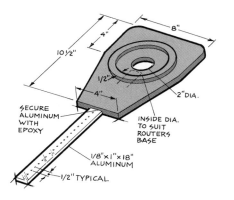

SECURE ALUMINUM WITH EPOXY

10½"
8"
4"
4"
½"
2" DIA.
INSIDE DIA. TO SUIT ROUTERS BASE
⅛"×1"×18" ALUMINUM
½" TYPICAL

Nothing will form a circular groove, cut openings in wall panels, or make rounds for table tops like a router fitted with this easy-to-make circle guide (above). The guide shown will form circles up to 36 inches in diameter.

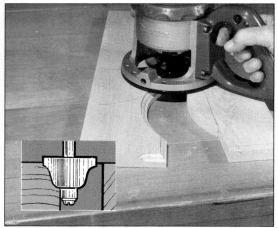

To cut dadoes, fit a plunge bit into the router. The bit's point enables it to pierce the wood while the router is lowered to sit on the work. Use a straightedge to guide the cut (left). To cut a stop dado, clamp a block on the straightedge to control the cut length. If you want to hollow out part of a block—something you might do when making a tray, for instance—attach an extended base to the router so it can span a wider area than the regular base will allow (center). A bit with a pilot (inset, right) can be used to shape curved as well as straight edges. Whenever you are using a pilot, be sure to insert a scrap block from the workpiece under the router's base on the side away from the work. This will go a long way toward keeping the router level. For an abridged list of commercial accessories, take a look through the table above.

Here are some basic tips for using a router:

● Grip the router firmly when you turn it on and as you feed it.

● Give it time to come up to full speed before making careful, initial contact with the wood.

● Keep the tool level. If necessary, put a scrap piece under the router's base on the side away from the work.

● Because bits turn clockwise, feed left to right. This is an ideal way to keep the cutter moving with the work.

● Cut with the grain whenever possible. You'll have to ignore this rule when doing freehand work, of course. Compensate by feeding slower and not forcing the blade—this will give you better control of the cutter and prevent any scorch marks from appearing on the wood.

All routers, no matter how powerful, are limited in how deeply they can cut and in their feed speed. You don't have to be a pro to realize you're taxing the tool when the cutting speed drops considerably or when burn marks appear on the wood or bit. Keep the bit working, but be sympathetic with the router's limitations. The more wood you're cutting, the slower your feed should be. Sometimes it's better to repeat a pass, cutting deeper the second time, to get the full shape or groove depth needed.

If you must stop during a cut, move the router away from the cut at a right angle. When you're ready to start again, slide the bit back into the groove, slightly short of where you left off—*by R.J. De Cristoforo. Drawings by Gerhard Richter.*

hidden hinges

I'm fascinated by all the devilishly clever hinges that give hardly a hint of their existence. You may not have seen them, but increasingly they are hiding in top-quality commercially made cabinetry. Now a wide variety of these hinges is available to you in retail stores.

The concealed hinges I've selected can be sorted into six types (see table). Some are more expensive than regular hinges, and some look complicated, but they are not that difficult to install. Most came with good instructions; some did not. A few had none. Some do not allow for adjustment after they're installed; others allow as much as 3/16-inch movement in three directions.

You have to do some freehand mortising to install a few of these hinges. And you need special drill bits for many. The multipivot (or European), face-frame, and lid hinges shown call for the use of a 35-mm flat-bottom bit to make the holes, but you can use a 1⅜-inch bit. It's risky to use spade bits: The starter point may be long enough to break through the face of the wood. Forstner-type bits are better: They do not chip on entry, they

cut very smoothly, and they have a short starter point.

The fully concealed cylinder hinges (often called Soss hinges) require holes bored with 10-, 12-, and 14-mm bits. You can substitute 25/64- and 15/32-inch bits, respectively, for the first two, but if you don't have a fractional drill close to 14 mm, you should buy the metric bit. Armor Products and The Woodworkers' Store (see addresses) sell metric bits—*by Phil McCafferty. Photos by Greg Sharko.*

SOURCES OF HIDDEN HINGES
Abra, Inc., Box 1086, Bloomington, IN 47402; **Armor Products,** Box 445, East Northport, NY 11731; **Constantine,** 2050 Eastchester Rd., Bronx, NY 10461; **Craftsman Wood Service Co.,** 1735 Cortland St., Addison, IL 60101; **The Fine Tool Shops, Inc.,** Box 1262, Danbury, CT 06810; **Klockit,** Box 629, Lake Geneva, WI 53147; **Leichtung, Inc.,** 4944 Commerce Pkwy., Cleveland, OH 44128; **National Builders Hardware,** 1019 S.E. 10th Ave., Portland, OR 97214; **Woodcraft Supply Co.,** Box 4000, Woburn, MA 01801; **The Woodworkers' Store,** 21801 Industrial Blvd., Rogers, MN 55374; **Woodworker's Supply of New Mexico,** 5604 Alameda Rd. N.E., Albuquerque, NM 87113.

Forstner-type bits (author's has multiple cutters) are best to drill flat-bottom holes; drill press or jig is a must.

Multipivot, or European, hinges are ideal for carcass (box) cabinetry. One piece screws to cabinet side or partition; the other fits in flat-bottom hole in door. Installed (left, rear) is Hettich hinge for overlay doors; it allows 90-degree door opening.

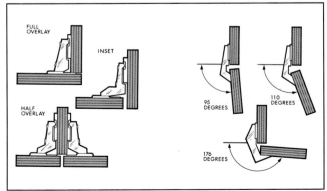

In front is 176-degree Grass hinge for inset doors. Drawings above illustrate overlay and inset doors and various opening angles available.

Fully concealed (often called Soss) hinges mount in edges (rear) or in edge and face, and open up to 180 degrees. At front, from left: Soss heavy-duty die-cast mortise-type; Brev machined-brass cylinder-type; Soss stamped-mortise-type. Cylinder-type fits bored holes; mortise-type requires bores plus shallow inletting. These hinges are not adjustable; install with extra care.

Automatic spring hinges are heavy-duty, utilitarian hardware. They face-mount without mortising. Spring action holds door (overlay or inset) closed without catches. Use on overhead doors and on side doors in campers and vans.

Lid, or fall-flap, hinges open so that lid is flush with surface to which it's hinged. When lid is closed, one hinge edge shows. ONI hinge (left) is metal; Hettich (right) has plastic housing. Both require 35-mm flat-bottom holes.

Invisible hinges for face-frame cabinets mount either on the front of the frame (left) or the edge (above). Both screw to the frame surface but require flat-bottom holes drilled in the door. These hold door closed without a catch.

Single-pivot Mico hinge (top) has nylon roller that cams into recess to hold door (overlay or lip) closed without catches. It requires 1/4-inch slot that breaks through edge of door. Hettich single-pivot hinge (above) is for hanging inset doors from cabinet top and bottom. Pivot pins rotate in nylon bushings that fit into holes you drill in top and bottom members. Hinges are tiny, unobtrusive, and adjustable; doors are easily removable by loosening four screws.

SOME HIDDEN-HINGE MANUFACTURERS

Type	Brand	Approx. price per pair ($)	Use	Materials and finishes	Size(s)	Comments, special features	Sources
Single-pivot	Hettich	2–5	Inset doors	Zinc- and nickel-plated steel	1″ × 1″	Adjustable	The Woodworkers' Store and Woodworker's Supply of New Mexico
	Mico	1–1.80	Lip and overlay doors	Nickel- and dark-copper- plated steel	1½″ × 2″	Self-loaded- closing types for lip and overlay doors ⅝″ and ¾″ thick	Armor Products and National Builders Hardware
	Roto-Hinge (see text)	0.80–1.50	Folding furniture, louvers. Lazy Susans, inset and overlay doors	Plated steel, hardwood	⅜″, ½″, ¾″, 1″ dia. × ⅜″, 9⁄16″ length	360-deg. swivel	Abra, Constantine, Leichtung, and Woodworker's Supply of New Mexico
Multi-pivot (European)	Blum	5–10	Half-, full-overlay, and inset doors	Nickel-plated steel	35-mm bore	Types for 95-, 110-, and 176-deg. opening, plus self-closing types; adjustable	The Woodworkers' Store
	Grass	7–10	Half-, full-overlay, and inset doors	Nickel-plated steel		Types for 100- and 176-deg. opening; spring closure; six-way adjustable	Constantine, National Builders Hardware, and Woodcraft Supply
	Hettich	3–8	Half-, full-overlay doors ⅝″–1¼″ thick	Nickel-plated steel, brown and white plastic		90-deg. opening; adjustable	Craftsman Wood Service and The Fine Tool Shops
		3.50–9	Half-, full-overlay, and inset doors	Nickel-plated steel, white plastic		Types for 96- and 168-deg. swing; spring closure; adjustable; min. door thickness 9⁄16″, max. ¾″	Constantine
Face-frame	Blum	5.50	Overlay doors with face frame	Antique-brass- plated metal	35-mm bore	Attaches to edge of face frame; types for ¾″ and 1½″ overlay available; adjustable	The Woodworkers' Store
	Grass	6		Antique-brass- and nickel-plated metal		Attaches to front of face frame; adjustable	The Woodworkers' Store and Woodworker's Supply of New Mexico
Lid (flap)	Hettich	3	Drop-down lids, doors, and flaps	Nickel-plated steel, brown plastic	35-mm bore	Adjustable	Constantine
	ONI	6–8		Nickel- and brass-plated steel		For heavy-duty applications; adjustable	Craftsman Wood Service and The Woodworkers' Store
Fully concealed	Soss	4–6	Folding doors and leaves, inset doors with sufficient frame thickness	Brass-plated zinc and steel	½″-dia. posts	Cylinder-type for ⅝″ -or-thicker doors	Constantine and Craftsman Wood Service
		5–9		Brass-plated steel	⅜″ × 1″ plate, ⅜″ × 1¹¹⁄16″ plate	Mortise-type	Constantine and The Woodworkers' Store
		7–12		Brass-plated zinc and steel	½″ × 1¾″ plate, ½″ × 2⅜″ plate, ⅝″ × 2¾″ plate	Mortise-type	Constantine, Craftsman Wood Service and Woodworker's Supply of New Mexico
	Various	3–6		Brass, brass-plated steel	10-mm posts for ½″ wood, 14-mm posts for ¾″ wood, 16-mm posts for ⅞″–1″ wood	Cylinder-type	Constantine, Klockit, National Builders Hardware, and The Woodworkers' Store
Automatic- spring	Synco	3–5	Drop flaps, overhead doors, overlay and inset doors	Chrome-plated steel	1⅞″ × 4¾″	Spring-loaded closure; 90-deg. opening; mounts on surface	Armor Products, Craftsman Wood Service, and The Woodworkers' Store

jointing on a disc sander

Wood cut with a saw usually is not accurate, smooth, or square enough for cabinetry work and other glued assembly, even if the cutting was done on a radial-arm or table saw. You can spend your time tinkering with adjustments on your saw to keep it as accurate as possible, or you can use the saw (as many woodworkers do) to cut the stock slightly oversize, then clean up the surface and bring the stock to accurate dimensions with other tools.

After blanking work on a table saw or radial saw, I now take the work to my 12-inch, bench-mounted disc sander for final fitting. The sander is fast and quiet. Using the miter gauge on the sander table, I bring the ends of boards to very accurate length without splintering and with an angle of exactly 90 degrees—or whatever is required. Then I dress the edges of the stock with a freehand technique that is surprisingly easy and accurate—with practice. It even works for large plywood panels.

I do these jobs on my disc sander, despite the fact that I have a perfectly good jointer in my shop. The jointer's rotating blades could do most edge dressing well, indeed, but they can't handle end grain or knotty and wild-grain woods. Nor can a jointer be used safely with stock shorter than 12 inches, narrower than 3/4 inch, or less than 1/2 inch thick. For all these reasons, I seldom use my jointer.

How to joint on a sander

You can joint the long edge of a workpiece on a disc sander by passing it across the face with a steady motion. But it must not pass quite straight across. You want the wood to contact the disc on the downward side only. If it contacts the upward side, you will get sawdust in your face at the least, and the workpiece in your mouth if you lose control of it. With a flat disc and a straightedge on the wood, touching only the down side might seem impossible. Actually, you will have very light contact on the upward side, but only the down side will be cutting.

I accomplish this with a strictly freehand technique, using sound and feel to guide me. With this method you feed the work from the down side. As the work is fed across the disc, you can feel and hear at which point it is in working contact with the disc and at which point it isn't. As you move the wood, you keep the working contact on the down side. It takes some practice to learn how to do this—just as it takes some practice to get an even cut on a jointer.

There are other ways to use a disc sander for jointing. Some woodworkers clamp a wood fence to the table and run the workpiece between the fence and the disc. The work has to be fed past the up side of the disc to make contact with the down side. The fence must be angled slightly to keep the work clear of the disc's up side. That forces the sanding to be done by the rim of the abrasive disc, which produces the worst possible scratch pattern.

Another approach is to use a sanding disc with a slight conelike bevel (no more than 2 degrees). This seems an obvious solution to the problem of contacting the down side of the disc while clearing the up side. But I'm leery of the beveled sanding disc. The major problem: getting a flat piece of abrasive paper securely glued to the conical disc. For this reason I haven't tried it. I might be a bit oversensitive on this point; I was once hit over the eye with a freshly stuck-on abrasive disc that flew off when the sander was turned on. (Consequently, I don't use stick adhesive anymore. I use Sears Disc Cement No. 2220.)

Plywood can be squared, even if panel is so large you can't see actual sanding; you can judge by feel and sound.

End-grain sanding to length can be done automatically on Shopsmith sanding disc; it has quill control and feed stop.

To joint the long edge of work, you feed from downward side of disc, easing work flat against disc with steady motion.

As work crosses face of disc, press it lightly against downward side while grazing upward side for minimum contact.

As end of work passes center of the disc, you ease it out of contact—but without angling, which would round the corner.

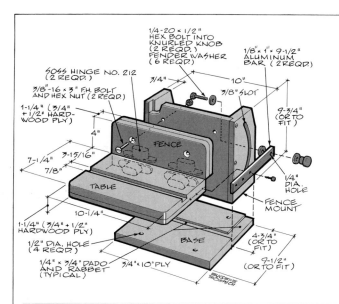

Each extension consists of two parts: a rigid vertical fence mounted on a base that is attached to the workbench, and a hinged table. The hinging is critical because the tables must tilt to match the tilt of your sander table. Ordinary leaf hinges can't be used because the knuckle would get in the way of the work. I used No. 212 Soss hinges (see diagram), which are completely recessed. The bases must be sized to fit your sander.

After cutting the parts, you assemble the bases. Glue and screw the baseboard and fence mount; attach the brackets temporarily with screws only. Glue the tables, and rout the miter-gauge clearance slots; glue the fences, and drill and countersink holes for the mounting bolts. Drill and clean out mortises for the Soss hinges using the template that comes with them. This must be done very accurately, either on a drill press or by horizontal boring on a Shopsmith. After mounting the hinges, check their operation. Shim the hinges so that the edges of the table and fence are closest together when the table is at 90 degrees.

Clamp the table-fence assemblies to the bases, and position them at the sides of the sander so the faces of the fences are flush with the face of the abrasive on the disc. Mark hole locations in the bench for either lag screws or machine through bolts; drill and mount the bases. Shift the clamped position of the table-fence assemblies so the tables are flush with the sander table (at 90 degrees), and drill through the fence mount.

Unclamp the table-fence assemblies, attach the aluminum bar-stock arms to the tables' sides, and bolt the assemblies to the bases. Trace the arc of the holes in the arms with the tables moved to 45 degrees up and down (or to match the pivot range of your sander table). Unscrew the side brackets and saw 3/8-inch-wide slots for the table-position locking bolts. Reassemble the brackets, check operation with bolts in the slots, then complete assembly with screws and glue. Varnish and wax the tables, and they're ready for use.

End-grain and plywood jointing

The bench disc sander is the one tool in your workshop that will surface end grain without splintering. The required accessory: a miter gauge. For accuracy, I set the miter gauge at 90 and 45 degrees, using a drafting triangle against the abrasive disc rather than depending on the gauge calibration or stops. I also use the triangle to set the tilting sander table perpendicular to the disc.

The miter-gauge positions narrow work accurately against the disc, but it is useless when you're squaring wide boards or plywood panels. Here, too, freehand sanding offers better control. The technique I use is to check the workpiece with a square, then take a pass across the disc with english applied to the work to correct the error. If you sand the workpiece with the high side up, the disc will apply the english. Using this method, you will be surprised at how fast you can get the touch necessary to square boards and plywood.

You can modify a disc sander for jointing long pieces and edging large plywood panels by adding in-feed and out-feed extensions equipped with fences. The fences guide the work on and off the disc and must be set accurately. The in-feed fence should be positioned approximately 1/32 inch behind the disc, and the out-feed fence should be flush with the disc surface. You must find the exact position of the in-feed fence by trial and error. Tables should have slots to clear (but not guide) the tongue of the miter gauge. The sidebar explains how to build them—*by Thomas H. Jones. Drawings by Eugene Thompson.*

12-INCH DISC SANDERS

Manufacturer	Model	Included	Recommended motor hp (1,725 rpm)	Shipping weight (lbs.)	Price ($)
Powermatic Div. of Houdaille Ind, Inc. McMinnville, TN 37110	35-B disc sander	Basic machine; no motor or controls	¾–1½	105	536
		Basic machine with stand; no motor or controls	¾–1½	206	613
Rockwell Power Tool Div. 400 N. Lexington Ave. Pittsburgh, PA 15208	31–122 abrasive finishing machine	Basic machine; no stand, motor, or controls	1	60	364
Sprunger Bros. Box 1621 Elkhart, IN 46515	DSF-21 disc sander	Complete with stand, motor, switch, and miter gauge	½	80	270
	DS-1200 disc sander	Basic machine; no motor, miter gauge, stand, or switch	½	40	165

eight elegant edges with layered laminates

For years, those dark, unsightly lines along counter-top edge seams have been the price you paid for the convenience and durability of plastic laminates. Save for this drawback, laminates provide one of the easiest routes to a professional-looking woodworking project. Simply glue and screw together a few pieces of particle board to form a core, and cover it with laminate: You can rapidly complete a piece of work as slick as anything you can buy in a store. But still, there are those dark edge-seam outlines to mar the effect.

Well, things have changed. The new laminates with full-depth color and no dark backings make it possible to produce work even slicker than you're likely to find in a store.

The trend toward "color-through" laminates, whose surface color runs all the way through to the rear of the sheet, started with Formica Corp.'s Colorcore; then Wilsonart followed with Solicor. R. J. DeCristoforo featured both in a chapter in last year's *Do-it-Yourself Yearbook*. Now Pioneer offers a similar product called Pionite Melcor (see listing of manufacturers). There's a premium for these new laminates, though: They will cost you from two-and-a-half to three times more than the earlier laminate materials.

Originally, the color-through laminates were developed to eliminate those dark lines, thereby improving durability by increasing the thickness of the wear layer of the laminate.

Along the way, however, designers have discovered new tricks you can do with the color-throughs to produce eye-catching edge treatments. Some of these techniques are described in the captions. But first, some general points:

Use a low-visibility contact cement when working with these laminates. Formica recommends its No. 100 or 140 cement; Wilsonart, its No. 500. The thickness of the glue line is critical to a neat job, so be sure to apply a thin, even layer of adhesive with a paintbrush or solvent-resistant roller. Also remember that, as in any project, using the right tools can make all difference. Here, you'll find that carbide-tipped tools make cutting much easier —*By A.J. Hand.*

Edge treatments you can make

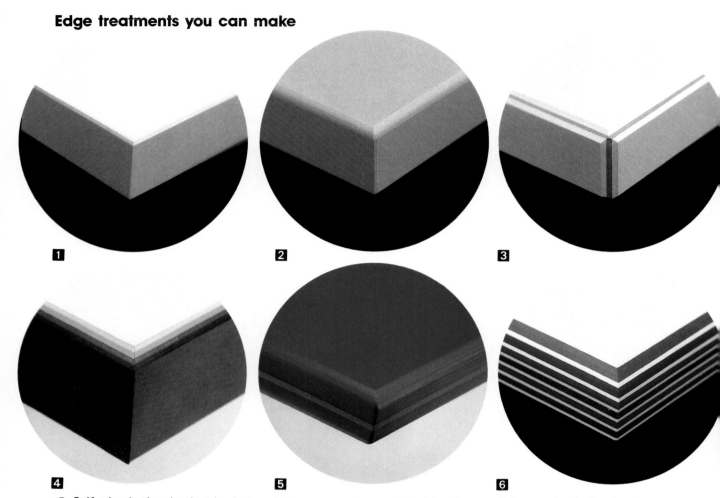

1 **Self edge is the simplest** laminate edge treatment of all. In most cases you'll use the same color material for both the top and edge banding. For contrast, I used Formica Colorcore in Desert Beige for the top and Cloud Blue for the edge banding.

The first step is to apply the edge banding. Put a double coat of cement on the edge of the substrate, allowing sufficient drying time between coats. A single coat will do for the edge banding. When the cement is tacky to the touch, place the edge banding in position. Trim the banding flush with your router, then fix the laminate to the top with a thin, uniform coat of cement on both surfaces. Position the laminate, and press it down firmly all around. For the neatest seams, apply extra pressure along the edges with a special edge-rolling tool, or squeeze the top down with a clamp and a block of wood to distribute the pressure and protect the laminate. Just tighten the clamp down on the block, release it, slide it along the edge a few inches, and repeat.

Trim the top with a router fitted with a bevel-trim bit, then rub the trimmed edge with lemon oil to restore it to full color and luster.

2 **Rounded edge can be produced** using the same techniques described for the self edge (1). The only difference is the choice of the router bit used for final trimming. Instead of a bevel-trim bit, use a rounding-over bit with either a 5/32- or 1/8-inch radius. Avoid using a bit with a radius larger than 5/32 inch or you'll cut all the way through the laminate and reveal the substrate. I used Dusty Jade Colorcore for this treatment and trimmed it with a 5/32-inch bit.

3 **Pinstripe edge** has a smart, contemporary look, and it's almost as easy to produce as the self edge (1). To start, apply a strip of edge banding in your choice of contrasting color to the edges of your work. Here I've employed Copper Rose Colorcore. Once it is in place, scuff-sand its smooth face with 80-grit paper to improve gluing adhesion. Using the same color as the top, cement another layer of edge banding right over it. Here, it was Silver Colorcore. Now trim both bands with a flush-trim bit. Apply the top laminate as before.

Finally, trim the edge with a 45-degree chamfer bit. Be sure to adjust the depth setting on your router to get the right effect. Set it too shallow, and you won't reveal the pinstripe; if you set it too deep, you may go all the way through to expose the substrate. It's a good idea to build a small mock-up of your edge treatment with scraps of laminate so you can do some test cuts on it and adjust your router accordingly.

4 **Shaded edge** gradually moves from a light shade at the top through ever-darkening bands in the same color family. For this sample, I started with Colorcore in Vanilla for the top, then graduated through Wheat, Sand, Ginger Brown, and Pumpernickel. There are several ways to achieve this effect, but here's the easiest:

Contrary to normal practice, apply your top laminate first. Next, apply a strip of edge banding in the next-darker shade using contact cement. Scuff-sand the face of this strip, and apply contact cement on the next-darker band. Sand and glue up a third band. Keep this up until all the colors are in place, then trim with a 45-degree chamfer bit and rub the machined edges with lemon oil.

An alternative procedure is to glue up the edge banding as a complete unit before cementing it to your work. This saves time because all strips can be glued at once—and all dry at the same time. Just scuff-sand all but the outermost layer of edge banding. Apply cement to mating surfaces, let them dry, and then assemble them.

The *drawback* to this technique is that you'll have to miter the banding units where they meet at corners. Applying the strips one at a time allows you to use simpler overlapping joints. You can also use a clear epoxy instead of contact cement. This can create very tight, invisible seams between strips, but it also requires great care and dozens of clamps.

5 **Bullnose pinstripe edge** requires plenty of work. To start, determine how many layers of laminate it will take

7 **8**

Laminate the edges and top as described for the self edge (1). Then take a ³⁄₈-inch ball-bearing rabbet bit and set it to cut a ³⁄₈-inch square rabbet. Make a test cut on a scrap of wood to check your settings, and then cut a rabbet into the top edge of your work. *Important:* If you cut this rabbet in the usual manner—feeding the router against the rotation of the bit—you will almost certainly chip the edge banding. Instead, start by taking a very light cut while feeding the router *with* the bit rotation. In other words, feed the router from right to left as you face your work. This cut need only be deep enough to penetrate the laminate. Also, don't try for a full cut, or the router will dig in and run on you. Just make a light pass. Then turn around and feed the router against bit rotation in the usual manner to complete the rabbet without fear of chipping.

Once the rabbet is cut, glue ³⁄₈-inch-square strips of hardwood into the rabbet with white adhesive. Miter the strips at all corners. When the glue is dry, trim the hardwood fillet with a chamfer bit. If you'd like a softer edge, you can use a rounding-over bit. For this example, I used Hunter Green Formica and an ash fillet.

8 **Formed hardwood edge** can be created with any of a variety of router bits. I used a "classical" bit here, but an ogee, cove, roman ogee, or rounding-over bit will also give good results. To begin, glue a strip of hardwood (I used walnut) to the edge of your work. Trim it flush on top with a flush-trim bit. Then apply edge banding (Wheat Colorcore here) in the usual manner. Next, laminate the top (I used Vanilla Colorcore). Finally, rout the edges using the edge-forming bit of your choice. Finish the hardwood with two or three coats of tung oil. *Note:* If this type of edge becomes damaged, you can renew it by rerouting it with your bit set a fraction of an inch deeper.

---

to build up to the desired thickness of your work. I used 12 layers of Spectrum Blue Colorcore for this job, plus two layers of Spectrum Red, and wound up with edge banding ³⁄₄ inch thick. Note that this thickness does not include the layer of blue for the top. Once you have determined the number of strips required, rip them about 1 inch wide on a table saw. Scuff-sand all smooth faces to increase adhesion, then contact-cement the strips into a neat stack. True up the stack by trimming about ¹⁄₈ inch off both edges on your table saw. A good triple-chip carbide blade works best for cutting this laminate stack.

Cut the finished edge-banding stack to the necessary lengths, miter any corners, and cement the pieces in place. Make sure to keep the top edge of the stack flush with the top edge of your work. An easy way to do this is to place your work face down on a smooth surface and simply slide the edge banding into position,

forcing it down tight against the work surface.

Once the edge banding is in place, install the top sheet of laminate. Then trim the edge—top and bottom—using a rounding-over bit. Here, I used a ³⁄₈-inch-radius bit, about right for the finished work thickness. Rub the machined edges with lemon oil.

6 **Candy-stripe edge allows endless** color combinations, but here I used a bright blend of Colorcore in Spectrum Red, Spectrum Blue, and White. The procedure is exactly the same as for the bullnose pinstripe (5), except here you finish off the edge with a larger ¹⁄₂-inch-radius rounding-over router bit.

7 **Chamfer fillet edge** puts the rich accent of hardwood along the edge of your work. If you do it as shown here, you won't even need to use the more costly color-through laminates. Conventional laminates will work just as well because the edges of the sheets remain covered.

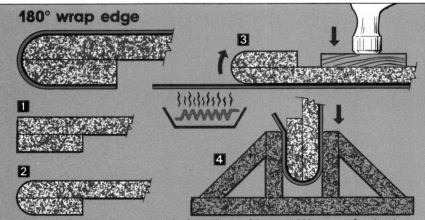

Conventional laminates can be heat-formed into a 180° wrap edge (top): 1) attach the particleboard strip to the bottom of the counter-top edge; 2) round off the edge, then apply contact cement to bonding surfaces; 3) position the counter top on laminate, leaving enough excess for wrap, apply pressure, and heat the laminate to 313° F; 4) slide the assembly into the forming fixture (made of scrap), remove it, and trim the edges.

Strips of laminate for a stacked edge banding are laid side by side for application of clear cement with a brush.

SOME MAKERS OF PLASTIC LAMINATES
Formica Corp., 155 Rte. 46 W., Wayne, NJ 07470; **Pioneer Plastics,** Div. of LOF Plastics Inc., Pionite Rd., Auburn, ME 04210; **Wilsonart** (Ralph Wilson Plastics Co.), 600 General Bruce Dr., Temple, TX 76501.

low-voltage yard lighting

Like most homeowners, I have an impulse to push back the night to make my house safer and more inviting. But the only real gesture I'd made in that direction was having my gas company install a post lantern in front of my house a few years ago. When the company recently enclosed a notice with my bill to alert me that the yard light was now costing me about $100 a year for gas, I took action. Rather than replace the lantern with an expensive 120-volt fixture

that would have involved conduit and buried cable, I converted the post lamp to operate with automotive bulbs (see drawing).

While I was at it, I made some more low-voltage fixtures that run off a photoelectric-control 12-volt power pack. The revamped post lamp seems almost as bright as it was when it burned gas, and with my other lights I've enhanced after-dark safety and security.

I've also reviewed what's commer-

cially available in outdoor lighting and have used a selection of these units for some striking effects in front of my house and in my backyard. The following pages explain how.

Low-voltage (L-V) units are not only safer and easier to install, they cost less to operate. One manufacturer estimates that a typical six-light set at current average electrical rates requires only a half-cent's worth of electricity per hour. And depending on the transformer you choose, you can

After dark, the stairs to a patio (left) or deck (above) can be hazardous, especially for guests not familiar with your turf. Hi-Lights units come with stakes that can be pushed into the earth at the sides of steps. These can be augmented with wall-mounted floodlights, as shown. Photo at right shows lawn lights and floods from RAB Electric.

Custom designing L-V lighting

PHOTO BY MALIBU

"Lightscaping" is the art of dramatizing your home and yard with the subtle special effects of outdoor lighting, while at the same time enhancing safety and security. Here are some procedures and tips that will help you plan and install the right system for your yard.

It's obvious that a well-lighted yard is a deterrent to prowlers. Also, you protect your family and guests by illuminating dark steps and other trip hazards such as uneven brick and flagstone walks.

Start by walking around your property in daylight and sketching a fairly large-scale and detailed layout showing trees, buildings, walks, etc. Note the locations of outdoor receptacles or protected places where transformers could be placed. Take another walk after dark with a flashlight, simulating floodlights and low-level lights with its

beam. See how light might play up under trees or shrubs. Identify all the places where lights would enhance safety.

● Floodlights highlight architectural aspects of your house, illuminate the exterior (photo, left), and accent trees and shrubs. Placed so as to "sweep" a wall, they dramatize textures such as masonry and rough-sawn wood.

● Globe lights around the perimeter of an outdoor spa or pool cast overall soft light to create a serene atmosphere. Their diffused light is also enough to light access areas, such as between a house and garage.

● Mushroom lights direct light downward to accentuate rocks and flowers in a garden and to detail shrubs or plantings. At the same time they can outline a pathway.

● Walk lights are most effective along pathways for illuminating steps or defining drives and patio perimeters.

At this point in planning, you need to know the wattage of bulbs and the capacity of the transformers available. Depending on the size of your planned installation, you might need more than one transformer. Check the specs; most are in the neighborhood of 100-watt capacity. Check the wattage specs of the bulbs you want to use. If you are planning to use eight 12-watt bulbs, you will need a transformer that can handle no less than 96 watts, and so on.

Purchased light sets should specify the bulb wattages. If you make your own, here are approximate specs: No. 89 single-contact bayonet-base automotive bulbs, seven watts; No. 93, 13 watts; No. 1004, 12 watts; No. 1034 or 1073, 23 watts; No. 1141, 18 watts; No. 1156 or 1157, 27 watts; No. 1195, 36 watts. The No. 4414 sealed-beam units you might buy from an L-V supplier should be marked for wattage—probably in the 11- to 17-watt range. Normal No. 14 wire from an L-V supplier should not exceed a 100-foot run. If it's convenient to locate a transformer in the middle of an area to be illuminated, run two directions equally from the transformer.

be pretty selective about the amount of time your system operates.

Whether you select from the good-looking and well-made lighting kits and fixtures on the market or make your own as shown on the following pages, the appeal and advantages of L-V systems are the same. The electrical voltage is reduced from 120 to a shock-free 12 volts by a transformer that incorporates a switch or timer device to control the lighting period. Wiring and mounting fixtures beyond the transformer not only eliminates the hazards of 120-volt circuits, it's also less time consuming. And you can do it all yourself, without bringing in a professional electrician.

To make your own L-V units, you'll need to buy components at an auto-supply store or department. For accent fixtures and subtle lighting, use single-contact bayonet-base bulbs and sockets. For floodlights, buy No. 4414 sealed-beam units at auto stores or sealed-beam replacement units (regular or halogen) from L-V lighting suppliers.

By all means, buy your L-V transformers from an L-V supplier, too, rather than trying to adapt doorbell transformers for the purpose. The latter are light-duty units that aren't weather resistant. And use an L-V supplier's high-quality hookup wire instead of regular two-conductor wire.

Fixture-making materials include PVC fittings, plastic dishes, translucent food jars and containers, and lumber that weathers well—such as redwood or pressure-treated pine.

Also handy for L-V lights are auto-accessory courtesy, backup, hood and trunk, and marking light fixtures. These come fully assembled (bulbs included) and are either water resistant already or are easily made so with a dab of silicone sealant.

Automotive sockets have only one wire lead because the socket would be grounded to the car body to complete the circuit. So you'll have to provide a wire to complete your circuit by fastening it to the socket with a wire lug and screw, or by soldering.

Even though low voltage is forgiving, take care to weatherproof any fixtures you make so the electrical contacts won't get rained on or stand in water. Plastic food containers are ideal for lamps because they have watertight snap-on or screw-on lids.

Where it's necessary to splice the wires outside a fixture in your custom-built system, strip and clean the connections, then twist the wires firmly together and coat them with electrical solder. Then be sure to wrap any exposed connection tightly with electrical tape.

It's best to make these final connections after you complete all hookups so that if the nighttime effect isn't quite what you want, you can fine-tune it by shifting locations of selected units. And bear in mind that if you don't want to expose your fixtures to the rigors of winter, you can design a system that you can bring indoors for seasonal storage. The easy flexibility of such an L-V system will let you try for a different effect next summer, in case you're not satisfied.

Before attempting to convert a gas lantern to low voltage, contact your local utility for assistance in terminating the gas service to the fixture. And be sure the light is fully cooled before you start work—*by Phil McCafferty. Drawings by Gerhard Richter.*

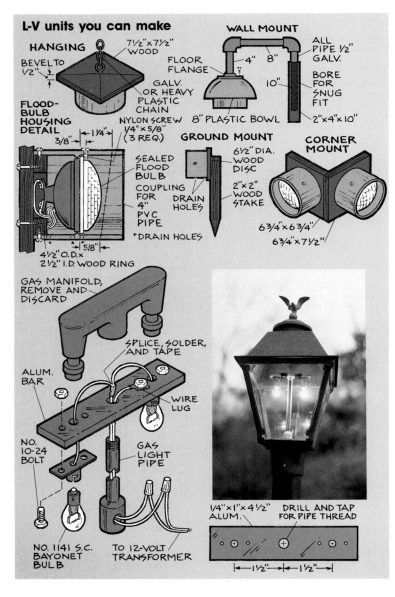

L-V units you can make

What's new in L-V equipment you can buy?

Smart new designs, fluorescents, remote photoelectric controls, more choice of control features, halogen bulbs, bulbs that make foliage look more natural: These are some things to look for in the outdoor-lighting section of home centers.

• Lunalite and Malibu offer floodlights with either regular sealed-beam lamps or halogen lamps. The more efficient halogen units are whiter and brighter, so they provide more illumination per watt than do incandescent lights. This means you can get more light for less power cost. Or, if you prefer, you can put more lights on a string.

• Nightscaping offers solid-copper floodlight fixtures with high-efficiency, 6,000-hour halogen lamps with a selection of beam angles. The color of these bulbs is said to enhance the foliage they illuminate. Malibu also offers top-of-the-line metal fixtures in both floodlight and tier-style accent lights. Nightscaping now offers multi-mirrored lamps in 20- and 50-watt sizes that permit improved control of beam spread from a more compact fixture. This is the first exterior use of MR16 lamps.

• RAB offers its three- or four-tier lawn lights in six- and 10-inch diameters and in a choice of housing colors: bronze, black, and green. RAB also has a full line of floodlights, spike lights, and a LightAlert security spot that turns on and off automatically when you step into and out of its range.

• Hi-Lights' new low-level accent lights have unique quick-disconnect posts. The feature allows you to unplug the unit so you can mow or trim a bush without having to work around the fixture.

• Hi-Lights' new timer-transformer has a "HI/LO" switch so you can operate at low power for added economy or for subdued effects. Lunalite has a new reduced-size, weatherproof transformer with a remotely positionable photocell that gives you more control of the on-off cycles. Malibu offers a wide choice of control units—manual, automatic timer (you preset the times you want the lights on), photo-cell (on at dusk, off at dawn), or various combinations. Malibu also offers its Welcome Home light—a stake unit with a plug-in power pack that turns the light on at dusk and off at dawn. Sears has a portable plug-in light with a similar photoelectric control that you can hang anywhere you need it.

• Most new non-flood fixtures use tiny new baseless bulbs that plug into special sockets. Some "sealed-beam" units are actually peanut bulbs inside a sealed clear-plastic envelope.

Major suppliers of the low-voltage lighting equipment mentioned above are: DRI Industries (Hi-Lights), 11100 Hampshire Ave. S., Bloomington MN 55438; Loran (Nightscaping), 1705 E. Colton Ave., Redlands CA 92373; Lunalite, 5300 Shoreline Blvd., Mound MN 55364; Malibu Div., Intermatic, Intermatic Plaza, Spring Grove IL 60081; RAB Electric Mfg. Co., 321 Rider Ave., Bronx NY 10451; Sears, Roebuck and Co., Sears Tower, Chicago IL 60684.

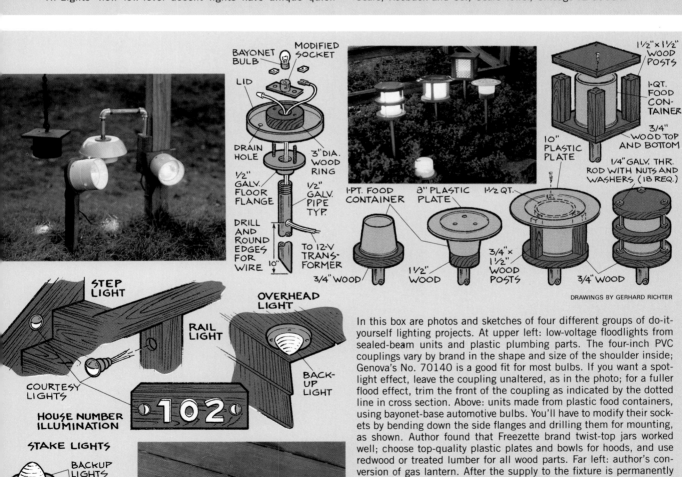

DRAWINGS BY GERHARD RICHTER

In this box are photos and sketches of four different groups of do-it-yourself lighting projects. At upper left: low-voltage floodlights from sealed-beam units and plastic plumbing parts. The four-inch PVC couplings vary by brand in the shape and size of the shoulder inside; Genova's No. 70140 is a good fit for most bulbs. If you want a spot-light effect, leave the coupling unaltered, as in the photo; for a fuller flood effect, trim the front of the coupling as indicated by the dotted line in cross section. Above: units made from plastic food containers, using bayonet-base automotive bulbs. You'll have to modify their sockets by bending down the side flanges and drilling them for mounting, as shown. Author found that Freezette brand twist-top jars worked well; choose top-quality plastic plates and bowls for hoods, and use redwood or treated lumber for all wood parts. Far left: author's conversion of gas lantern. After the supply to the fixture is permanently terminated, remove the mantle-manifold unit and replace it with the two-bulb holder shown. The pair of No. 1141 bulbs should use only about 36 watts and should last more than 1,000 hours. The bulbs cost just a few cents more than replacement gas mantles. In the photos and drawings at near left are examples of 12-volt automotive light fixtures that can be adapted for outdoor-lighting use. Like other auto lights, most of these will require the addition of a second wire for hookup. These small units are easy to mount in snug sockets drilled in posts, railings, stringers, and house-number boards.

cookie-cutter concrete

I won't say it was easy. But pattern-stamping a concrete patio at my son's home was no tougher than it would have been to hand-trowel a slab to a supersmooth finish. And for only about $200 more than we'd have spent on that plain slab, Doug and his wife, Leanna, have a colored, grooved patio that looks as if it's laid with expensive clay tiles. And I ended up with a pair of pattern-stamping pads that can be used again and again.

You can do pattern-stamping, too. What used to be a pro-only job can now be tackled by do-it-yourselfers using new plastic stamping pads available in a variety of designs (see box). These outsize cookie cutters create concrete sidewalks, driveways, and patios that appear to be paved with tile, brick, or stone. They can also be used indoors for house, basement, and garage floors. When done well, only an expert can tell that grouted, pattern-stamped concrete isn't the real thing.

For the most part, a pattern-stamped slab is prepared in

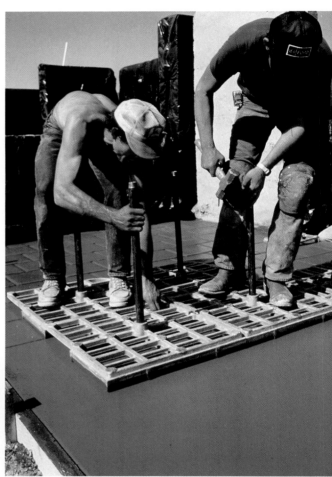

Large working surface of aluminum stamping pads (above) allows professional crew to complete large job before concrete stiffens. Vertical pipes act as handles for moving pads. Patio stamped by the author (left) and jigsaw like surface at San Diego mall (below) suggest the range of patterns.

the same way as a plain one. The usual needs of concrete slabs—such as uniform support, proper jointing, careful edging, and complete curing—all apply. The thickness of the slab is no different than for plain slabs.

There are some differences, however. For one, the forms should be laid out in multiples of the size of the stamping pads (allowing an extra 1/16 inch per foot for float, or movement of the pads as they are impressed in the soft concrete). Thus, the inside measurement between the forms of a 12-foot-wide patio slab should be 12 feet 3/4 inch.

Smoother mix

A pattern-stamped slab requires a somewhat different kind of mix than a plain slab. Because large stones might get in the way of the stamping pad's blades, a cement-rich, small-aggregate mix is used. It should be made with a maximum coarse-aggregate size of 1/4 inch. If you order ready-mix, tell your dealer that you are planning to pattern-stamp. Also say that you want the mix to contain enough fines and an aggregate gradation to make a workable, easily finishable slab. The dealer likely will increase the normal cement content.

Air entrainment is important to prevent water from separating and weakening the concrete. Specify 7 1/2-percent air entrainment, plus or minus 1 percent. For a protected slab or one built in a mild climate, specify 3 percent air entrainment.

Although it is usually best not to use additives in concrete, you may need the additional finishing time that one or two additives can provide. Normal concrete begins to set 1 1/2 hours after mixing—faster on a hot, dry day. (Don't try pattern-stamping in that kind of weather. Wait for a cool day, or work early in the morning.) To take some of the pressure off the stamping operation, you may want your dealer to add a water-reducing retarder to the mix along with a small amount of superplasticizer. This combination gives a high-slump condition that remains workable for two to three hours.

Expect to pay a little more than you would for a standard mix. The concrete pump and operator to place the mix between the forms will also cost another $80 or so—definitely worthwhile considering the time it will save.

Because you are trying to obtain a match with natural paving materials, you will be coloring the slab. The best approach is to use two applications of dust-on coloring. Any color that would look natural in real paving material may be chosen for pattern-stamped paving. We used a brick-red oxide coloring pigment in our dust-on mix.

You should get started on the coloring as early in the life of the slab as possible. This means dusting it on *before* bull-floating (smoothing the surface with a long-handled float immediately after strike-off). The air entrainment in the mix will help prevent water from bleeding to the surface and getting in the way of your early finishing.

Ordinarily you'd apply the first coat of color *after* bull-floating, but we saved a whole floating by doing it first. Then came the second dust-on application, which we troweled using a magnesium float.

As soon as the concrete has cured enough so that impressions do not fill in, you can begin stamping. In our case, the concrete was ready by the time we'd finished the coloring and floating. To make impressions, you position the pad and then pound it with a dead-blow hammer (Stanley Tools makes several sizes; see box) to set the blades about 1/2 inch in the concrete. To minimize movement of the pad, pound first in the center and then around the edges. Avoid pounding over an unsupported corner, though; that could break the plastic. Because the concrete will be setting

Slab to be stamped is prepared in usual way. Bull-float immediately after strike-off to maximize stamping time.

Author's crew tried two stamping methods. Here, stamper positions one pad while standing on another.

Working from knee board permitted greater care in positioning pads, but area under board needed extra float.

while you work, making impressions will require somewhat more pounding as the day progresses.

Around the edges of the slab there will be places where the pads won't fit. There, it is necessary to hand-tool the grooves using chisellike grooving tools that come with the pads. If done correctly, there is no visible difference between the tool-stamped and pad-stamped grooves.

Because the color layer is quite thin, the stamp-pad blades may punch through in it in places, exposing gray concrete at the bottom of the grooves. You can remedy this by dabbing a slurry of water and dust-on coloring into the grooves with a paintbrush. You do this the following day, after the slab is strong enough to hold your weight. Be sure to damp-cure your slab for five days. Don't cover it with a sheet of plastic, as that tends to make colored concrete look blotchy. A spray-on membrane curing compound is best. The compound will degrade within a month to leave the slab cured and bright. You can get it from a concrete supplies dealer.

Two stamping techniques

Our pattern-stamping crew—Doug; Leanna's father, Bob Hunt; and I (Leanna hand-tooled while we pounded)—tried two methods of working with the stamp pads (see photos). Bob preferred working from knee boards as he stamped. The results he achieved commend this technique, but because the area under the boards required a quick once-over with the magnesium float, he worked more slowly than Doug and I did. Our technique was to stand on one pad while pounding another. Our portions showed a few misalignments that Bob's did not, though.

Either way you work, if you get the first pad correctly aligned with the house or other master line, the others will pretty well follow suit. The second stamp pad is set against the one already in place and lowered with its edges aligned. To disguise slight irregularities, try to arrange the pattern so that long lines run across the line of sight.

A good rule of thumb for how much area of slab to tackle in one day is 100 square feet per worker. This rule worked for us. We began pumping at 10:30 A.M. and finally put our tools away at 5:30 P.M., tired. Without the additives, our patio would have gone partly unstamped. Next time, I'd make the 450-square-foot area a two-weekend project and forgo the retarding additives.

One reason for that became obvious the next morning. A normal mix would have set hard enough to walk on by nightfall, but our slab stayed slightly tacky. During the night several dogs dropped by to investigate and left paw prints all over the rear portion of the patio. By morning the concrete had hardened, preserving the prints like dinosaur tracks. Fortunately, we were able to hide them by brushing on a slurry made from leftover dust-on coloring.

Despite such problems and the hard work of pattern-stamping, I'd gladly do the job again. Tired or not, the beauty you build in as you work provides a satisfaction that inspires you until the last portion has been stamped. Doug and Leanna love the rustic, handmade look of their patio. So does everyone else who sees it—*by Richard Day.*

Pads for pattern-stamping concrete

 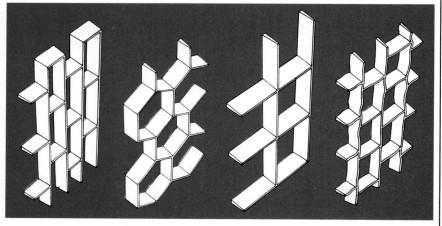

Pattern-stamping pads are available in either aluminum or plastic. Professionals use aluminum pads, but at well over $200 apiece (at least two are needed), these are too costly for most do-it-yourself projects. It may be possible to rent a set of aluminum pads, but they are not readily found at rental yards. Plastic pads cost about $72 each, including a pair of hand tools for completing the pattern in spots where the full pad can't fit. Properly handled, the plastic pads should last through a number of projects, longer if you're careful not to pound on them too hard.

We used Brickform plastic stamping pads (above, left) for our project. They are foam-injected to be rigid and stress-free yet resilient. They weigh just 7 pounds each—considerably less than metal pads. The blades on the stamp pads make 1-inch-deep impressions when the pad is fully pounded down. (We found it difficult to get a full-depth impression, however, and settled for half-depth grooves.) All four sides of the pads are made to match up with another pad, so you can move in any direction no matter where you start. For convenience, the pads have molded-in grab handles and optional mounts for easier-working extension handles. Or they can be ganged by fastening them to an optional gang module. This minimizes float and misalignments.

Brickform stamping pads are available from many concrete-products suppliers in brick, hexagon-tile, square-paver, and cobblestone patterns (drawings, left to right). Or you can order them by mail from Goldblatt Tool Co., 511 Osage, Kansas City, KS 66110. For pounding, use only a 3- or 4-pound dead-blow hammer, not a regular hammer. The Stanley Compo-Cast Soft Face hammer ($25) is an example of the proper tool. Irregular patterns like the cobblestone (right) greatly ease the task of pattern alignment.

Instructions with the stamp pads show them used with polyethylene sheeting over the concrete to produce a pillowed effect. While we liked the looks of the rounded edges, we decided that spreading poly sheeting evenly over the fresh slab would be too difficult and thus stamped it bare. Some pillowing resulted anyway. Perhaps it would be easier to use poly on a narrower, more accessible slab such as a sidewalk or narrow driveway—*R.D.*

installing surface wiring

As you get involved in various remodeling projects around your home, sooner or later you might want to run electrical wiring across walls or ceilings that are diffi-cult to get behind or—even more problematic—along solid masonry walls made of brick, concrete, or stone block.

Try concealing the new wiring with surface-mounted channels and fittings. It's the only way to both le-gally and attractively extend house wiring in such cases. Trimmer ver-sions of these normally commercial

Off-white color of surface wiring blends into mortar joints of brick wall (above).

Chiseling into wall to conceal wiring would be difficult or impossible.

In this case, surface wiring may be the only way to add a new ceiling fixture.

and industrial fittings are now availa-ble in hardware stores.

The Wiremold Co. (60 Woodlawn St., West Hartford, CT 06110) makes a line of surface-wiring materials it calls the On-Wall Wiring System. Available in prime-coated steel and plastic (the latter is a brand-new prod-uct) these pieces are off-white in color and can be painted to match any room's color scheme.

Installing surface wiring is simple, but getting the best results requires thorough planning. In a good installa-tion the wiring is inconspicuous. Straight lines and neat corners are a must. It's also best to blend the mate-rial into the background by painting it or applying wallpaper, unless its off-white color happens to match the ex-isting surface. Using these products requires little in the way of tools; you

Wiremold's Sure-Snap system elimi-nates need to snake wires through chan-nels from either end. Instead, plastic

covers snap on after wires are placed in channels. Parts can be painted with latex-base paint.

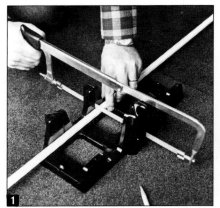

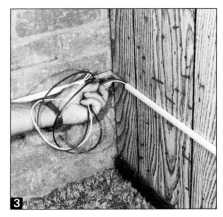

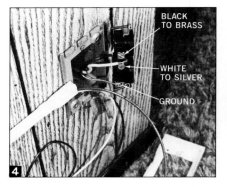

BLACK TO BRASS

WHITE TO SILVER

GROUND

Use miter box or vise and 32-tooth-per-inch hacksaw to cut channels (1). Mark path of channel on wall, and attach clips to wall (2). Keep channel runs parallel or next to moldings or baseboards. Once metal channels are installed, push wire from elbows in both directions into boxes (3). With plastic channels, lay wire in place, then snap on covers. When mounting boxes, use pliers to twist out opening where channel enters box (4). After new receptacles and switches are in place, connect to existing system (5)—with power shut off. Then attach wires as shown.

probably have all of them in your home toolbox.

Planning ahead

The Wiremold system consists of channels, which come in either ½- or ¾-inch widths, and various elbows and adapter fittings (see drawings). Measure and sketch out the job before you buy the materials to be sure you get the right quantity of fittings and channels.

Start by turning off the power to the existing receptacle where you'll pick up the power supply for the circuit addition, then measure to the locations of the switch boxes, receptacles, or ceiling fixtures that you intend to add. The existing receptacle must have two unused terminals to start the new wiring run; if it doesn't, you'll have to replace it with one that does. Also, to use Wiremold's system, the existing wiring *must be grounded* so that the new exposed wiring will be grounded, too.

If the existing receptacle has a third (round) opening in addition to the two flat openings and if there is a third wire leading to the grounded (green) screw lug on the receptacle, you can assume the system is grounded. Some older two-wire systems might be grounded to the metal

switch boxes, again by a third wire in the cable. For complete safety, check for ground with a plug-in tester.

As you take these measurements, note carefully the position of each bend. There are several configurations of Wiremold elbows. Inside and outside elbows permit turns around corners; conventional flat elbows guide the wiring through turns on a flat surface. The elbow covers snap off so you can push the wire straight through a channel from point to point rather than having to snake it around bends.

When you're shopping, remember to get screws and clips to attach the fittings and channels. Electrical components such as covers, switches, and receptacles will also be needed.

Once you've decided on your fittings, you must also choose between the ½-inch-wide A system and the ¾-inch-wide B system. If you've added any conventionally wired receptacles to your home, you've probably worked with flexible plastic-sheathed cable (type NM, often called Romex), which is available at most hardware or building-supply stores. If you have some type NM cable around the house and are planning a relatively short run, you can use it in the B system.

In most cases, though, it's easier to

use type THHN, a skinnier insulated wire that is often used commercially —but you may have to go to an electrical-supply store to find it, unless you can get by with 14-gauge. Wiremold packages 14-gauge THHN wire as part of its system; however, this is suitable only when the receptacle you start from is wired with 14-gauge wire protected by a 15-amp fuse or circuit breaker. Most newer houses have larger 12-gauge wire, protected by 20-amp fuses or circuit breakers. If this is the case, you'll have to buy THHN 12-gauge wire or go to the wider B system so you can use Romex.

Installing the wiring

Start at the outlet where you will begin your circuit. Be certain that all power is turned off by removing the fuse or flicking the circuit breaker. Double-check the receptacle by plugging in a properly working lamp, or use a test light or volt-ohm meter to be certain there is no current in the line. Then remove the cover plate from the existing outlet, and remove the screws that fasten the receptacle to the old box. It's not necessary to disconnect the wiring.

Now slip the base of an extension box over the outlet, and screw it to the existing wall box. Measure to the next fitting, being certain to account for

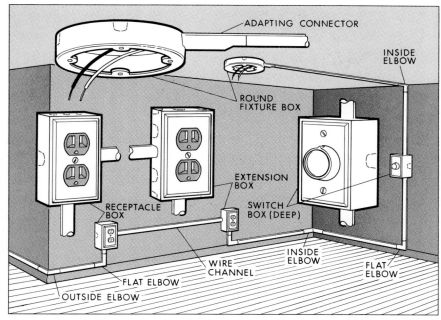

The components in this drawing are the building blocks of a surface-wiring system.

the beveled tongues of the fittings and the adapting connectors used on switch or outlet boxes. Cut the wire channel to the correct length with a fine-toothed hacksaw, and file off any sharp edges or burrs. Install mounting clips along the channel path about every 2½ feet. Inserting the tongue of the next fitting base into one end of the wire channel, slide the other end into the tongue of the installed box or fitting. Then snap the channel into the clips, and fasten the new fitting to the wall or ceiling.

Be sure that the path of the wiring channel is straight and runs level with any molding or baseboard to present a neat appearance. Continue to build the system, fitting by fitting, until you have reached the end destination. Just repeat the sequence of mounting the fitting, cutting the channel, fastening mounting clips, then attaching the next fitting as you

move along the surface of the area being wired.

Once all the fittings and channels are mounted on the wall or ceiling, the conductors are put into place. You will always have a black (hot) wire and a white (neutral) wire. In most cases you will also have a third (green) wire as the grounding conductor, which should be included throughout the system. Push the wire from one fitting toward the next through the wire channel. When an elbow is included in the run, start wiring at the elbow, and push wire in both directions to reduce the distance that the wire has to be pushed and to avoid having to run the balky conductors around corners. Leave approximately 6 inches of wire extending from each outlet box where you intend to attach a receptacle or switch. These devices and their covers are connected in the conventional manner.

Often you may be able to simplify a surface-wiring job by concealing part of the wiring. For example, if you're installing a ceiling fixture, you may be able to fish wires through the wall but not above the ceiling. In that case you'd run surface wiring from the ceiling outlet box to the hole through which the wall wiring emerges (see sidebar).

A final word of advice: when your wiring project is completed, don't be offended if no one notices your work. That's the sign of a first-class job—*by Evan Powell.*

Special applications for on-wall systems

When I needed a separate circuit for a range-hood microwave oven, I had to run it from an existing kitchen outlet on a concrete-block wall. My electrician and I worked out the method shown in the photo at right, using a professional system known as Metalmold. It's wider than Wiremold and isn't primed white. Most of the run could be made through an appliance closet by feeding the channel through chiseled notches. When the doors are closed (the unhinged edge of one door must be notched to fit over the channel), all's concealed except short runs on either side, photographed here to blend with the walls.

In the photo at far right I'm installing a paddle fan (foreground) from a new outlet in dropped ceiling. Cables had to reach this outlet from two widely separated wall switches (a dial to control fan speed, and a switch for the light kit). The adjacent wall was structural masonry, so I drilled a hole through the ceiling at this wall and fed up two runs of Romex cable, fishing them out through the larger hole for the outlet box. When all connections were made, I was left with two exposed cables running parallel down the wall, so

I cut two lengths of ½-inch Wiremold channel to size, screwing a pair of clips behind each run of Romex. This let me snap the two channels side by side over the Romex. It's a tight fit because this size channel is not intended for Romex, but the slimmer effect of adjacent runs is neater. A dab of patching compound filled the ceiling hole for an unobtrusive installation.

These ideas may suggest original ways to use surface wiring to solve problems in your own home—*Al Lees.*

Lapped up the side of the tub platform (top), Tarkett's Response vinyl flooring creates an elegant, seamless approach to the step-up bath. Careful cutting produces the compound curves needed to fit vinyl coving into an inside corner (above left). Outside corners (above) are patched, but beveled joints on precision-fit patch are nearly invisible.

seamless flooring

Professional installers of sheet floor covering are a close-mouthed group. I discovered this when I sought advice on coving the floor covering up the wall instead of butting it at the base. If you run the flooring up the wall, you don't have to install those dull-looking vinyl baseboards. Coving also dispenses with dirt-catching corners—and it gives a rich, unified look to the room.

But ask a professional installer for tips on cutting the compound curves required, and you get a quizzical look. These pros work by eyeballing the cuts, and it takes a lengthy apprenticeship to learn the technique.

Because I wasn't interested in learning the job as a vocation, rather in doing it successfully in my home, I worked out patterns for the critical cuts. The patterns can be adapted to most installations—but remember, not all corners in rooms are square, and not all walls are purely plumb. Cut your patterns a bit oversize to allow for shaving for a perfect fit.

Begin the job by making a paper pattern of the floor's perimeter, cutting so the edges are about ½ inch away from all vertical planes. Mark all areas—inside and outside corners and projections—where you'll need a cutout pattern.

Next spread out the floor covering in a space that's large enough for it to flatten, then tape down the perimeter pattern. Where you want the floor covering to cove up the wall (see diagram), mark the cut line on the flooring about 3½ inches away from the paper-pattern edge.

Scale up the corner cutout patterns, and test-fit to the actual corners before marking the pattern on the flooring. I used a felt pen for this job—the broad line provided enough extra material to shave for precise fitting when installing.

Before laying the flooring, you should also prepare the support for the coving. To give the flooring shape and support, professionals cover the joint between the floor and wall with

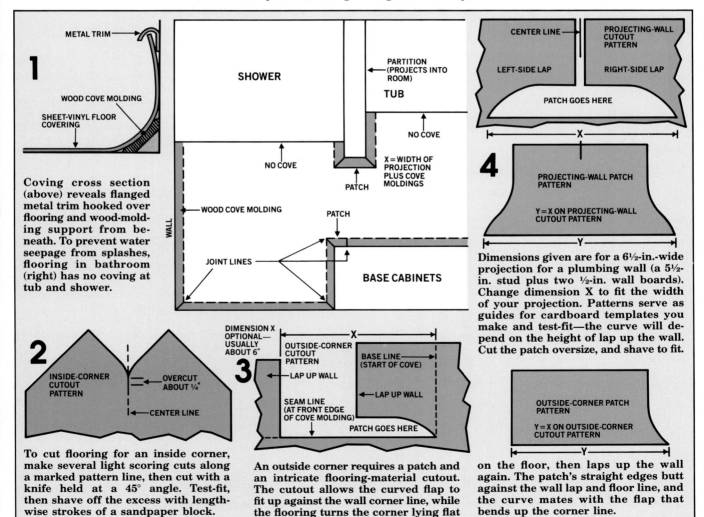

1 Coving cross section (above) reveals flanged metal trim hooked over flooring and wood-molding support from beneath. To prevent water seepage from splashes, flooring in bathroom (right) has no coving at tub and shower.

2 To cut flooring for an inside corner, make several light scoring cuts along a marked pattern line, then cut with a knife held at a 45° angle. Test-fit, then shave off the excess with lengthwise strokes of a sandpaper block.

3 An outside corner requires a patch and an intricate flooring-material cutout. The cutout allows the curved flap to fit up against the wall corner line, while the flooring turns the corner lying flat

4 Dimensions given are for a 6½-in.-wide projection for a plumbing wall (a 5½-in. stud plus two ½-in. wall boards). Change dimension X to fit the width of your projection. Patterns serve as guides for cardboard templates you make and test-fit—the curve will depend on the height of lap up the wall. Cut the patch oversize, and shave to fit.

on the floor, then laps up the wall again. The patch's straight edges butt against the wall lap and floor line, and the curve mates with the flap that bends up the corner line.

a wood cove molding, mitering it at the corners and nailing it in place. The miters don't have to be perfect, but don't leave big gaps. If you err, use wood dough as a filler.

To clamp the coving in place and cover its raw edge, use aluminum trim, available in silver or bronze at flooring-supply stores, which also sell the molding. When nailing trim to the wall, set it against a line drawn about 3¾ inches up from the floor, and drive nails at the base of the slots. This lets you tap the trim down to cover the flooring after it's installed.

Miter the trim carefully at all inside corners, but you can bend-miter it around outside corners, as the pros often do. Use a square file to form a V at the bend area. Then bend the material to form a 90-degree corner. If this system seems bothersome, just use the cut-and-fit method everywhere.

A popular preference among installers is a common utility knife with interchangeable blades. Straight blades and those with a hook are the most useful—but keep a supply on hand. You'll find that dull blades will cause problems.

Most of us hold a knife too timidly. Grip it firmly, enclosing it in a fist with the thumb extending a bit so it can act as a depth gauge. You can use a straightedge on the straight cuts, but you must work freehand on the curves, so it's a good idea to do some practice cutting on scrap material.

Make a light scoring cut first, then repeat it to emphasize the cut line. Lift the material, and follow the scored line with a through cut. It helps to have a board under the material for support close to the cut line.

Carefully follow the marked line with several scoring cuts, and make the through cut while holding the knife at about a 45-degree angle. This is necessary so mating edges at joints will fit correctly. Don't worry about cutting the exact angle at this point—you can shave and fit the patch as you go along.

You can shave off excess with a knife, but a more cautious method is to work with a smooth file or with sandpaper wrapped around a small block. Stroke away from the surface if filing, lengthwise if using sandpaper. Take it easy—you won't be able to add material if you overdo.

Don't cut the patches until you're ready to place them, but scale up the patch patterns and make a cardboard template for shaping the inset piece.

Keeping the material flexible is important—I let the covering sit in the sun for about ten minutes before laying it. Then I rolled the material and placed it in the room, allowing it to adjust to room temperature for an hour. Next step: unroll half the flooring and adjust it to fit against one wall; then unroll the second half. I used a heat gun (a hair dryer will do) for this procedure, especially at joint areas and where the material rolled up the wall.

Now fold back half of the material and apply the recommended adhesive on that half of the floor, but don't spread it where the sheet vinyl goes up the wall. Repeat for the second half of the floor.

Once the flooring is laid, anchor the perimeter that laps up the wall. Apply adhesive to the back of these loose edges only. Press the flaps against the wall, then tap down the metal trim to secure them. At outside corners, test-fit the cardboard patch, then use the template as a cutting pattern. Trim the patch so joints butt tightly (see drawings), then use seam sealer to keep joint edges together and prevent dirt and moisture from entering—by R.J. De Cristoforo. Drawings by Nina Wallace.

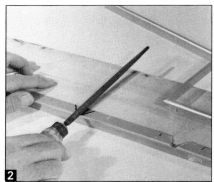

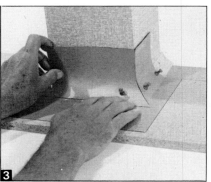

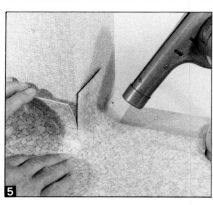

Wood cove molding nailed to the floor supports the vinyl flooring lapped atop it. Lip of the tap-down aluminum trim holds the cove in place (1). To miter the trim at outside corners, cut a notch in the flange, then file out a V-shape in the flat section (2). To fit flooring around a projecting wall, you must first test-fit cardboard templates (3), then cut a patch by gently scoring along a straightedge (4). Cut the curves, being sure to bevel edges for a smooth fit. Heat the flooring to make it flexible for fitting (5). Trim the patch, then apply adhesive to the molding and slip the patch in place. Final step is to seal the seams with sealer (6).

marble tile goes diy

"It looks like marble," my neighbor said. She tapped the beige-tiled bar top, and added with surprise, "It even feels like marble."

I assured her that my formerly stained, laminate-covered bar top *is* now topped with Italian Travertine marble. And I'm surprised, too.

In my do-it-yourself experience, nothing is ever as easy as it sounds. But HearthStone Designer Tiles are indeed simple to install—and the results are even richer than the pictures suggest. The key is Ultrabond, a far more powerful adhesive than most found on stick-on tiles.

Alan B. Shute, president of Hearth-Stone (Hearthstone Way, Morrisville, VT 05661) first developed the system for himself. Shute was trying to install a marble-tiled bathroom but was

Classic deep-veined Carrara marble tiles, bonded to the wall by a dry-set adhesive, create an elegant foyer (preceding page). The white tiles produce an equally dramatic sink vanity and backsplash (left). Rich honey-beige Travertine marble tiles are stunning yet practical on a kitchen backsplash (right). When used for backsplashes and counter tops, the substrate should be sealed with polyurethane. A carton of 40 white or beige tiles covers 10 square feet and costs $89.50.

daunted by the traditional thick, mortar-bed-setting method.

"The mortar sagged and slurped over everything. We couldn't keep the test tiles in place long enough to set. What a mess," he recalls.

Shute then tried a thin-set mastic adhesive. "The stuff dries too fast and won't let go if you goof," he says.

So HearthStone developed Ultrabond. Five small pads of the adhesive will attach the 6-inch-square marble tile to almost any flat surface, including old ceramic tile and plastic laminate. "We don't recommend its use over wallpaper or any sheetlike wall covering," says marketing director Keith Walker. "The tile will stick all right, but its weight may pull down the covering."

The mirror-polished, precisely cut HearthStone tiles come with either a beveled or square-cut edge. No grout is used with the tiles, but HearthStone advises installing beveled-edge tiles on walls exposed to moisture and sealing the joints with transparent vinyl caulk. Both caulk and a kit of simple tools are available.

"Use the straight-cut tiles for your bar," advised project director David Colburn. "It makes a flat surface with no dirt-catching depressions."

After preparing the bar top, I tried out different layouts for the Travertine tiles. They were beautifully matched in color and grain—but there were subtle differences that could either be ignored or played up, depending on where I placed them.

The 22-by-48-inch bar top took 32 tiles; cutting eight tiles at the two-thirds mark gave me the right size for back and side rows. I did all cuts first. HearthStone's directions are quite clear (see photo), but the job takes practice. Some of my edges came out a bit ragged, but I simply smoothed

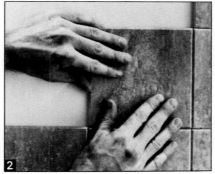

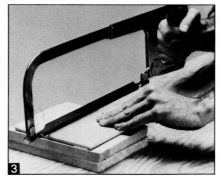

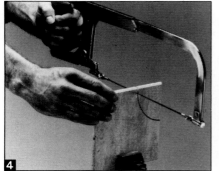

Super strong adhesive pads (1) bond with firm pressure, so position tiles gently (2) before pressing. To trim, support the tile on wood blocks (3), and use a straightedge (not shown) to score deeply with a tungsten-carbide hacksaw blade. Then rest the tile on a table edge, and press gently to break cleanly. Cut curves (4) and holes using a tungsten-carbide wire blade applied with light pressure. Syringe-applied bead of vinyl caulk seals a backsplash (5). Tools and caulk are available from HearthStone. Author (below) sprayed clear lacquer to protect the surface.

them with a file. I rounded the corner pieces by slicing off small pieces, then filing. HearthStone supplies extra adhesive pads for trim pieces.

With the cuts made, laying the tile was as easy as promised. I positioned them all first, then laid one course at a time, starting with the left side and continuing with the front row I placed

each tile down lightly, pressing firmly when I was sure it was placed correctly. Twice I used a putty knife to pry up a tile and reposition it. After laying the first two courses, the job became simple and speedy. I just aligned each tile's edges, pressed it down, and pulled it against the adjoining course.

Colburn advised against using the vinyl caulk on the bar top: "Constant scrubbing might lift it out." But he suggested I protect the surface by sanding it lightly with a fine grit, then spraying on clear lacquer. A coat of heavy-duty auto wax should work as well—*by Susan Renner-Smith. Photos by Greg Sharko and the author.*

expensive plumbing repairs you can do yourself

Considering the prices charged by plumbers, all plumbing repairs *they* make are expensive. That's reason enough to get your feet wet and tackle plumbing problems yourself.

I mean that part about getting your feet wet figuratively, of course. The purpose of fixing a leak or clogged drain—the two plumbing problems you may face—is to keep things dry.

Water leaks can spout from around threaded removable fittings such as trap clean-out plugs and faucet packing nuts; faucet nozzles; nonremovable fittings such as tees and elbows; and cracked pipes. Chances are you'll be able to fix any of these using a relatively simple repair that's dirt-cheap.

Removable fitting leaks

All it may take to stop a leak at a threaded fitting is tightening the fitting, but do it with finesse. Otherwise you may bend a part, strip threads, or tighten things up so much you'll have one heck of a time getting the fitting loose if that becomes necessary.

If tightening doesn't work, your next move depends upon the fitting you're dealing with. Let's say it's a trap clean-out plug (fig. 1). Lay a towel over the sink, tub, or shower drain opening to stop sewer odor from penetrating the house. Once water is drained, the odor is no longer blocked.

Place a pail beneath the trap and attach a pipe wrench to the plug. Turn the plug counterclockwise to remove it. Be prepared for the water that will gush out.

Here's the critical part: That plug and trap must be 100 percent dry before you apply joint compound or Teflon thread tape to the plug threads, else the drip will continue. The surest way is to wipe the plug and as much of the trap interior as you can reach with rags or paper towels and then let them air dry for two or three days. Stuff a rag into the trap drain hole to keep gases from escaping. During that time, of course, you can't use the sink, tub, or shower.

An alternative method that's faster, but not as sure, is to fire up a propane torch and move the flame over the trap. You'll probably see smoke emanating from the drain hole—that's steam. Be careful not to hold the torch in one spot too long and to keep flame away from surrounding combustibles such as wood beams and drywall. Remember, too, that if you leave even a small pocket of water, the repair may not take and you'll have to start over.

When things are as dry as you can get them, wrap Teflon thread tape or smear joint compound around the threads of the plug; then, carefully insert it into the trap, hand-tighten, and turn with a wrench until it's real snug. After a couple of hours, remove the towel from over the drain opening and pour water down the drain. Wait 10 or 15 minutes, return to the plug, and run your finger around it. Not wet? You've just saved yourself $30 or more for a plumber's call.

Compared to leaky traps, a leak from around a compression-faucet packing nut is child's play. Compression faucets are those with two handles—one for cold water, the other for hot.

If water leaks from around the handle or bonnet (that's the decorative cover under the handle), turn off water to the faucet by closing the shut-off valve. Remove the handle and bonnet, if one is used, and unscrew the packing nut by turning it counterclockwise. This assumes that you can't stop the leak by tightening the packing nut.

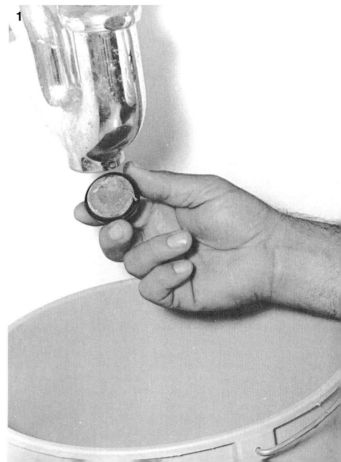
1

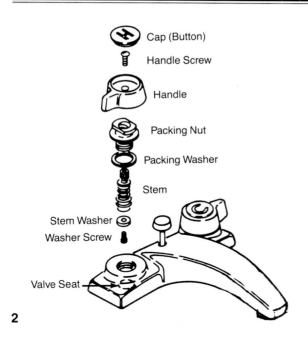

Cap (Button)

Handle Screw

Handle

Packing Nut

Packing Washer

Stem

Stem Washer

Washer Screw

Valve Seat

2

Workings of a typical compression faucet.

If there is a packing washer or O-ring at the top (fig. 2), take it with you to the hardware store and replace it with another of equal size. That'll stop the leak.

If there is no packing washer or O-ring, buy some self-forming packing (it's graphite in string form), wrap it around the stem, and screw the packing nut back on. As you tighten the nut, the self-forming packing will compress and stop water from leaking.

Repairing a leaking faucet

If water drips from the nozzle of a compression faucet instead of around the handle, you're dealing with a worn stem washer or damaged stem tip (fig. 2). Remove the stem and replace the washer and screw. If there is no washer, there may be a cap that snaps over the tip of the stem. This faucet is known as a high-hat faucet. Pull off the cap and get another. If there is neither a washer nor a cap—just a metal tip that has corroded—get a new stem.

Suppose you replace a washer or cap, or install a new stem, but it doesn't stop a leak from the faucet nozzle. Could the faucet be worn out? It's possible, but more likely a pitted valve seat is preventing the washer, cap, or stem tip from seating fully.

Instead of replacing the faucet, get a valve seat dressing tool, insert it into the faucet so the cutter rests against the valve seat, and turn it a few times until you feel no resistance on the tool (fig. 3). Fill a syringe with water from another sink and flush out the metal particles that remain from the resurfacing. Then, reassemble the faucet and try it out.

Leaks from stationary fittings

You can stop most leaks from around stationary fittings with an epoxy compound available at plumbing supply stores. The key to making this repair stick lies with the area being clean and dry. Do it when you're home alone, because the water's going to be off for awhile.

Turn off the main shut-off valve, and drain the home water system unless the pipe in question is outfitted with

a shut-off valve. To make this repair, the fitting and pipe or pipes screwed to it have to be void of water.

Wipe around the fitting with a towel; then, light up a propane torch and work the flame over the area for several minutes, using the precautions discussed earlier. Watch the trouble area for five minutes. Does any water drip from the fitting during that time? If even a drop appears, apply more heat with your torch. If the fitting is leak-free, clean corrosion from around it with steel wool. Then, spread a liberal quantity of epoxy around the fitting with a putty knife. Let dry, then turn on the water.

Frozen and cracked pipes

Pipes don't just up and crack for no reason. Usually, that reason is lack of precautions in cold weather. Water in a pipe that's exposed to the cold will freeze and cause ice to place stress on the pipe, which will crack.

If you know that one or more of the pipes in your house is vulnerable and hear that temperatures in your area are going to plunge, don't take any chances. Get some heat temporarily applied to the pipe or pipes.

If there's no way to arrange heat—not even a photoflood lamp rigged up near the pipes—turn on the water in a couple of sinks and let it flow at a slow rate. This old-time farmer's trick often works.

If you still find there's no water flowing from faucets, thawing frozen pipes quickly may prevent cracking. To tell which pipe is blocked, turn on one faucet after another. If there's no water from all faucets, the main feed pipe is the culprit. If water flows from all but one, the branch pipe to that sink is the one that needs attention.

The quickest way to thaw a pipe is with propane torch. Other ways are with a hair dryer, a photoflood lamp, heating pad, or by wrapping rags around the pipe and pouring

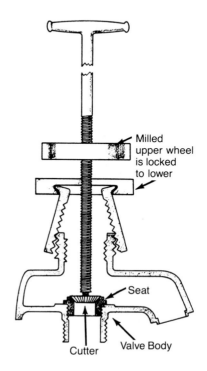

Milled upper wheel is locked to lower

Seat

3

Cutter

Valve Body

Valve-seat grinding tool.

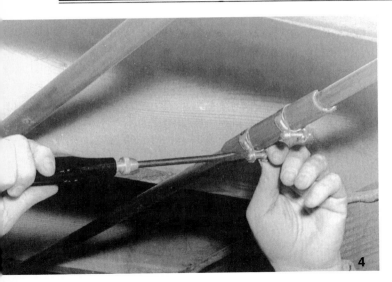

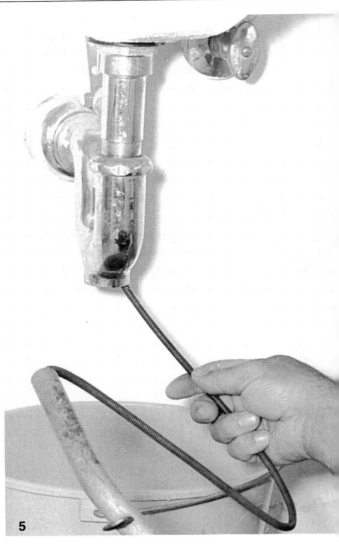

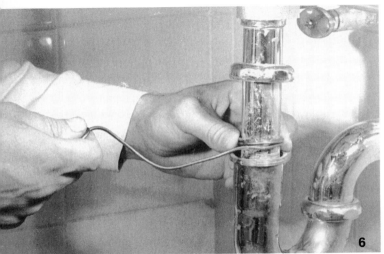

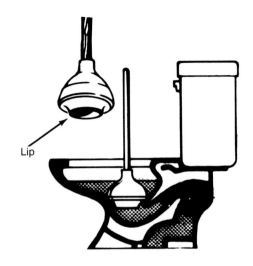

boiling water over it. Whichever method you use, first open a faucet served by the pipe.

What if the pipe is already cracked? Turn off the water valve and thaw the pipe if it's still frozen. Then, try the following simple repair method, which should work if the crack isn't too big.

The first repair is made with a length of hose slit lengthwise so it can be formed into a collar (fig. 4). The hose should be long enough so each end overlaps the break in the pipe by about 3 inches. You also need two hose clamps. Use stainless steel if the pipe is metal to avoid galvanic reaction, which causes rust. If the pipe is plastic, any kind of metal clamps will do.

Wrap the hose around the break in the pipe. Place clamps around the hose on each side of the break and tighten snugly, stopping short of crushing the pipe. Turn on the water. If there's no seepage from the ends of the hose, you're home free.

If you do get seepage, turn the water off again and get a pipe clamp from your plumbing supply dealer. This is a long, one-piece clamp. With hose in place, place the clamp over the hose so it's centered right over the break in the pipe, and tighten the clamp bolts. If this doesn't work, you'll have to replace the section of pipe.

Lip

7

Special toilet plunger differs from the usual sink plunger with its fold-out lip, designed to bring increased pressure to bear on the clogging material.

Here's a problem those living in cold climates may run up against if they have wells. Suppose you get in the shower one morning or are shaving. When you open the faucet, water flows for a few seconds and then stops. You check the water pump pressure gauge at the water storage tank and it reads zero.

Is the pump shot? Maybe, but chances are it's not if the water pump control housing is lying where it's been subjected to the cold. The breaker points inside the housing may be frozen in the open position. Open a faucet or two, take off the housing cover, and apply heat from a hair dryer to the points until they start moving. The pump will go on, the gauge needle will shoot up to show normal pressure (25 to 40 psi), and water will begin flowing again.

Clogged drains

Nine times out of ten you shouldn't have to call a professional to unclog a drain. The tenth time is if tree roots have gotten in the main drain leading from the house to the sewer or septic tank; then, a power auger is needed. You can rent one, but this kind of repair is usually best left to a professional.

Methods for unclogging a sink drain involve using a plunger, chemicals, and an auger. Try a plunger first. It's the easiest, cheapest, and safest method and will usually work if the clogging condition isn't too severe.

For maximum effectiveness, bail water out of the sink so only enough is left to cover the cup of the plunger. Be sure to stuff a rag in the sink overflow opening to increase the pressure exerted on the clogging material.

Try a chemical drain opener next if the drain remains blocked. Whether you use a liquid or solid, remember that chemical drain cleaners are caustic and are dangerous if not used properly, so follow instructions.

If things are really blocked, get a drain (not a toilet) auger. Insert the auger through the drain opening until it hits the blockage; then, rotate the auger in one direction to break the clogging material into bits.

If you can't get the auger through the drain opening, work at the trap. With a pail under the clean-out plug, remove the plug, insert the auger through the hole, then do your stuff (Fig. 5). Spread joint compound or Teflon tape around threads before you reinsert and tighten the plug. If there is no clean-out plug, remove the trap and insert the auger. When you reinstall the trap, use packing around trap nuts to seal threads and prevent leaks (Fig. 6).

The easiest way to clear a toilet clog is with a plunger that has a fold-out lip, which fits snugly into the opening (Fig. 7). A drain, or sink, plunger doesn't have this lip.

If a plunger doesn't work, skip right to a toilet auger. Like a plunger used for toilets, a toilet auger differs from one used to clear sink drains. Don't bother with chemicals; there's no way for them to reach the clog unless you flush the toilet, which you can't do.

Replacing drains

An unexpected problem that can be costly to fix arises when a metal sink drain pipe or trap corrodes through and begins to leak. The repair is easy. Just follow the steps shown in figures 8 through 11.

Notice that plastic drain pipe, trap, and fittings are shown as the replacement parts. They are easier to install than metal. And unlike metal, plastic can't corrode, so the repair should be permanent—*by Mort Schultz.*

To replace a trap, use Channel-type pliers or an adjustable pipe wrench to carefully loosen drain trap nuts (fig. 8). Apply penetrating solvent if needed. Plastic fittings couple directly to metal threads (fig. 9). Play it safe—take old metal fittings along and compare with plastic before buying. You'll find the job as simple as it looks (figs. 10 and 11).

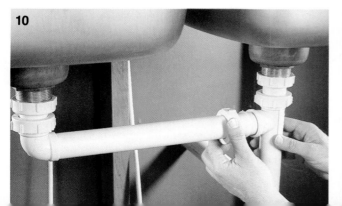

repairing plastic auto-body parts

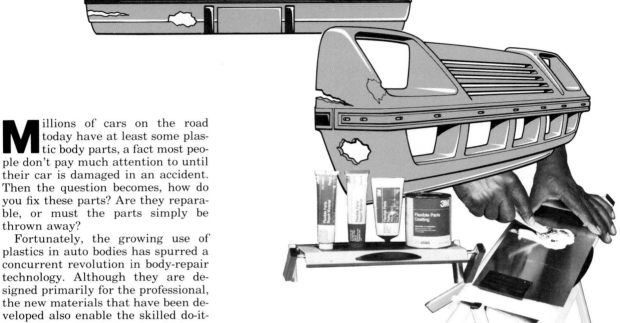

Millions of cars on the road today have at least some plastic body parts, a fact most people don't pay much attention to until their car is damaged in an accident. Then the question becomes, how do you fix these parts? Are they reparable, or must the parts simply be thrown away?

Fortunately, the growing use of plastics in auto bodies has spurred a concurrent revolution in body-repair technology. Although they are designed primarily for the professional, the new materials that have been developed also enable the skilled do-it-yourselfer to perform many body repairs successfully.

To learn what's new in repair techniques for plastic body parts, I visited 3M Company's technical center, in St. Paul, Minnesota, and talked at length with Rod Otzenberger, technical services supervisor for 3M's Automotive Trade Division. A major supplier of body-repair materials, 3M has worked closely with car makers in developing techniques for repairing today's plastic body panels.

Otzenberger explained that there are dozens of plastics now in use for auto-body parts. The Pontiac Fiero (see diagram) is a rolling sampler of some of the more widely used plastic materials. They include:

● Reaction injection-molded unrethane (RIM): Often referred to simply as urethane, this rubbery plastic is used for body panels at the front and rear of many domestic cars. It is flexible and resists minor impacts well. Because it is soft and can be easily molded, it has allowed designers to build sleek, aerodynamic cars that can also meet U.S. and Canadian bumper-impact standards.

● Reinforced reaction injection-molded urethane (RRIM): This ure-thane is reinforced with glass fibers or flakes to make it stiffer than RIM, so it can be used for large vertical panels —for example, the doors and fenders of the Fiero.

● Sheet-molded compound (SMC): This hard plastic is similar to the glass-fiber material used in boats. It consists of glass fibers embedded in a thermosetting plastic resin. It is often used for large, flat panels, such as the hood, deck, and roof of the Fiero and Corvette. SMC is even found on the new Cadillac Fleetwood Seventy Five Limousine, where it is used for the rear doors, hood, and roof insert.

● Other plastics found in car body parts include acrylonitrile butadiene styrene (ABS), nylon, polyvinyl chloride (PVC), polypropylene, and polyester. Still others go by such trade names as Honda Polymer Alloy or General Electric's Xenoy.

Which plastic is it?

Many of these plastics can be easily repaired. A few cannot. "One of the major difficulties in making a repair is first identifying what plastic you have," says 3M's Otzenberger. "Even the experienced professional has problems with this, especially on older cars."

Recently, General Motors and other car makers began stamping parts with a code indicating the type of plastic used. "While this information is on the parts, many times it's hard to find, because it's stamped on the inside," Otzenberger says. "You may even find two adjacent parts where one is reparable and one is not." Otzenberger suggests looking in the car maker's service manual for information on the types of plastic used on the car, and whether they can be repaired.

Such confusion is likely to continue as more and more plastic parts are used. "Steel isn't likely to roll over and die," says Otzenberger, "but I think many of the manufacturers are looking at Fiero-type construction for a model or two. We're going to see more of them."

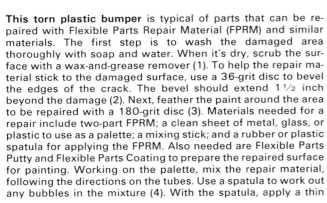

This torn plastic bumper is typical of parts that can be repaired with Flexible Parts Repair Material (FPRM) and similar materials. The first step is to wash the damaged area thoroughly with soap and water. When it's dry, scrub the surface with a wax-and-grease remover (1). To help the repair material stick to the damaged surface, use a 36-grit disc to bevel the edges of the crack. The bevel should extend 1½ inch beyond the damage (2). Next, feather the paint around the area to be repaired with a 180-grit disc (3). Materials needed for a repair include two-part FPRM; a clean sheet of metal, glass, or plastic to use as a palette; a mixing stick; and a rubber or plastic spatula for applying the FPRM. Also needed are Flexible Parts Putty and Flexible Parts Coating to prepare the repaired surface for painting. Working on the palette, mix the repair material, following the directions on the tubes. Use a spatula to work out any bubbles in the mixture (4). With the spatula, apply a thin

first coat of repair material to the damaged area. Keep applying coats until the material is built up slightly above the surface (5). After the repair material has cured, level and contour the area of the repair with 80-grit sandpaper followed by 180-grit sandpaper. A hand block will keep the paper flat against the part. Low areas appear as dark spots; fill them with another layer of repair material (6). After the surface has been sanded as smooth as possible, minor scratches and pinholes can be filled with Flexible Parts Putty. Apply it with a spatula, just as FPRM was applied. Next, wet-sand the area with 400-grit sandpaper, using a sanding block to help keep the finished area smooth and level (7). Finally, seal and prime the repair with two coats of Flexible Parts Coating. Wet-sand the area again with 400-grit paper, then paint. Follow the paint manufacturer's directions, and be certain to use a flex agent, if specified (8), to prevent cracking.

One plastic to watch out for is ethylene propylene copolymer, which is used on front-end body parts of GM J-cars and many Japanese cars. It looks very much like RIM, but at this time there is no way to repair it. Damaged parts have to be replaced. On GM cars the code markings on these parts include the letters EP.

Repair techniques

Fortunately, new repair materials can fix even extensive damage to most common plastics. 3M's Flexible Parts Repair Material (FPRM), Otzenberger claims, will fix most plastics, including RIM, RRIM, SMC, ABS, PVC, polyester, some nylon, and the Honda Polymer Alloy used for the fenders, lower doors, rocker panels, and quarter panels of the Honda CRX. It also can be used to make cosmetic repairs on the new Xenoy plastic bumpers on the 1985 Ford Escort and Mercury Lynx. "We have done quite extensive testing to qualify the material for a variety of plastics," says Otzenberger.

Some manufacturers still suggest using epoxy or polyester body putty to repair cracks or holes in SMC and other glass-reinforced plastics. But Otzenberger claims that FPRM can make more reliable repairs and is easier to use than these traditional materials.

Fixed well enough to sell

To demonstrate how FPRM is used, 3M technician Sidney McGee repaired several different plastic panels. One demonstration involved the badly damaged bumper from a late-model Ford Mustang.

The part was in such bad shape that a salvage-yard operator had given it to McGee for nothing. "I asked him if he'd buy it back if we fixed it," McGee said. "He agreed he would." Looking over the finished part later, I was impressed with the quality of the repair. "I hope he has his checkbook ready," McGee chuckled.

Keep in mind that although 3M products were used in the demonstration photos, other suppliers may have similar plastics-repair products in their lines. When shopping, be sure to pick up how-to and safety literature from the suppliers.

Supplies for the repairs described here are too specialized for most discount stores to carry. Instead, check large auto-supply stores, which often carry full lines of body-repair materials and tools. In many areas there are jobbers who specialize in these supplies. Although these stores cater to

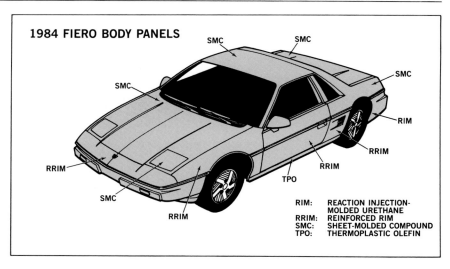

1984 FIERO BODY PANELS

RIM: REACTION INJECTION-MOLDED URETHANE
RRIM: REINFORCED RIM
SMC: SHEET-MOLDED COMPOUND
TPO: THERMOPLASTIC OLEFIN

Pontiac Fiero has body parts of various plastics. Panels dismount for repair.

professionals, the counter people are usually happy to help a well-informed car owner.

Fixing big holes or cracks

A minor puncture in a plastic panel can be sealed from behind with autobody repair tape, but larger holes or cracks must be reinforced with a fiberglass patch applied to the back side of the part. In some cases, you may have to remove the part from the car to get at the damaged area.

To ensure good adhesion, wipe the area where the patch will be applied with solvent, then sand it with a 50-grit disc. If necessary, use tape or clamps to hold the damaged pieces in place. Next, cut two pieces of fiberglass cloth large enough to extend about 1½ inches beyond the damaged area.

Following the directions on the tubes, mix the FPRM on a clean sheet of metal, glass, or plastic. Then apply a ⅛-inch layer of the material to the back of the panel, coating the entire area the patch will cover.

Put the first fiberglass patch in place. Then apply a second layer of FPRM, and press the second patch in place over the first. Immediately cover this patch with enough material to fill in the weave, and allow the repair to cure for 20 to 30 minutes at 60 to 80° F. Now you can begin repairing the front side of the part.

Painting pointers

Two special steps must be taken when painting parts made from a soft plastic like RIM: The repair areas should be sealed to prevent bull's-eyes, and a flex agent must be mixed into the paint so it will adhere to the part without cracking.

Bull's-eyes occur when solvents in the paint swell the microcellular foam plastic. The result is that the repair is visible through the final paint finish—even though it was filled and sanded perfectly. To prevent bull's-eyes, seal the repair area with Flexible Parts Coating. Apply two coats, with ten minutes' drying time in between. After 45 minutes of final drying time, wet-sand the repair with 320-grit paper.

Most paint companies supply a flex agent for use with their paints. Be certain that you get the right agent and that you follow instructions—and safety precautions—to the letter. Some paint-flex agents contain isocyanates, which are extremely hazardous. A respirator approved by the Occupational Safety and Health Administration (OSHA) is usually required to work with this substance.

You will also need a compressor and a spray gun to apply the paint. If you don't have a spray gun or can't borrow one, a small body shop may be willing to do the job. But keep in mind that most painters won't guarantee against problems under the primer unless the body work was performed by a professional whom they know.

Fortunately, at least two companies—Bondo and Swiss—sell flexible black paint in a spray can. This allows repair of black bumpers without spray equipment.

As with any body-repair procedure, you should wear work gloves to protect your hands while grinding and sanding. Wear plastic gloves while mixing and applying FPRM. And wear safety goggles (not glasses) to keep sanding dust out of your eyes— *by Thomas Wilkinson. Drawings by Russell von Sauers.*

troubleshooting the charging system

It's late. You're tired and hungry. But home is only a few miles down the road, and the car is parked just in front of you. You climb in, turn the key, and . . .

You know the rest of this sad tale: a dead battery. At best, you hear a momentary "ticking" sound as each cell gives its life on your behalf. And the inevitable silence to come is broken only by your thoughts of tow trucks, jumper cables, phone calls, and a cold dinner.

Buy a new battery? You could, but if the problem is elsewhere—in your car's charging system—you'll have made a costly mistake that will likely reward you with another cold dinner tomorrow night.

The battery is designed for one job: to provide a short, high-current output to start your car. But it works like a checking account. Every time you start your car, you make an electrical withdrawal. Once the engine is running, the charging system then redeposits replacement energy for the next start. If it doesn't, or if there is a constant energy draw while the engine is not running (as from a trunk light that doesn't go out), the battery eventually discharges completely.

Diagnosing a dead battery is easy. But finding the cause of the problem takes time, tools, and, most important, a logical sequence of tests. Your first test, of course, is on the battery itself. If it passes, you go on to check the car's charging system. Here's how it's done.

Start with the battery

Before performing any tests on the battery, charge it or be sure it has been charged. (Wear safety goggles when working around a battery—especially when you attempt to charge or boost one. A spark can cause it to explode.)

Your first check is to make sure that the battery will accept a charge. Many modern maintenance-free batteries have a built-in eye or hydrometer that indicates the state of charge by color: Green is OK, black means a discharged battery, and yellow indicates that the battery is beyond recharging and must be replaced.

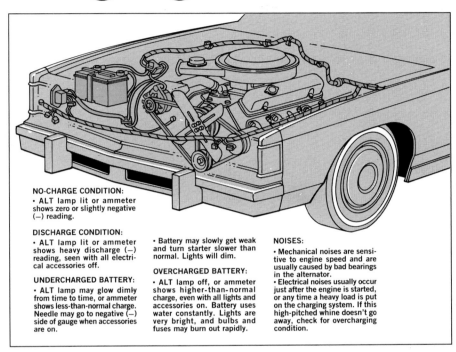

NO-CHARGE CONDITION:
• ALT lamp lit or ammeter shows zero or slightly negative (−) reading.

DISCHARGE CONDITION:
• ALT lamp lit or ammeter shows heavy discharge (−) reading, seen with all electrical accessories off.

UNDERCHARGED BATTERY:
• ALT lamp may glow dimly from time to time, or ammeter shows less-than-normal charge. Needle may go to negative (−) side of gauge when accessories are on.

• Battery may slowly get weak and turn starter slower than normal. Lights will dim.

OVERCHARGED BATTERY:
• ALT lamp off, or ammeter shows higher-than-normal charge, even with all lights and accessories on. Battery uses water constantly. Lights are very bright, and bulbs and fuses may burn out rapidly.

NOISES:
• Mechanical noises are sensitive to engine speed and are usually caused by bad bearings in the alternator.
• Electrical noises usually occur just after the engine is started, or any time a heavy load is put on the charging system. If this high-pitched whine doesn't go away, check for overcharging condition.

Older wet-type batteries with removable caps can be tested using a hydrometer. A 50-point difference in hydrometer readings between any two cells is reason enough to replace the battery. Colored electrolyte (grayish or reddish instead of clear) is another tip off.

If the battery checks out OK, your next test determines how well it holds a charge. The most reliable check is to use a carbon-pile load tester across the battery. This is basically a heavy-duty variable resistor used to simulate a steady load. For the test, it's adjusted to draw three times the battery's ampere-per-hour rating for 15 seconds. (Check the battery or owner's manual for the rating.) The battery voltage during the test should not drop below 9.5 volts.

If you don't have access to a carbon-pile tester, a load test can be done using the car's starter and a voltmeter connected across the battery posts (see drawing A). Pull the coil wire (so the car won't start), crank the engine for 15 seconds, and watch the meter. If its reading drops below 10 volts

while the engine is cranking (assuming the starter is OK), the battery should be recharged and retested. If it fails again, replace the battery.

Be sure the battery is charged before performing a load test. Otherwise, even a perfectly good one will fail. If it accepts a charge and passes the load test, you know the problem is elsewhere.

Finding current drain

You've opened the trunk. A convenience light comes on to help you see. You close the trunk, but the light stays on because of a defective switch. Result: The battery goes dead due to the slow—but steady—current draw of the light.

It doesn't take much: Current draw from any improperly working accessory will slowly but surely discharge the battery. A quick check will tell you if that's the problem; a little detective work will pin down the cause.

To test for a current draw, remove the negative battery cable and install an ampere meter in series with the terminal and disconnected cable (see drawing B). Any current flow will register on the meter. If you don't have an ampere meter, you can use a simple 12-volt test lamp between the battery terminal and the battery cable. Generally, any current flow that will light a 12-volt lamp will kill a battery.

Test your hookup by turning on the headlights. The ampere meter should show the current draw, or the test lamp should light. (If you're using a test lamp, the headlights or any other high-current accessory will not function when turned on. Only the test light will glow.) Now turn the headlights off, and check that all other accessories (and the ignition switch) are off. If you have a clock, remove its fuse. With everything off, there should be no drain.

If there is, you have found the problem: Something is discharging the battery. But what? To find it, you'll have to systematically check every accessory. If removing or disconnecting a particular accessory eliminates the drain, you've found the cause. Repair or replace it.

Disconnect (or remove) the trunk light, for example. If this eliminates the drain, its switch will have to be replaced. If the drain is still present, try the glove-compartment light, then move on to the fuse panel and try removing one fuse at a time until the meter drops or the test lamp goes out. Items such as electric seats generally work off circuit breakers. Try working the seat switch to see if it sticks in the "on" position, and do the same with electric-window switches. Station-

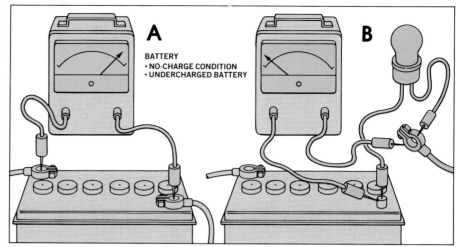

A
BATTERY
• NO-CHARGE CONDITION
• UNDERCHARGED BATTERY

B

wagon rear-door-window motors are a frequent cause of intermittent battery failures, as are cigarette lighters that stick.

Check the cables first

If your battery is in good shape and is not being discharged by a current draw, it's likely that the charging system is not recharging the battery as you drive. But before checking—or changing—any expensive component such as the alternator or regulator, begin with the cables.

The charging-system wiring must have tight, clean connections. Check the connections from the battery to the starter and on to the alternator and bulkhead connector. Many perfectly good batteries and starters have been replaced because the cable to the

starter simply was corroded or loose, causing a temporary open circuit.

Dirty battery terminals will create a circuit resistance that may block the flow of recharging current from the alternator. Remove the cables, and clean their terminals and the battery posts with a terminal-cleaning brush (drawing C). But be careful: Battery posts are more fragile than they look and can easily be damaged. Never try to twist off a terminal; use a battery-terminal puller.

Alternator and regulator woes

The alternator generates the electrical current needed to recharge the battery; the regulator controls the amount. If anything interferes with this process, the battery will eventually discharge.

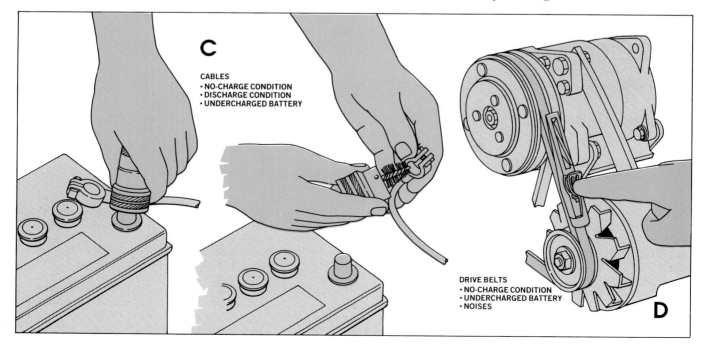

C
CABLES
• NO-CHARGE CONDITION
• DISCHARGE CONDITION
• UNDERCHARGED BATTERY

DRIVE BELTS
• NO-CHARGE CONDITION
• UNDERCHARGED BATTERY
• NOISES

D

Even something as seemingly insignificant as a loose alternator drive belt (which seems to be turning the alternator pulley at idle) can sufficiently reduce the current output of the alternator. (The red alternator light will not glow.)

The V-belt tension is extremely important and should be checked frequently. One way to check it is simply to hold a ruler alongside the belt and measure how much the belt deflects when pressed down with your thumb. Your car's factory manual will tell you how many inches are allowed. Another way is to use a belt-tension gauge (drawing D). Gates Rubber Company offers a "Krikit" V-belt tension gauge (#91107) for about $20. Twist the belt to check its walls for signs of cracking. A shine is indicative of a slipping belt.

In any situation where the battery has gone dead, it is wise to perform an alternator-output test. The idea is to measure the voltage and current the alternator sends to the battery. Normally, an alternator will maintain about 14 volts in the system (with the engine accelerated to about 1,500 rpm) and send about a 10-ampere charge into the battery soon after starting.

Frequently, an alternator malfunction occurs when one or more of the alternator diodes become shorted, causing the battery to receive alternating current instead of the direct current it needs. Another potential problem is a shorted or open stator, a condition that reduces or eliminates charging voltage.

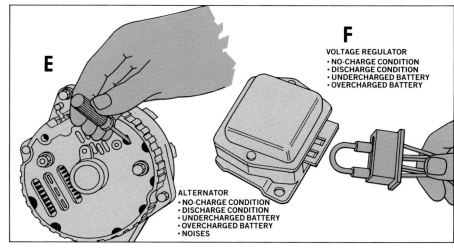

One way to find these problems is to use an inexpensive tester, such as Suntune's CP7620 charging-system tester (about $22), that can indicate a shorted diode or stator and can reveal a low-charged battery or charging-system-component failures.

Another way is again to use a carbon-pile tester across the battery terminals. This loads the system, forcing the alternator (and regulator) to pass the maximum output. A voltmeter is connected between the regulator's battery ("B") output and ground, and an ampere meter is placed in series with the regulator and battery. On a good alternator, the output should be within 10 percent of its voltage rating (check the specification for the particular make and model).

If the alternator does *not* maintain the specified voltage, it should be further tested by "full fielding." This test simply bypasses the voltage regulator to determine if the trouble is in the alternator or the regulator.

On popular GM Delcotron alternators with internal voltage regulators, you merely insert a small screwdriver into a D-shape hole in its back (see drawing E). A good alternator will charge when "full fielded" (and with the engine racing) to within about 10 percent of its rated capacity (check the owner's manual for capacity and rpm). A defective alternator will have a lower-than-specified or zero output.

To test other systems, the external alternator must be disconnected and a jumper installed between the alternator field wire and, depending upon the car, the battery connection ("B") or ground (drawing F).

If the alternator passes this test, it's likely that the voltage regulator is at fault. Since the regulator controls the alternator output, it can either prevent charging or cause the voltage output to be so high that it will literally boil the electrolyte out of the battery (and eventually destroy the alternator). Glaring lights, frequent lamp burnouts, or a rotten-egg odor are often tip-offs to an overcharging alternator, as is a heavy accumulation of powdery white crusts on the battery tray.

External voltage regulators often malfunction because they are not properly grounded or because the ground strap between the engine and the fire wall has become disconnected. Check those possibilities before you replace the regulator—*by Bob Cerullo. Drawings by Russell von Sauers.*

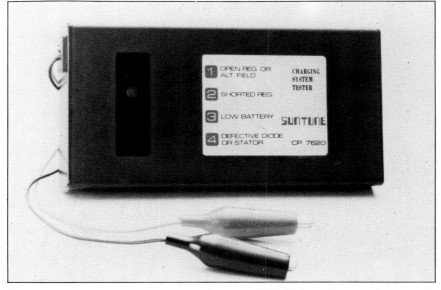

Charging-system tester, such as this Suntune CP7620, is an inexpensive yet valuable tool. LEDs show status of battery, alternator stator and diodes, and regulator. A carbon-pile load across the battery is not required for its use.

troubleshooting drum brakes

Every time I work on a car's brakes, I reflect on what a simple, efficient device the disc brake is—as shown in my chapter in last year's *DIY Yearbook*. But when I get to the rear wheels, I grumble once again at how many more parts make up a drum brake. There are also several possible arrangements of the drum brake's hardware, so it's easier to get confused and make a mistake while repairing them.

This is a guide to what to look for when you check the condition of your car's drum brakes. I'll tell you how to inspect and replace brake drums and shoes, and how to avoid the common pitfalls of drum-brake service.

Off come the drums

Your inspection of the brakes' mechanical condition begins with removing the rear wheels and brake drums—after you have placed the car on a pair of sturdy jack stands. Getting the drums off is sometimes the hardest part of the job. Frequently a rusty ridge builds up on the drum's edge. To remove a drum like this you must first back off the brake adjuster with a brake-adjusting tool. This allows the brake shoes to pull back clear of the drum. Often a rear drum will rust to the axle flange at the drum's center opening. The application of penetrating oil and a few hammer taps will usually free it.

With the drum off, you have a clear view of the brake shoes and hardware. This first view is important; make a picture of it in your mind before you take anything apart.

There will generally be an accumulation of grayish dust clinging to the brake shoes and hardware. This dust may contain asbestos, which can cause health problems. Always use an approved dust mask when you clean off the brakes. Avoid breathing or ingesting any of the dust, which should be disposed of in a sealed plastic bag. Use a brush to clean brake parts, not an air hose.

Types of brakes

Observe the type of drum brake you are servicing. Many full-size U.S.-made cars use a duo-servo, anchor-type self-adjusting brake on the rear wheels (see drawing). It can be identified by the star-wheel adjuster at the bottom and the fixed anchor pin at the top. Self-adjuster linkages may use levers or cables. Either way, the movement of the brake shoe turns the star wheel enough to spread the shoes outward toward the drum.

Many small cars, such as the Chevrolet Chevette, Ford Escort and Lynx, Chrysler K-cars, and imports like Honda, use nonservo rear drum brakes. These have an obvious difference: Instead of a star wheel, they have a fixed anchor plate at the bottom (see drawing).

Your first concern should be to check the thickness of the friction material on the brake shoes. There should be at least $1/32$ inch of material above the rivet heads on riveted linings. If the linings are bonded to the shoes, they should be at least as thick as the steel shoes. Measure the lining at its thinnest point. It's false economy to ignore brake linings that are worn. Once the rivet heads or brake-shoe metal make contact with the drum, rapid damage occurs. Grooved or scored drums are the result of failure to replace worn linings soon enough.

Next, check for leaking wheel cylinders. Replace a cylinder that weeps any fluid. Also look for grease leaking from the rear axle onto the brake backing plate and brake shoes. If the rear-axle grease retainer is leaking, it must be replaced before you install new brake linings. Remember to look at the back of the brake plate. Make sure the steel tubing going into it is in good condition. Check all hydraulic tubing and hoses going to both rear wheels. Sometimes rust and abrasion from a rubbing exhaust pipe can damage brake tubing.

If you have noticed a pulsing of the brake pedal when the brakes are applied, a rear drum may be out of round. This can be caused by frequent brake overheating (on long mountain descents, for example) or by application of the parking brake to a too-hot drum. The shoes applied inside it prevent the hot drum from contracting back to its normal round shape as it cools.

Over a period of time brake drums—particularly wide ones—may become bell mouthed; that is, the drum distorts, preventing full contact with the shoes. A bell-mouthed drum can cause brake fade, weak braking, and premature wear on one side of the lining. If the drums are not too distorted, the solution to both this problem and to out-of-roundness is having the drums machined on a brake-drum lathe by a good automotive machine shop.

Servicing drums

It is sound practice to machine the brake drums whenever new linings are installed. Machining takes off a thin layer of the drum's surface metal, leaving an even yet slightly roughened surface to help break in the new shoes. Every

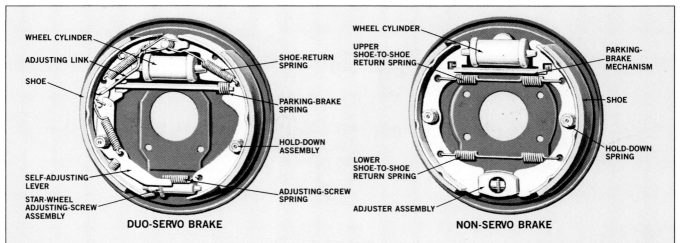

WHEEL CYLINDER

ADJUSTING LINK

SHOE

SHOE-RETURN SPRING

PARKING-BRAKE SPRING

HOLD-DOWN ASSEMBLY

SELF-ADJUSTING LEVER

STAR-WHEEL ADJUSTING-SCREW ASSEMBLY

ADJUSTING-SCREW SPRING

DUO-SERVO BRAKE

WHEEL CYLINDER

UPPER SHOE-TO-SHOE RETURN SPRING

PARKING-BRAKE MECHANISM

SHOE

LOWER SHOE-TO-SHOE RETURN SPRING

HOLD-DOWN SPRING

ADJUSTER ASSEMBLY

NON-SERVO BRAKE

When pressure is applied to brake pedal, entire duo-servo brake assembly (above left) moves against drum. Force is transferred from primary brake shoe through star wheel to secondary shoe. This is known as servo action. Primary shoe is always closer to front of car and may have shorter lining. In this system secondary shoe provides 70 percent of stopping force. In non-servo brakes (above right), forward shoe—often the longer one—does most of the work.

drum must be carefully measured before cutting; removing too much metal is unsafe and can result in overheating or drum distortion—even a broken drum. Generally, it is unsafe to remove more than 0.06 inch of metal from the drum surface. Many drums have a cutting limit stamped into the metal. It is also a good idea to keep the inside diameters of the rear drums within 0.01 inch of each other.

You must also inspect each drum for cracks—they become more visible after machining. Cracks may develop at the bolt circle or at the outside of the brake flange. Discard a cracked drum.

Sometimes the extreme heat generated during braking causes a change in the metal of the drum itself. The result is bits of steel in the cast-iron drum surface. These hard spots can cause rapid lining wear, chatter, or a hard brake pedal. Normal machining will not remove the hard spots; they must be ground using a special cutter with a grinding-wheel head. In extreme cases where the hard spots run deep into the metal, you'll have to get a new brake drum.

If you install new brake linings, be sure to buy only those of the best quality. Cheap brake-lining friction material may not be able to withstand the extreme heat buildup that braking generates.

The same heating and cooling cycles that can distort a brake drum also act on the brake return springs. Lively return springs are important; always install new ones when you replace the linings. Another necessary investment is a brake-spring tool. Attempting to remove a brake return spring with pliers or other makeshift tools can lead to serious injury. I know a mechanic who almost lost his eye when a pliers he was using to install a brake spring slipped.

Examine the self-adjusting mechanisms carefully. Make sure the star wheels are lubricated; work them by hand to be sure they move freely. On nonservo brakes, make sure the adjusting levers are working. Once the new shoes are installed, check your handiwork against your mental picture, a shop manual, and the untouched brake on the other side of the car.

Your shoes are on backward

The error I see made most often by nonprofessionals is reversing the brake shoes. Usually I find that the primary, or forward, shoe is properly installed on the left rear wheel but incorrectly located on the right rear wheel. It's important to remember that the right-rear-brake setup is a *mirror* image of the opposite side. When I suggest that it is wise to disassemble only one brake at a time so that you have the intact brake as a reference, you must not take this to mean the two sides look exactly alike. A good way to remember how the brakes should look on either side is to consider drum rotation: Visualize an arrow at the top of the brake pointing in the direction the drum rotates when the car is moving forward. The primary shoe will always be at the point of the arrow.

Finally, before you reinstall the drum, check that the parking-brake cable is working freely. These cables often seize with rust. Apply penetrating oil to solve this problem while you have access to the mechanism. After the wheel is on, use your adjusting tool to adjust the brake until it begins to drag. Then back off the adjuster so the wheel rotates freely when the brake is released—*by Bob Cerullo. Drawings by Ray Pioch.*

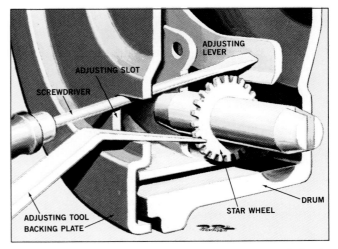

ADJUSTING LEVER

ADJUSTING SLOT

SCREWDRIVER

ADJUSTING TOOL

BACKING PLATE

STAR WHEEL

DRUM

Adjusting tool turns star wheel through access slot in backing plate of hub. Screwdriver releases adjuster lever.

install a knock eliminator

The blood is just beginning to flow back from my head. For what seemed like hours, I lay under the dashboard of my vintage 1978 Chevy while my wife, Marilynn, drove along Interstate 80 at her usual breakneck pace. Why the automotive gymnastics? I had installed a Carter Engine Knock Eliminator (EKE) under the dash, and to adjust the control unit's sensitivity I had to turn a screw recessed in its housing. Next time, I'll be sure to install the control unit on *top* of the dash.

Ping is a serious troublemaker for the mechanics in my shop. That's because peak engine performance occurs at a point just before engine detonation. If we tune an engine for top performance, customers often complain about ping. If we de-tune to eliminate ping, drivers complain about poor pickup and fuel economy. The EKE makes for a self-monitoring ignition system that advances for fuel economy and performance, then retards to prevent detonation.

Installing the unit's Electronic Control Unit (ECU), or "black box," is simple. It can be mounted on the engine fire wall, on the inner fender, or inside the passenger compartment. Simply drill four holes for the ECU's attachment screws and mount the unit. (Because adjustments may be necessary, keep my awkward position in mind when you select a location.)

The next step is mounting the detonation sensor. The sensor is like an electronic ear. Engineers call this type of device an accelerometer. This one is tuned for vibrations in the 6,000-Hz range, which is the frequency emitted during spark knock. The tip of the sensor can be screwed into any USS 3/8-16 threaded hole in either the intake manifold or cylinder head. If a hole of this size isn't available, the sensor can be mounted by using a simple bracket supplied with the kit. Naturally, the mounting location should be as close to a combustion chamber as possible.

Knocking out knock

When a knock occurs, the piezoelectric diaphragm within the sensor converts the sound into electrical pulses. These pulses are received by the ECU, and the spark is retarded proportional to the strength and frequency of the knock. Timing is retarded just enough to eliminate the knock and for only as long as the knock lasts.

The most difficult part of the installation is the wiring. The wires in the harness should be connected according to the diagram that's appropriate for your vehicle (see drawings). My Chevy has a high-energy-ignition system, which meant splicing three wires into the distributor wiring. The entire job took just over an hour.

After the basic installation, I mounted a toggle switch under the dash to open the circuit between the sensor and the ECU. Although it's not part of the recommended installation, the switch gives me a way of comparing performance with and without the knock eliminator. I also installed a special meter on the dash that indicates the amount of retard occurring when the ECU is reacting to knock.

Checking the system's operation was easy. I clipped on the leads from

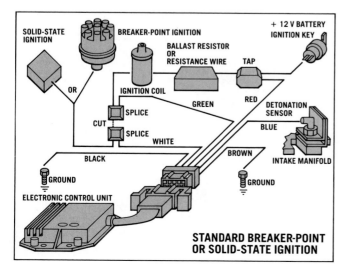

STANDARD BREAKER-POINT OR SOLID-STATE IGNITION

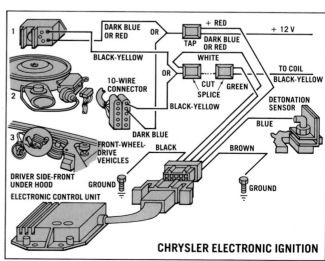

CHRYSLER ELECTRONIC IGNITION

my timing light, then lightly tapped near the sensor with a small metal hammer. The timing retarded itself automatically. When I stopped tapping, the advance returned to normal.

Each owner has to adjust the system for the grade of fuel used and the amount of knock (if any) he's willing to tolerate.

Then I took an extensive road trip and tried various grades of fuel, from 86 to 93 octane. With the more-expensive high-octane fuel, the retard meter's needle barely moved, except for a degree or two on some steep hills. However, with the lower-octane fuels the needle was quite active, jumping up to 15 degrees at times. Further-

more, each time I flipped the cutoff switch, I could hear the loud report of abnormal combustion.

What were my conclusions after testing this device? The EKE did greatly reduce knock and ping. It enabled me to use lower-octane unleaded fuel in an older engine that generally performs better on unleaded premium fuel.

I averaged 16 mpg for the 2,200-mile road trip. With a saving of 10 cents per gallon using unleaded regular instead of unleaded premium, I estimate that the EKE's $114 purchase price would be recovered in roughly 18,000 miles.

Engine protection

But more important, my engine was protected from engine-damaging detonation that can occur even when using premium fuel—or when pulling a trailer or other load. Of course, there was a slight loss in power when the sensor detected a knock. On a level road, the power loss was hardly noticeable, but it became a bit more obvious when traveling uphill.

The EKE can be used on four-, six-, or eight-cylinder negative-ground, spark-ignition engines (breakerless and contact points). The exceptions are the General Motors V6 models with odd-firing ignition and the Wankel rotary engines.

Because the EKE momentarily alters the factory timing curve, I asked the folks at Carter whether its use was legal in all states. J. Joseph Muller, Carter's patent attorney, assured me that the device is legal in every state, including California—*by Bob Cerullo. Drawings by Russell von Sauers.*

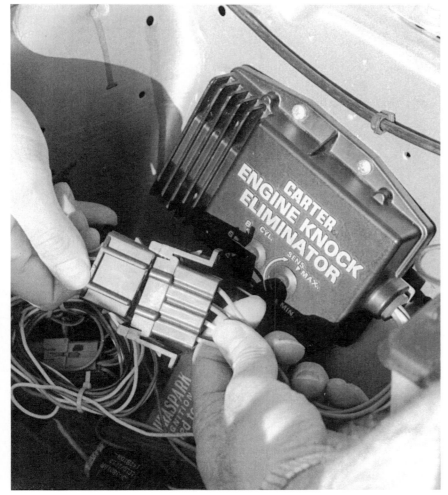

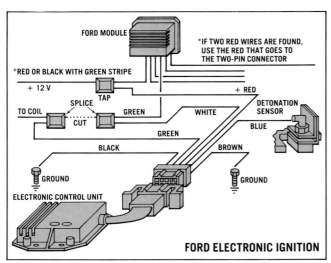

FORD ELECTRONIC IGNITION

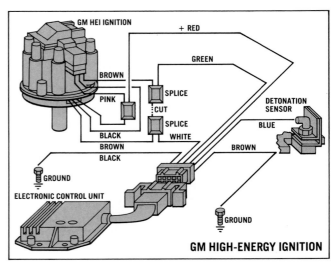

GM HIGH-ENERGY IGNITION

keeping your car heater hot

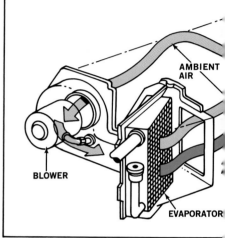

I was having dinner with an old friend one cold, rainy Sunday when a phone call from fire-department headquarters summoned him to a multiple-alarm blaze raging at the other end of town.

He invited me along for the red-lights-and-siren dash to the scene of the fire. As we raced through city traffic, I noticed the windshield slowly fogging up despite the fact that the defroster blower was on "high." Even with my frantic efforts to wipe the windshield clear, we were losing our forward vision. Luckily, we reached the fire without my friend having to hang his head out the side window to see where he was going. The ride had been frightening.

After the fire was under control and my friend returned to the car, I offered to take a look at the problem. He explained that he had reported the condition to the fire department's repair shop, but the city-owned car was returned with a memo stating that nothing was wrong with the heater or defroster.

A few days later in my shop, I placed a thermometer in the path of the discharge air coming from the car's heater-defroster. The reading was 125° F—more than hot enough. The airflow from all the defroster louvers was strong when the control was moved to the "defrost" position.

I then thought that the problem might be extraneous moisture in the defroster system. It's symptomatic of a leaking heater core for steam to discharge from the defroster ducts once the car has warmed up. But there was no steam, no odor of antifreeze, and no coolant dripping onto the passenger-compartment floor.

There was nothing left to do but get to the core of the problem. I removed the car's heater element and rigged up an air hose so the heater could be pressurized and tested in a tank of water. Sure enough, there was an al-most imperceptible stream of escaping air bubbles, indicating a tiny leak. Although not visible as a coolant leak, it was spraying water vapor into the defroster airstream, and the vapor was condensing on the windows. A new heater core solved the problem.

Heater and defroster problems are seldom as difficult to solve as this one, but they all require careful and thoughtful diagnosis. Here are some common heater-defroster problems, with tips on how to troubleshoot and repair them.

Leaks? Thermostat problem?

For the heater to work properly, the engine must be fully warmed up and coolant must be flowing through the heater core. (The heater core is like a miniradiator through which air is forced by a blower.) The first place to check when there is insufficient heat is the radiator. A low coolant level caused by a leak will prevent an adequate amount of coolant from reaching the heater core. The best way to check for leaks is with a cooling-system pressure tester.

The thermostat plays an important part in getting the engine warmed up quickly. It also determines how quickly you'll get heat inside the vehicle. If the thermostat has been removed or remains in the open position, it will take much longer for the engine to reach its proper operating temperature.

To test the thermostat, place it in a pot of cold water along with a thermometer. Heat the pot on a stove-top burner. As the water starts to boil, watch for movement of the thermostat valve and note the temperature at which it happens. The normal thermostat-opening temperature should be stamped on the thermostat's body.

How to find blockages

Generally, there are two heater-core hoses. One hose feeds hot water into the core; the other returns cooled discharge water to the engine. The best way to determine whether the core is being fed a sufficient supply of hot coolant is to carefully touch each of the hoses. Both hoses should be about the same temperature. If one is hot and the other merely warm, there's a blockage, which can be caused by a defective heater valve, a kinked heater hose, or a clogged heater core.

The heater valve controls the flow of coolant to the core. The way to spot a defective valve is to touch the hoses on the inlet and outlet sides of the heater valve. The valve is usually defective if the inlet or outlet side is cool.

But before you replace a suspect valve, check a few other things. First, make sure the mechanism that operates the valve is working. If it's a vacuum-operated valve, make sure the vacuum signal to the valve changes when the system is switched from "off" to "heat." It's important to note that there are two types of vacuum-operated heater valves. One is normally open; the other is normally closed. If a normally open valve has been installed where a normally closed valve belongs, hot coolant will be introduced into the core only when

AMBIENT AIR

BLOWER

EVAPORATOR

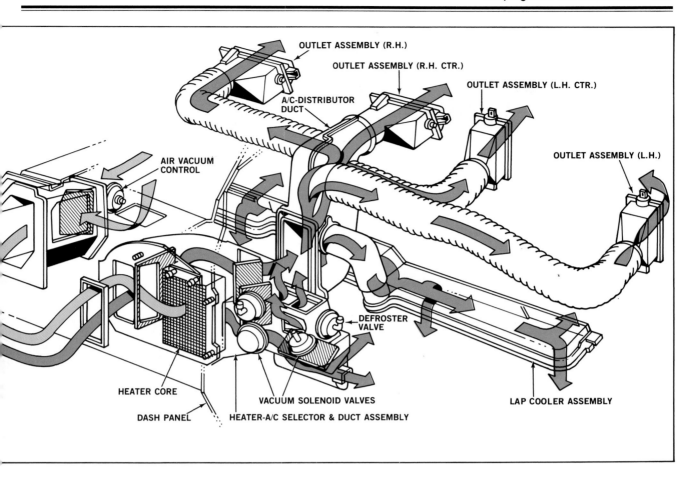

OUTLET ASSEMBLY (R.H.)

OUTLET ASSEMBLY (R.H. CTR.)

OUTLET ASSEMBLY (L.H. CTR.)

A/C-DISTRIBUTOR DUCT

OUTLET ASSEMBLY (L.H.)

AIR VACUUM CONTROL

DEFROSTER VALVE

HEATER CORE

DASH PANEL

VACUUM SOLENOID VALVES

HEATER-A/C SELECTOR & DUCT ASSEMBLY

LAP COOLER ASSEMBLY

the system is switched off. When the switch is in the "on" position, the valve will be closed.

Some heater valves are controlled by a cable attached to the temperature-control lever. Make sure the cable is operating properly by having a helper move the temperature-control lever from "hot" to "cold" while you watch for movement in the valve. There also should be some resistance in the lever; if it's too easy to move, the cable may be disconnected or broken. An excessive amount of resistance may mean the cable is bent.

If you still have doubts about the valve after these checks, bypass it by installing a short length of pipe. The valve is defective if the bypass gives you heat.

Frequently, coolant won't flow through a heater core because the core itself is clogged with rust or radiator sealer. If the clogging matter will flow, a core sometimes can be cleaned without being removed. Carefully remove both heater hoses. If the hoses have been baked on by prolonged high temperature, cut them off short. Then, slice longitudinally and peel the remaining pieces of hose off the pipe to avoid breaking it.

Next, purchase two short lengths of heater hose and attach them to the inlet and outlet pipes. Install a garden-hose adapter (available at any hardware store) in the open end of the outlet hose. Using garden-hose water pressure, try short bursts of water to flush out the clog. (Make sure the heater valve is open.) Start with the discharge side of the core, and switch the garden hose back and forth between the inlet and outlet sides.

Here's another trick that may work when all else fails to clear a clog. Temporarily reverse the car's normal heater hoses. This reversed flow may dislodge more of the clog after a few days of operation. Be sure to place the hoses back in their correct positions.

Vacuum? Electrical?

If the heater core's hoses were both approximately the same temperature when you felt them, the problem may be inside the heater assembly. Most modern heaters, especially the climate-control type, use what car makers call mode-and-blend doors. These are doors within the heater assembly operated by small vacuum or electric servomotors. If a vacuum hose or

small wire is disconnected in any climate-control system, the heater door will remain closed. So although the core may be boiling hot, no heat will enter the passenger compartment.

Generally, the most exotic heater-control problems are caused by a disconnected or clogged vacuum line at the source of the vacuum supply. Before you attack a servomotor- or vacuum-operated heater-control valve, make sure the main vacuum hose is properly connected to the engine's intake manifold and to any vacuum-reservoir tanks. Vacuum tanks usually look like large, black tomato-juice cans or black plastic balls.

Vacuum hoses to the heater and air-conditioning systems are routed just like electrical wiring, and schematic diagrams are available for almost all cars.

Electrical problems involve either the switching system or blower motor. For heat to enter the cabin, air must be blown through the heater core. If you switch on the heater but don't feel air discharging from the lower heater duct, try moving the switch to another mode. If the blower operates in any other position, the trouble is restricted to the switching system.

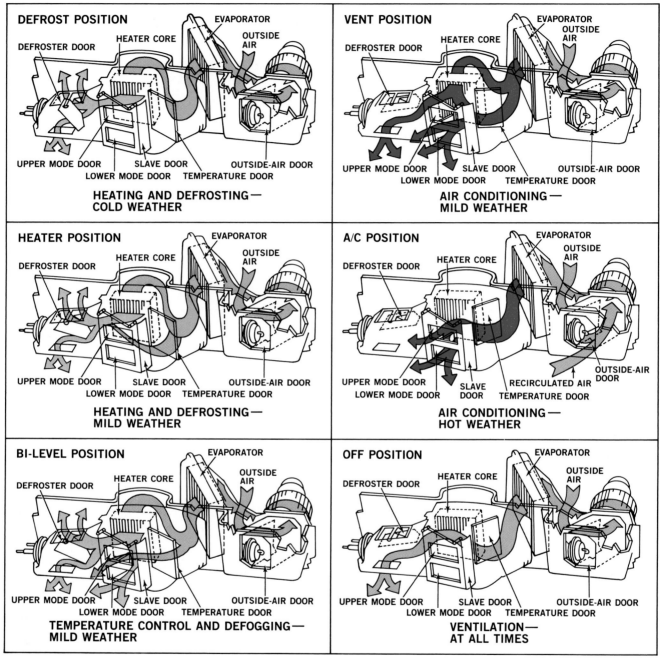

DEFROST POSITION — EVAPORATOR, OUTSIDE AIR, HEATER CORE, DEFROSTER DOOR, UPPER MODE DOOR, LOWER MODE DOOR, SLAVE DOOR, TEMPERATURE DOOR, OUTSIDE-AIR DOOR

HEATING AND DEFROSTING— COLD WEATHER

VENT POSITION — EVAPORATOR, OUTSIDE AIR, HEATER CORE, DEFROSTER DOOR, UPPER MODE DOOR, LOWER MODE DOOR, SLAVE DOOR, TEMPERATURE DOOR, OUTSIDE-AIR DOOR

AIR CONDITIONING— MILD WEATHER

HEATER POSITION — EVAPORATOR, OUTSIDE AIR, HEATER CORE, DEFROSTER DOOR, UPPER MODE DOOR, LOWER MODE DOOR, SLAVE DOOR, TEMPERATURE DOOR, OUTSIDE-AIR DOOR

HEATING AND DEFROSTING— MILD WEATHER

A/C POSITION — EVAPORATOR, OUTSIDE AIR, HEATER CORE, DEFROSTER DOOR, UPPER MODE DOOR, LOWER MODE DOOR, SLAVE DOOR, RECIRCULATED AIR, TEMPERATURE DOOR, OUTSIDE-AIR DOOR

AIR CONDITIONING— HOT WEATHER

BI-LEVEL POSITION — EVAPORATOR, OUTSIDE AIR, HEATER CORE, DEFROSTER DOOR, UPPER MODE DOOR, LOWER MODE DOOR, SLAVE DOOR, TEMPERATURE DOOR, OUTSIDE-AIR DOOR

TEMPERATURE CONTROL AND DEFOGGING— MILD WEATHER

OFF POSITION — EVAPORATOR, OUTSIDE AIR, HEATER CORE, DEFROSTER DOOR, UPPER MODE DOOR, LOWER MODE DOOR, SLAVE DOOR, TEMPERATURE DOOR, OUTSIDE-AIR DOOR

VENTILATION— AT ALL TIMES

If the blower does not work in any mode, check the heater's fuse. A bad blower motor is probably at fault if the fuse is intact. You'll need a 12-volt test lamp to troubleshoot this gremlin. With one lead from the lamp grounded, probe the wire at the heater blower. With the heater switch in the "on" position, 12-volt current should be arriving at the blower and the lamp should light, indicating either a bad motor or poor blower-motor ground.

If the test lamp doesn't light, trace the wiring back to the control switch and relays in the circuit between the motor and heater control. Blowers that operate only at low speeds usually have a defective high-speed blower relay or control switch. If the low-speed modes can't be selected, it's probably the blower-motor resistor block. On most cars, this is located on the heater-air-conditioner housing under the hood.

Even the most sophisticated heater-defroster control systems yield their secrets to careful, logical troubleshooting—and GM's C-cars, which use the new Soft Touch air-conditioner control, have a self-diagnostic feature.

Finally, there are two important points to remember when doing heater-defroster repair: Disconnect the battery, and don't force anything. If something doesn't come out easily, you've probably missed a bolt or forgotten to remove an obstruction. A little too much muscle can result in a leak. Considering the many steps required in a heater-core removal, it's not the kind of job you'll want to do twice. So be gentle, and be sure of your diagnosis—*by Bob Cerullo. Drawings by Russell Von Sauers.*

diy guide to auto a/c

Although occasional A/C breakdowns occur, if you know how your A/C system works, can do routine maintenance, and can learn a logical troubleshooting sequence, you can reduce or eliminate expensive repairs.

Annual checkup

Your early-season A/C checkup should start from the driver's seat. Switch on the system, and check that the fan blows air in each of the switch positions (more on the fan later). Move the control levers to make sure the air-circulation system works in the defrost, heat, and A/C modes. Use your hand to feel for cool airflow at the A/C discharge louvers. Insert a thermometer into the louvers. After the system has had a chance to cool the interior (about five minutes), the mercury should read below 50° F.

Shut down the engine, and raise the hood. Check the A/C belt tension. A slipping belt will significantly reduce the compressor's efficiency. Check the belt's condition by twisting it to expose the V-section. A glazed surface means it's time for replacement. Inspect the A/C hoses for any accumulation of dirt or oil, usually a sign of a leak. Be sure you wear goggles when you inspect any pressurized system. Check all hose fittings for tightness—but be careful not to overtighten. Never tighten or loosen a fragile A/C fitting with a single wrench. Always use a backup wrench. Look the lines over for chafing. Then run your hand carefully along the underside of each hose to check for cuts. Replace any damaged or swollen hoses. (For this, you'll have to discharge the system by relieving the pressure through the service fittings, which look like tire valves. Just depress the valve with a screwdriver—*but don't let the refrigerant [R12] touch your skin.* See the "Working safely" box.)

Inspect the A/C condenser. Remove any accumulated leaves or debris from the cooling fins. Keep a sharp eye out for oil leaks or stains, as these are tip-offs to a slow leak in the condenser and indicate that replacement may be in order.

If the system in your car is equipped with a sight glass, remove the plastic cap and check for bubbles in the window. A system that is cooling should have a clear sight glass after operating for about 15 minutes. If bubbles are still present after warm-up, a partial charge of R12 is needed. If the system is not cooling and the sight glass is clear, it probably needs a complete recharge. (This requires complete evacuation of the system by a good-quality powerful A/C vacuum pump before attempting to recharge with refrigerant.)

The A/C systems on many of the newer models don't have a sight glass. A cycling clutch orifice-tube system is typical of these A/C systems. Recharging such a system is usually guesswork, but there are two ways of making sure the system is fully charged. The first is to fully discharge the system and have it evacuated, and then recharge with the factory-specified amount of R12. The second method is to use a device made by TIF Instruments (9101 N.W. 7th Ave., Miami, FL 33150) called an electronic sight glass. (All the equipment mentioned in this article is expensive, perhaps too expensive for you to purchase for such limited applications, but you should know about its existence and function.) The TIF 4000 (see photo) uses ultrasonics to measure the state of refrigerant charge in the evaporator's lines by means of two sensors clamped to the outside of the metal lines.

The risk in recharging the system without a sight glass or gauge is that you'll overfill with R12. A police captain I know thought a bomb had gone off under his hood, and ran for cover when his overcharged A/C system blew a pressure-relief valve. A/C systems work best with the specified amount of R12 for your car.

Troubleshooting

So you've checked over your A/C system, but when you turn it on, it doesn't work efficiently. Now what?

First, make sure the A/C blower is working. If not, check the fuse. If that's good, use a test lamp to check for power at the blower-motor electrical connection. If current is arriving, the lamp will light. This indicates either a defective blower motor or an open blower-motor ground.

If the lamp does not light, you may have a defective blower-motor switch, a defective blower-motor relay, or a break in the circuit between the fuse and the blower motor.

Next, check the compressor: It must be turning for the system to function. I've seen even professional mechanics waste a great deal of time trying to cure a sick A/C system without ever checking the compressor's clutch. The outer part of the compressor's pulley turns with the belt. But for the compressor to function, the inner section of the pulley must also be rotating. That means the electromagnetic clutch must be energized. If the inner-pulley section doesn't rotate when you switch on the vehicle's A/C, probe the electrical connector at the clutch coil with a test light to determine whether power is arriving. If the lamp lights, the clutch coil or its ground is faulty.

If the lamp doesn't light, trace back along the feed circuit to determine the fault. It could be a low-pressure cutoff switch. Other things to look for are disconnected electrical hookups, vacuum hoses, or control cables that operate selector-mode doors within the plenum chamber. It may help to get a diagram of the specific vacuum and electrical circuits used in your car's A/C system.

On any cycling clutch system, the clutch should click on and remain on until the system is cooling. Then it should begin to slowly cycle on and off. With the clutch working, the A/C should be cooling if R12 is flowing freely through the system, but its flow can be stopped by a number of different problems. A clogged filter in the receiver-dryer can do it. A blocked orifice tube or seized expansion valve might also be the cause. You may logically ask, How can a sealed system become clogged? Moisture is generally the answer. Water will freeze when it finds its way into the orifice tube or expansion valve. It may also act within the system to form a grit that clogs filters and tears away at the compressor's moving parts.

The way to tell whether or not your system has a clog is to measure the high- and low-side pressures with a set of manifold gauges. (These gauges are fairly expensive [$150 to $200] and can be dangerous to use—see safety box. You might want an experienced mechanic to interpret any readings you take.)

You install the gauges on the service fittings, each of which is usually covered with a small plastic, brass, or aluminum cap for protection, with the engine off. Close all the hand valves on the manifold set. The center hose connection should be capped or attached to a refrigerant cylinder. Now connect the high-pressure gauge hose to the high side of the system. This connection may be located on either the compressor or the muffler, or somewhere in the line between the compressor and the condenser. Connect the low-pressure-side hose to the low-side service port.

System pressures vary from model to model and with ambient temperature. If you decide to buy a set of gauges, don't wait until there's A/C trouble to use them. Install them and record what the healthy pressures are. Then you will have established an accurate baseline for a properly operating system.

What else could cause you to roast in your car? One of the most puzzling problems can be caused by the car's heater. The heater valve could be sticking open because it's defective or is connected to an inoperative control

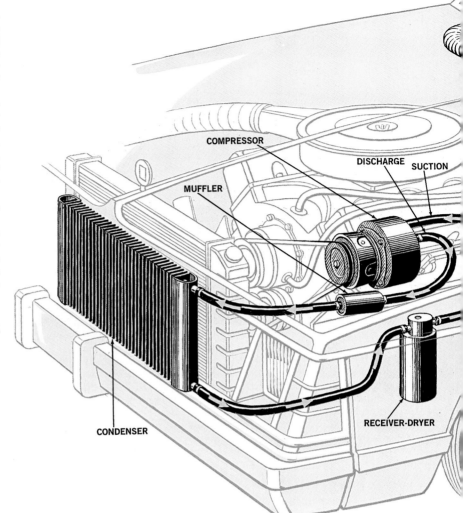

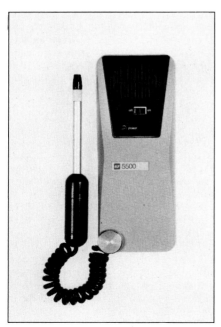

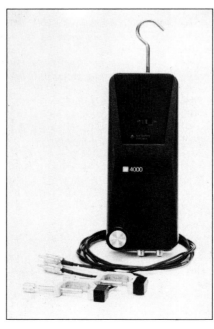

TIF 5500 leak detector's battery-operated pump detects leaks as small as a ¹/₂ ounce per year ($159.95). TIF 4000

($189.95) has two electronic ears that listen for the ultrasonic sound of a charged A/C system.

cable. Try clamping off the heater hose to prevent a flow of hot coolant to the heater core. If that solves your cooling problem, a defective heater valve is the culprit.

Another cause of malfunctioning A/C is a loss of R12. Some systems will lose a few ounces a year and may be impractical to repair. Finding the leak in other systems may require special equipment. (I never use dyed refrigerant for this purpose in my shop, and I can't recommend it.) One effective method is to use an electronic leak detector. The same TIF Instruments mentioned earlier makes one such device. The model 5500 Micropump leak detector (see photo) works like an electronic nose to sniff out R12 leaks. A small vacuum pump pulls air samples past the probe sensor tip. If a leak is detected, a beeper will sound.

Once you've discovered the location of the leak, you'll have to remove the

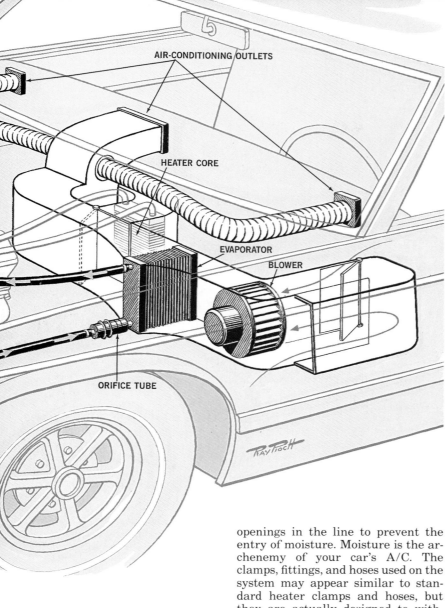

AIR-CONDITIONING OUTLETS

HEATER CORE

EVAPORATOR

BLOWER

ORIFICE TUBE

and work carefully, and you'll enjoy a cool summer—*by Bob Cerullo. Illustration by Ray Pioch.*

How it works

The principle

First: Although there's obviously something called heat, there's no opposite equivalent called cold. To make something cold, one removes the heat—in much the same way one can remove the light to make a room dark. The purpose of the A/C system is to absorb heat from the passenger compartment and move it outside the vehicle. This exchange of heat takes place at the evaporator.

At the evaporator, high-pressure R12 is metered into a low-pressure envelope. On leaving the metering device, this carefully regulated R12 starts to boil (its boiling point is minus 21.6 degrees F). As it changes from a liquid to a gas, it absorbs heat. This low-pressure refrigerant vapor, now carrying heat from the cabin, is drawn to the compressor. There it is compressed into a high-pressure, high-temperature vapor. The compressing action causes the refrigerant to have an extremely high temperature. At this point, the hot vapor passes into the condenser, a radiator-like device. As outside air passes through the fins of the condenser, the R12 vapor gives up its heat and condenses into a high-pressure liquid. It then collects in the bottom of the condenser until it is again metered into the evaporator.

This process works so well that unless some form of control is used, the evaporator would eventually freeze into a block of ice. One type of control simply shuts off the compressor by turning off the power to the electromagnetic clutch using a thermostatic or pressure-activated switch at the evaporator.

A/C mechanics

The mechanical heart of a car's air-conditioning system is the compressor. It's driven by a belt through an electromagnetic clutch. When 12 volts is applied across a switch to the coil within the clutch, the compressor engages. Cool low-pressure R12 is drawn into the suction side of the compressor and is pumped out the discharge side as a hot gas under high pressure. The hot high-pressure gas is piped to the A/C condenser, where it cools to become a high-pressure liquid. It then passes through the receiver-dryer, where it is filtered. Inside the receiver-dryer a desiccant absorbs small amounts of moisture. Next the liquid R12 passes through a metering valve called an expansion valve (on some systems a fixed orifice tube). The gas then passes into the low-pressure environment within the evaporator. The liquid rapidly changes into a gas and absorbs heat as it does so. This chills the walls of the evaporator. Passenger-compartment air passes across the evaporator's fins and is cooled. The blower pushes this air into the cabin to cool the passengers. The R12 exits the evaporator and is drawn back into the suction side of the compressor, and the cycle begins anew.

You should identify and familiarize yourself with the system on your car before attempting any maintenance.—B. C.

defective component. Keep in mind the kind of pressures with which you're dealing. Normal pressures can reach 350 psi—and higher when there's a system malfunction. Before you attempt to remove any lines, make sure the system is fully discharged as described previously. You should also be prepared to plug any

openings in the line to prevent the entry of moisture. Moisture is the archenemy of your car's A/C. The clamps, fittings, and hoses used on the system may appear similar to standard heater clamps and hoses, but they are actually designed to withstand far greater pressures.

If your system has lost its charge of R12, it may have also lost much of the refrigerant oil needed to lubricate the compressor. Check to see whether there is evidence of a lot of oil splashed in the compressor area. If there is, you'll need professional help.

Be patient in your system checkout

Working safely

Wear eye protection when working with refrigerants. Gloves and heavy clothing could help protect your skin from frostbite. Refrigerant inadvertently sprayed on the skin or in the eyes will cause the tissue to freeze. R12 is nonexplosive and nonflammable. It is also nonpoisonous—unless exposed to an open flame, when it converts to highly toxic phosgene gas. Nevertheless, avoid breathing R12 at all times. Do not transport containers of R12 inside the passenger compartment of your vehicle. Exposed to high temperatures, possibly generated by the sun's rays, the pressure inside could become high enough to burst the container walls. Keep in mind that any steam cleaning or welding near refrigerant components could result in an excessive pressure buildup and a line or component rupture. Check to be sure that all the connections are tight before charging the system. Don't replace A/C-type hoses or fittings with heater-hose or cooling-system clamps. If you're using a set of manifold pressure gauges, do not open the hand valve of the high-side pressure gauge while the system is operating (engine running). If the valve is opened and a refrigerant can is connected to the center hose on the manifold, 150- to 300-psi refrigerant gas will flow into the can, possibly causing it to explode. Be sure that the work area is adequately ventilated.—B. C.

the new cordless rechargeables

Last summer I embarked on a project that involved cutting five panels of ⅝-inch plywood and two panels of ¾-inch plywood into 90 pieces. I had a new Hitachi 6¼-inch cordless circular saw to try out and report on, and I showed it to my collaborator on the project, an experienced woodworker. "It may be useful for a few trim cuts," he remarked with a skeptical look at the small green plastic saw, "but we'll need a *real* saw for the serious cutting." So I borrowed a big, beefy circular saw with a reassuring AC cord.

Nevertheless, we decided to see what the cordless saw could do. After the first fast and effortless cut, my colleague began to look at the little saw with obvious respect. "Let's keep a record of how much we cut with it," he suggested. We used it throughout the day, recording 68 feet of cutting through ⅝-inch plywood. The last cut was as effortless as the first, and the battery did not need a recharge. Indeed, the cordless saw was so convenient that we did the entire project with it. The big AC saw never came out of its case.

Since then I've roamed stores and trade shows, perused catalogs, and talked with manufacturers to see what other cordless tools are available. The selection is astounding and ranges from inexpensive screwdrivers for light-duty use to heavy-duty pro tools for all-day use by tradesmen. Naturally, there's a wide difference in performance—and price. But I'm impressed with how well *most* of them do the job they were designed to do.

"Cordless tools are the fastest-growing segment of the tool market," says Ron Gronke, Skil's product manager for cordless tools. Although the technology isn't dramatically new, it has improved year by year.

"When we came out with our first cordless drill in the early 1960s, it had a 4.8-volt battery pack and produced 40 to 50 watts of power," says Richard Walters, Black & Decker's advanced-development manager for electromagnetic components. "Now our professional cordless tools have 9.6-volt batteries, and their power output is 100 watts. That compares with the lower end of AC products."

Most cordless tools use 1.2-volt nickel-cadmium batteries, massed to form battery packs from 2.4 to 9.6 volts (a few are even larger). When cordless tools first came out, recharging took 16 hours. Now all professional models I've found recharge in an hour. Some consumer models also have 1-hour chargers, others take longer, and some still take 16 hours.

The tools shown in the photos are representative of what's available but are by no means a complete collection. Black & Decker and Makita, for example, have extensive lines of cordless tools. Prices are manufacturers' suggested prices (they are often greatly discounted), including battery and charger unless noted. Two mail-order sources are Trend Lines (375 Beacham St., Chelsea, MA 02150) and U.S. General (100 Commercial St., Plainview, NY 11803).

Some tools bear more comment than caption space permits:

Screwdrivers and drill-drivers. In professional tool lines the drill-screwdrivers have ⅜-inch chucks, two or more speeds (low for driving screws, higher for drilling) plus reverse, and either 7.2- or 9.6-volt battery packs that slip out of the tool for recharging. That means you can buy a spare battery and have one charging while the other is powering the tool. Many pro drill-drivers have adjustable clutches, which let you set the torque to match your task. That minimizes the risk of twisting off screw heads, stripping threads, or damaging your work.

Consumer cordless screwdrivers and drill-drivers usually have ¼-inch chucks. Batteries typically range from 2.4 to 6 volts. Many come with charging stands that keep the battery charged all the time. Chuck speeds range from 130 to 300 rpm. That's fine for turning screws but slow going for drilling even small holes. The Makita M001 drill-driver, in the company's new consumer line, is an exception to most of these generalizations, however (see caption).

Circular saws. All three 6¼-inch saws shown use the same carbide-tipped slim-kerf Japanese-made blade, which helps account for their effortless cutting and lasting battery power. The Hitachi and Milwaukee saws use 12-volt lead-acid batteries; the Makita has a 10.8-volt nickel-cadmium type. "With lead-acid you get more power for the size of the battery," Hitachi engineer Roy Ishizawa told me. The trade-off: The lead-acid battery is warranted to last through only 200 charge-discharge cycles; a

typical nickel-cadmium will go through 1,000.

All cordless tools come with safety warnings, which should be read and heeded. Many of the tools are made of bright-colored plastic that children find attractive. Because they work without being plugged in, cordless tools can be more dangerous than AC tools. So play it safe; keep them locked away from curious young hands—*by V. Elaine Gilmore. Photos by Greg Sharko.*

MAKERS AND DISTRIBUTORS OF TOOLS SHOWN
AEG Power Tool Corp., 1 Winnenden Rd., Norwich, CT 06360; **Amercep,** 909 E. El Segundo Blvd., El Segundo, CA 90245; **Black & Decker** Consumer Power Tools Div., 3012 Highwoods Blvd., Raleigh, NC 27625; Professional Products Div., 626 Hanover Pike, Hampstead, MD 21074; **Robert Bosch Power Tool Corp.,** Highway 55 West, New Bern, NC 28560; **Gar-Tec Products,** 3603 W. 161st Ave., Lowell, IN 46356; **Hitachi Power Tools U.S.A. Ltd.,** 4487-F Park Dr., Norcross, GA 30093 or 7490 Lampson Ave., Garden Grove, CA 92641; **Makita U.S.A.,** 12950 E. Alondra Blvd., Cerritos, CA 90701; **Milwaukee Electric Tool Corp.,** 13135 W. Lisbon Rd., Brookfield, WI 53005; **Porter-Cable Professional Power Tools,** Box 2468, Jackson, TN 38301; **Ryobi America Corp.,** 1158 Tower Lane, Bensenville, IL 60106; **Sears, Roebuck and Co.,** Sears Tower, Chicago, IL 60684; **Skil Corp.,** 4801 W. Peterson Ave., Chicago, IL 60646; **Wen Products,** 5810 Northwest Highway, Chicago, IL 60631.

Cordless drill-drivers and screw-drivers: Hitachi D10D (1) has a 9.6-V battery, two speeds (300 and 1,000 rpm), and adjustable torque; $185. Ryobi BD-1020AR (2) has a 7.2-V battery and 300- and 600-rpm speeds; $148. Sears Craftsman 1112 (3) has a 7.2-V battery, a low-gear speed range of zero to 250 rpm, and a high-gear range of zero to 750 rpm; $100. Milwaukee 3/8-inch driver/drill (4) has a 7.2-V battery, a variable speed of 100 to 600 rpm (electronic feedback keeps the speed constant under load), and adjustable torque; $159. Wen 2222 (5) has a 6-V battery, two speeds (150 and 320 rpm), and charging stand; $50. Skil 2305 (6) has a 3.6-V battery and a charging stand; $38. Ikra 3.7-V screwdriver (7), imported by Gar-Tec, has a removable battery pack that plugs into an AC outlet; $60. Amercep Turbo Driver II (8) has a 3.6-V battery pack; $40. Makita M001 (9) has a 7.2-V battery pack and 600-rpm speed; $78. Black & Decker 9021 (10) has a 2.4-V battery and charging caddy; $55. AEG EZ502 (11) has a 2.4-V removable battery and an adjustable clutch; $90. Skil Twist (12), with a 2.4-V battery, can drive up to 500 screws on a charge, says Skil; $28.

Cordless saws: 4300DW Makita jigsaw (1) has a 9.6-V battery, a 2,700 stroke-per-minute cutting speed, and a base that can be reversed for flush cuts and angled for bevels; its specs say it cuts 39 feet of 1/2-inch softwood on a charge; $158. Black & Decker jigsaw (2) has a 9.6-V battery, 2,400 stroke-per-minute cutting speed, and is said to cut 30 feet of 1/2-inch softwood per charge; $183. Milwaukee 6 1/4-inch circular saw (3) has a 12-V lead-acid battery and 3,400-rpm speed. Its specs say it makes 80 cuts through 2×4s per charge; $195. Hitachi 6 1/4-inch circular saw (4) has a 12-V lead-acid battery, a 3,200-rpm speed, and is said to make 100 cuts through 2×4s per charge; $200. Makita 5600DW 6 1/4-inch saw (5) has a 10.8-V nickel-cadmium battery pack and 1,000-rpm speed. Its maker says it cuts 125 times through a 2×4 per charge; $224. Makita 3 3/8-inch circular saw (6) has a 9.6-V battery, 1,000-rpm speed, and cutting depth of 3/8 inch. Its specs say it cuts 32.8 feet of 1/2-inch plywood per charge; $65.

A miscellany of cordless tools: Makita 9035DW finishing sander (1) has a no-load speed of 6,000 orbits per minute, a 7.2-V battery, and 1-hour recharge; its switch must be depressed constantly to run; $128. Ikra (Gar-Tec) solder gun (2) uses the same 3.6-V battery pack as the Ikra screwdriver's (top left photo) and has a 3-W power rating; it's claimed to reach 500° F in six seconds, with a maximum temperature of 600°; $45 with battery. Amercep Turbo Solderor (3) has a 2.4-V battery and a 12-W power rating; it comes with a 120-V AC and 12-V DC charger (for car battery) and recharges in 10 to 12 hours; it's said to reach soldering temperature (480° F) in ten seconds, and can yield 250 spots of solder per charge; $25. Amercep 3.6-V Turbo Tool rotary hobby tool (4) has two speeds, 1,500 and 4,000 rpm (compared with Dremel's variable-speed Moto-Tool's 5,000 to 28,000 rpm), and recharges in 10 to 12 hours; $50. Hitachi impact wrench (5) has a 9.6-V battery, a ½-inch-square drive, and a 1,200-rpm no-load speed; it weighs 5.5 pounds, has 72.3 foot-pounds of torque, recharges in 80 minutes and is said to tighten 130 bolts on a charge; it's $220.

Specialty cordless drills: Makita DA3000DW angle drill (1) has a 7.2-V battery and 700-rpm speed, and is claimed to drill 300 ⁵⁄₁₆-inch holes in medium-hard wood per charge; $176. Black & Decker 1910 (2) has a 7.2-V battery, 65-W motor, 600-rpm speed, and high torque (41 foot-pounds) for drilling hard materials; $141. Black & Decker 1920 (3) has a 9.6-V battery, 100-W motor, and 1,850-rpm speed. It takes bits to ³⁄₈ inch for metal and masonry and ³⁄₄ inch for wood; $174. Porter-Cable 800 hammer drill (4) has a 9.6-V battery, 350- and 1,000-rpm speeds, and can be used as a hammer drill for masonry (6,300 or 18,000 impacts per minute) or as a straight drill for wood and metal; $195. Bosch 11213K rotary hammer (5), with a 24-V nickel-cadmium battery, is the most powerful cordless tool, says Bosch. It has a 780-rpm speed, delivers 3,600 blows per minute, weighs 7.7 pounds, recharges in 2 hours, and operates as a straight drill; cost—$399 with case.

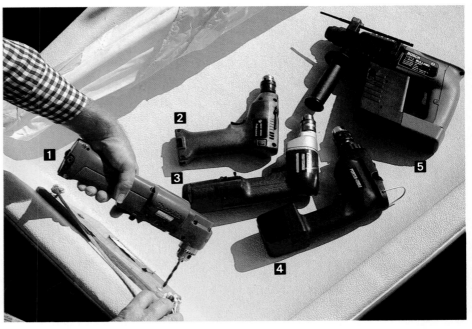

turntable table saw

At first glance the Norsaw 805 looks pretty much like a conventional table saw. But a second glance at the new Norwegian import dispels that notion:

● Motor and blade mount beneath a rotating turntable centered in the table top. You pivot the turntable into one position for ripping, move it 90 degrees for crosscuts, and position it anywhere in between for miters.

● Unlike most table saws, this one has roller infeed and outfeed tables.

● For crosscutting, the fence (indeed the whole infeed table) slides forward on rollers to feed the stock.

Putting these features to work efficiently takes some practice. To rip, for example, you lift a lever to raise the blade, then tighten a knob to lock the blade up. Next, you pivot the turntable so the blade is parallel to the fence. Then you slide the fence into position and lock it there. You feed your stock as you would with any table saw, although the roller tables make the operation smoother, easier, and safer.

To crosscut, pivot the turntable so the blade is perpendicular to the fence. Place your stock against the fence, and make your cut. If the stock is narrow, you can just raise the blade through it in an inverted plunge cut. For wider stock, lift the blade-elevation lever with your left hand and draw the fence and stock forward with your right hand. As soon as the cut is complete, lower the lever to drop the blade back below the table.

Bevel cuts are made in the same way, but with the blade tilted. Both of these cuts are unusually safe because the blade turns away from you and because you drop the blade below the table after every cut.

To cut miters, you pivot the turntable to the desired setting and make an inverted plunge cut. For compound miters, you tilt the blade as well. All miters must be made with a plunge cut—a convenience when handling long stock—but the 8-inch blade size limits your stock width to about 4 inches. That's the Norsaw's biggest weakness: It means the saw can't make the basic rafter cuts required for roof framing.

The 805, however, is the perfect jobsite saw for the professional trim carpenter. It is solidly built of galvanized steel, it's designed to stand unprotected in any kind of weather, and it sets up in just a couple of minutes. And although the saw is light and

Norsaw's blade is raised and lowered with a large lever (below table). Other controls include a turntable lock lever (front of table), elevation lock knob, and bevel lock knob (below table).

Infeed and outfeed tables make it easy to cut large stock. The saw is set to rip.

compact, it has remarkably large rip and crosscut capacities, handles full sheets of plywood with ease, and has the muscle to do real work.

In addition to muscle, the 805 offers precision. Its motor and bearings run with an almost eerie smoothness, and, with its quality carbide blade, cuts are just about perfect.

Understand, though, that the saw was designed for the thinking pro. For example, there are no stops on the turntable. You have to make your settings by eye on the miter scale. This may seem crude, but it's effective. I know from experience with trim work that few corners in a house are exactly 90 degrees. Thus, you are often setting your saw at angles other than 45 degrees. For work like this, stops just get in the way.

If you're looking for a job-site saw that can do typical trim work and handle big ripping and crosscutting jobs, the Norsaw 805 deserves consideration. If you'd also like to do rafter work, consider one of the 805's big brothers: these are the 12-inch 1203 ($1,975) or the 16-inch 1603 ($2,375) —*by A.J. Hand.*

NORSAW 805: SPECS AND CAPACITIES

Table Size	Weight	Motor	Blade Size	Max. Depth	Max. Rip	Max. Crosscut	Price*
17½ ×20 in.	80 lbs.	2.1 hp	8-in.-dia., ⅝-in. bore	2⅜ in.	35 in.	35 in.	$975

*Price includes infeed and outfeed tables; imported by Norsaw Inc., 344 West Cummings Park, Woburn, MA 01801

new-tech carbide cutters

Ioften wondered why we put those big chunks of expensive tungsten carbide on the face of saw teeth when most of the cutting is done at the top of the tooth," remarked John Edgerton, test-lab supervisor for Omark Industries. So Edgerton made some experimental circular saw blades with small carbide tips placed horizontally on top of the teeth instead. He was pleased with the blades' performance. That was three years ago.

Early in the summer of 1985, Black & Decker introduced a decidedly different tungsten-carbide circular saw blade. Dubbed the Piranha, it is a thin blade with curved carbide teeth and gullets shaped like fish hooks.

That August, Vermont American announced two new blades with peculiar dentition: the Laser X2, whose teeth have V-grooves down the face, and the Particleboard/Plywood (PB/P) blade with angled teeth. Though thicker than the Piranha, these blades, too, are relatively thin, producing kerfs well under 1/8-inch thick.

Obviously, it was time for Edgerton to dust off his experimental blade. Another thin-rim blade, Omark christened it the Credo 'Cuda for its March 1986 introduction.

What are the engineering reasons behind these thin (more or less) blades with their unconventional shapes? Are they really better than the traditional carbide blade—thick or thin—with vertical block-shaped teeth? I was dispatched to answer the first question, and the second was assigned to *Popular Science* contributor Phil McCafferty, an experienced workshopper. He shop-tested the new-geometry blades, along with some thin-rim Japanese imports with teeth of traditional shape, Vermont American's new low-price Handi-Duty model (thin, but of traditional tooth shape), and three from Freud—one thin premium blade and two standard blades from that maker's new contractor/do-it-yourselfer line.

Traditional carbide

Tungsten carbide is a dense, metal-like substance made by heating powdered tungsten and carbon black with a cobalt binder. It is extremely hard, which makes it ideal for cutting tools. When used as the teeth for circular saw blades, the tungsten carbide is usually formed into small blocks.

Tungsten-carbide teeth of saw blades come in surprising shapes. From left: Tsumura 7 1/4-inch, eight-tooth rip; Freud 9-inch planer; Black & Decker 32-tooth Piranha; Omark 10-inch, 40-tooth Credo 'Cuda; Freud 10-inch, 80-tooth fine; Freud 10-inch planer; Omark 7 1/4-inch, 20-tooth Credo 'Cuda; Black & Decker 7 1/4-inch, 18-tooth Piranha.

These are attached, typically by silver-brazing, onto the steel of the blade to form vertical teeth.

The exact shape, or grind, of a carbide tooth depends on the intended use of the saw blade: For crosscut blades the teeth are usually ground with sharp side points that will slice through wood fibers. Called alternate-top-bevel teeth, the points are alternately on the left and right sides of consecutive teeth.

The teeth of a ripping blade generally are ground flat on top so that each acts as a tiny chisel. Ripping blades usually have fewer teeth and larger gullets (waste-clearance channels between the teeth) to handle the larger chips created by ripping.

Combination (combo) blades, designed to handle crosscuts, miters, and ripping, may have alternate-top-bevel (ATB) teeth or may combine beveled teeth with a periodic flat ripping-type tooth (this is called a planer blade).

First fish

Black & Decker's new Piranha line has ATB teeth, but the faces of the teeth are curved (see photo). The combination of the curve and the beveled top produces a knifelike slicing action for smoother, faster cuts, the company claims.

The blade was designed by mechanical engineer Peter Chaconas. He began by analyzing existing carbide blades and concluded that they have some fundamental flaws. "My carpenter buddies constantly complain that carbide blades throw chips—big chips—in their faces," Chaconas told me. He determined that a thinner kerf would minimize that problem.

"Another problem I recognized was that the noncutting edge of an ATB

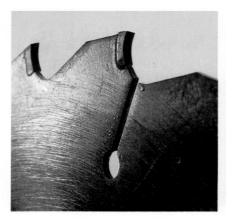

Piranha, Black & Decker's new combo blade, has curved tungsten-carbide teeth with sharp cutting points and large, round gullets that carry the sawdust out of the kerf, says the company. This is the 7 1/4-inch, 18-tooth model.

Credo 'Cuda, from Omark Industries, has horizontal carbide tips brazed to the tops of the teeth. Tooth arrangement plus the thin kerf of the blade add up to smoother, splinter-free cuts and less friction, the company claims.

V-groove, cast in the face of Vermont American's Laser X2 saw blades, gives each tooth two cutting edges and balances the cutting load, it's claimed. Smoother cuts and more efficient chip removal are also claimed for this blade.

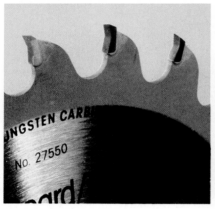
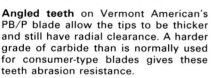

Angled teeth on Vermont American's PB/P blade allow the tips to be thicker and still have radial clearance. A harder grade of carbide than is normally used for consumer-type blades gives these teeth abrasion resistance.

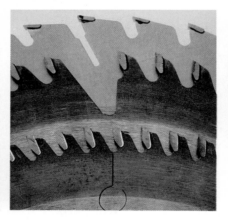

Freud's 80-tooth fine-finish thin blade (front) and planer blade (center) have block-shape carbide teeth. Note tooth size relative to Omark's Credo 'Cuda (rear). Also note the laser-cut expansion slot in the 80-tooth Freud.

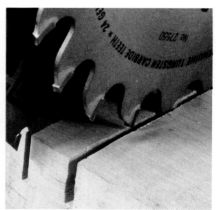

Thick and thin of the 7 1/4-inch blades tried: Tsumura blades cut the thinnest kerfs—0.082 and 0.084 inch. The Credo 'Cuda and Piranha were just slightly wider. Vermont American's PB/P blade cut the thickest kerf: 0.114 inch.

tooth may protrude laterally beyond the cutting edge of the tooth in front," he said, "so one side of that tooth would be dragged through the cut. That increases the force required to push the saw." To eliminate that drag, the noncutting side of the teeth are found well inside the kerf on the Piranha.

Finally, by analyzing the patterns of sawdust and resin deposits on the blades after use, Chaconas concluded that with standard carbide blades, chips tend to wedge between the blade and the kerf during the cutting rather than staying in the gullet of the blade until they can escape from the kerf.

"The combination of the large kerf width, dragging of the teeth, and the chips wedged in the kerf meant the blade didn't cut as freely as it should," Chaconas said. "That bothered me, especially for portable-saw use. Anytime you have to push harder, you in-

crease your chance of an accident."

The Piranha's large, round gullets are designed to cradle the chips while they're in the kerf. "As the tooth exits the workpiece, it creates a sort of vortex action that ejects the chips," Chaconas explained.

The net effect of the narrower kerf, reduced tooth drag, and chip control yields a blade that requires 50 percent less pushing force than does a standard carbide blade, Black & Decker claims. And that reduces the wear on the saw motor. "Motor wear is directly related to the amperage your motor requires," Chaconas pointed out, "and amperage draw is related to the required pushing force."

VA blades

While Chaconas touts the speed and ease of cut with Piranha blades, Mac McCord, vice president of engineering at Vermont American, emphasizes

the smoothness of cut of that company's new combination blade, the Laser X2.

"The smoothness of the cut is directly related to the speed of the blade, the feed rate of the material, and the number of teeth," explained McCord. "The first two being equal, a blade with more teeth will have a smaller chip load and, consequently, less splintering."

The Laser X2, with its V-groove teeth, has two cutting points on each tooth. Thus with the same number of teeth you get twice the cutting surface of a traditional ATB tooth grind. The V-groove also creates a double face bevel on each tooth, which forms sharper cutting points. That also contributes to the clean, splinterless cut, according to the company.

"The extra points on the Laser do mean that the cut will take a little more power," McCord admitted, "but at reasonable feed rates the difference should be too small to perceive."

Vermont American's new Particleboard/Plywood blade was designed to handle the abrasiveness of the binders in composition boards and to stand up to their hardness.

"We used a harder grade of carbide for the teeth than is normally used on consumer-type saw blades," McCord said. The angled tooth shape on the PB/P blade (see photo) is to enhance the stability of the blade.

The top 1/4 inch on the carbide tip has a molded-in forward slant, called the hook, or rake, angle. The greater the hook angle of the teeth, the more a saw blade tends to pull itself into the work. (Too pronounced a hook angle can cause a blade to bite into the wood too readily for easy control, especially on radial-arm saws.)

"By molding part of the hook angle into the carbide tips on the PB/P blade, we don't have to angle the steel teeth forward as much," McCord explained. By reversing that hook angle, the steel can form a broad base under the tips, providing better support for the cutting edge. "With the steel *below* the tips, they tend to be pulled through the cut; if the steel were *behind* the tips, they'd be pushed," McCord noted. A cutting edge is more stable when pulled than when pushed. "It's similar to pulling a string rather than trying to push it," he added.

The tooth design also aids chip ejection. "When the angle of the tooth reverses, it reverses the direction of the chip flow, which gets them started on their path out of the cut," McCord said. The end result of these features is that the blade moves fast and smoothly through dense materials without jamming or splintering the board, the company claims. And that puts less strain on the saw motor.

Second fish

Omark's Edgerton, like Chaconas, heard complaints about carbide blades spraying chips in carpenters' faces. His tests indicated that his experimental thin blade with horizontal teeth minimized the problem.

To see why, he spread a tough coating called machine bluing on his blade and on some standard carbide blades. As he used the blades, the spray of chips abraded the bluing in patterns that revealed just how the chips moved. "We also used a strobe light to look at chip spray," he said.

"In the old-fashioned blades the sawdust just boiled around inside the

gullet looking like it didn't know where it wanted to go. But in my blade the chips seemed to get out of the gullet right away and exited in the direction opposite the blade's rotation, as they do with steel-tooth saw blades."

Omark claims that the horizontal-tooth Credo 'Cuda cuts easier, produces less splintering, and has less tooth drag; thus the saw motor draws less amperage than with standard carbide blades.

Is thinner better?

The performance claims of these new-geometry blades also are made for thinner blades of standard shape. Black & Decker's Chaconas thinks the Piranha's thinness has a lot to do with its speed and ease of cutting, but lists chip control as a benefit of that blade's unusual form. Omark's Edgerton doesn't feel he can isolate the effects of tooth placement from those of thinness on the Credo 'Cuda blade.

Vermont American's McCord is not convinced that thinness is all it's cracked up to be. "It's a good talking point and does contribute to less power consumption," he commented. "If all other parameters are the same, you may detect less effort in cutting.

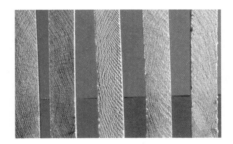

Oak samples show the cut quality of combo blades. From left: Freud, Piranha, Credo 'Cuda, Tsumura, Laser X2, and Handi-Duty. Handi-Duty and 'Cuda were 7 1/4-inch blades, thus did not cut as smoothly as the others, all 10-inchers.

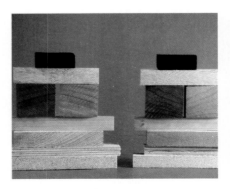

Carbide ripping blades are worth owning. Both Fine Tool (left samples) and Tsumura (right) blades are free-cutters.

But the wood saving claimed is irrelevant to the do-it-yourselfer."

McCord also mentions the disadvantage of thin blades: They're not as stiff. "With portable saws, guidance is never good," he said. "You get some deflection of the saw blade, and that's proportional to blade stiffness, which is related to thickness."

For similar reasons, Freud does not recommend its thin blades for portable saws or for cutting wood more than 3/4 inch thick, according to Barry Dunsmore, assistant vice president of Freud.

The engineers who designed the new-geometry blades give convincing reasons for the characteristics they built into their products, and have tested them against standard tungsten-carbide blades to back up their performance claims. But controlled, independent tests to verify those claims have not been done. Edgerton and McCord also point out that there will be variations in the quality of all consumer-type saw blades. Manufacturing tolerances are not generally tight enough to prevent that—*by V. Elaine Gilmore. Photos by Greg Sharko and Phil McCafferty.*

Shop-testing the new blades

I tried a dozen thin- and somewhat-thin-kerf carbide-tipped circular saw blades, including those with new tooth designs. I also tried two new moderately priced standard-kerf planer blades from Freud. I learned two things: Thin can be beautiful, and there's more than one way to make a good saw blade. Indeed, I didn't find a bad blade in the bunch.

Just what is a thin-kerf blade? If there is a dividing line between thin and standard carbide blades, it is probably around 1/8 inch. The table lists the measured kerf width of the blades I tested. I cut the kerfs in a block of maple, used feeler gauges (thin strips of metal) to

The Fine Tool and Freud 10-inch, 80-tooth blades give satiny edges. They cut slowly, and can burn on ripping cuts.

measure the kerfs, then measured the feeler-gauge stacks with a micrometer.

It would not seem fair, and probably wouldn't even be possible, to directly compare all these blades. So I looked at general quality, compared blades intended for the same task, and addressed some general and specific claims made by suppliers. I ran all the 7- to 7 1/4-inch blades on a portable saw, table saw, and radial-arm saw; I ran the one 9- and all the 10-inch samples on my table and radial-arm saws.

New-geometry blades

Though Black & Decker, Omark, and Vermont American approach the objectives differently, all their new combo blades have extremely sharp cutting edges and subtle ways of minimizing friction and improving chip removal. I found all to be fast-cutting blades with excellent all-around characteristics.

Although I did not abuse the blades or run them to destruction, I ran them all through enough tough hardwoods, resinous softwoods, plastics, and abrasive particleboard and plywood to feel satisfied that all three of these new designs are good saw blades.

Comparing the new blades with each other, I found some variation according to the material being cut. But on balance, I thought Vermont American's Laser X2 had a slight edge for cut smoothness, Black & Decker's Piranha cut with the greatest speed and ease, and Omark's Credo 'Cuda blade seemed to produce a bit less edge splintering. That held true for crosscuts, miters, and rips.

The thin Japanese blades imported by The Fine Tool Shops and Woodcraft Supply (Tsumura brand) produced just as smooth a cut as did the new-geometry blades, on average, but didn't go through the wood with quite the same speed and ease. Freud's standard-kerf combo planer blades also produced smooth cuts, but seemed to cut with less speed and ease than did any of the thinner blades.

I've heard of concern about the trueness and stability of thin blades so I checked all for flatness and runout against several conventional carbide blades. I found essentially no difference in quality in these areas. If you force the cut or use a blade that's dull, certainly a thin blade will be more susceptible to buckling than a heftier model, but I don't work that way.

Can you sharpen?

Rivals have maintained that the unconventional blades—the Piranha, Laser X2, Credo 'Cuda, and PB/P—are impossible to sharpen. After talking to the manufacturers, a major maker of saw resharpening machines, and three sharpening shops, here's what I learned.

The Piranha can be reground on the tooth tops. A diamond wheel with a special radius would be required to regrind

the face of the teeth. Black & Decker does not intend the faces to be reground. The Laser X2 can be reground on the sides and tops of the teeth. It is not intended that the V-groove tooth faces be ground—indeed they are not ground in manufacture: The shape is molded into the carbide inserts before sintering.

The horizontal top surfaces of the Credo 'Cuda's carbide tips are nearly flush with the blade body. To resharpen, it might be necessary to slightly relieve the steel blade body behind the tips. Omark recommends grinding the face instead.

With its V-hook configuration, Vermont American's PB/P blade could be face-ground down to where the angle reverses. Top and side grinding would be standard.

You'll note that all of these unconventional blades have small teeth. Thus

you're not going to be able to resharpen them many times. Given the long life of carbide blades and the modest cost of most of these, resharpening may not be cost-effective anyway.

Claims are made that thin-kerf blades are quieter than others. They do seem quieter to me; nevertheless, I wouldn't run a saw without hearing protection. Among the 7- to 7 1/4-inch blades I tried, I'd rate the Handi-Duty and Piranha the quietest. The two 10-inch, 80-tooth blades (one from Freud and the other the Tsumura blade) are really quiet, especially the Freud. Its expansion slots are finely cut with a laser (see photo), which reduces blade noise, the company says.

Also, for smoothness of cut, the two 80-tooth blades were slightly superior. They generally produced satiny cuts that would not require sanding before forming a glue joint—*Phil McCafferty*.

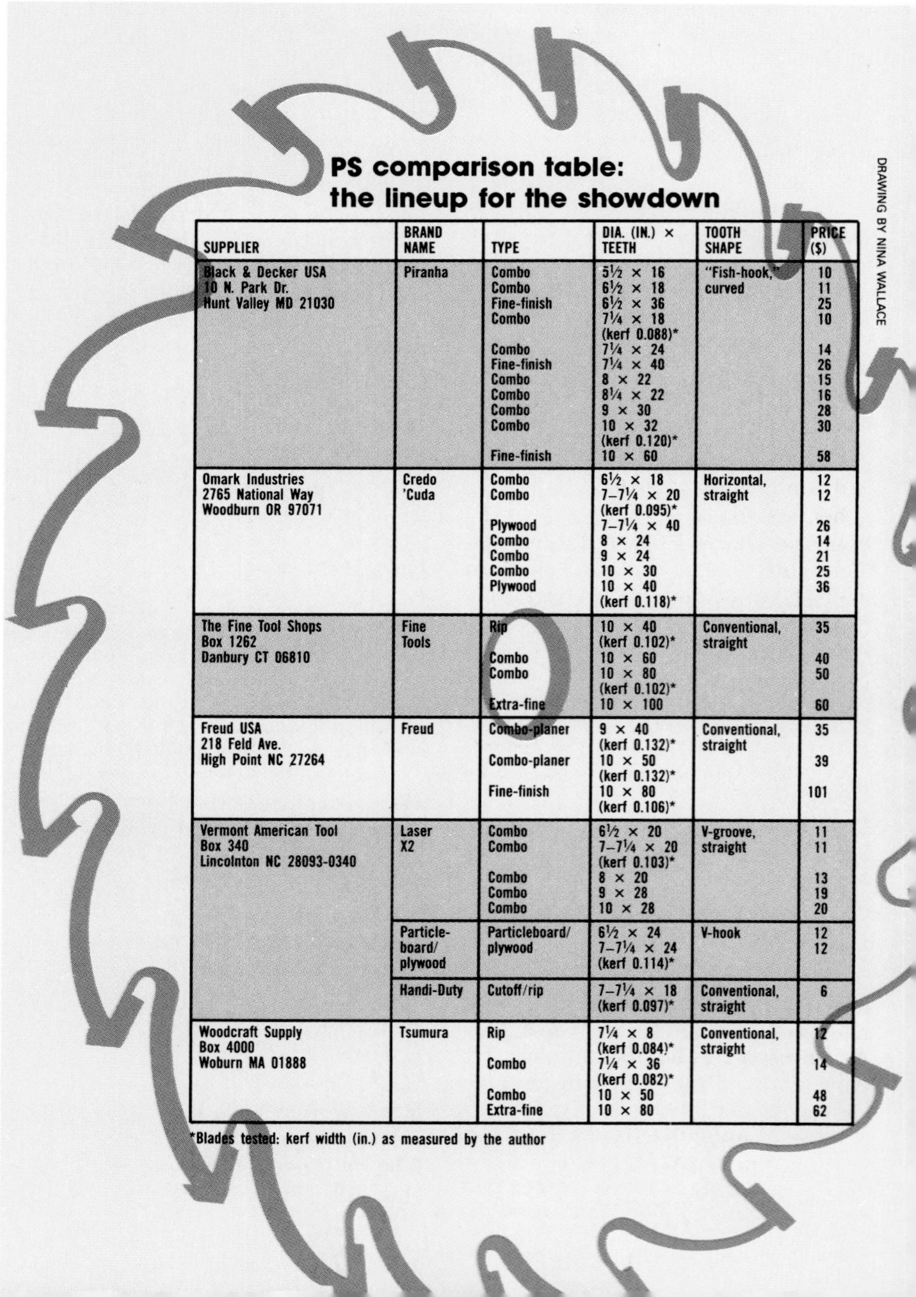

PS comparison table: the lineup for the showdown

SUPPLIER	BRAND NAME	TYPE	DIA. (IN.) × TEETH	TOOTH SHAPE	PRICE ($)
Black & Decker USA 10 N. Park Dr. Hunt Valley MD 21030	Piranha	Combo	5½ × 16	"Fish-hook," curved	10
		Combo	6½ × 18		11
		Fine-finish	6½ × 36		25
		Combo	7¼ × 18 (kerf 0.088)*		10
		Combo	7¼ × 24		14
		Fine-finish	7¼ × 40		26
		Combo	8 × 22		15
		Combo	8¼ × 22		16
		Combo	9 × 30		28
		Combo	10 × 32 (kerf 0.120)*		30
		Fine-finish	10 × 60		58
Omark Industries 2765 National Way Woodburn OR 97071	Credo 'Cuda	Combo	6½ × 18	Horizontal, straight	12
		Combo	7–7¼ × 20 (kerf 0.095)*		12
		Plywood	7–7¼ × 40		26
		Combo	8 × 24		14
		Combo	9 × 24		21
		Combo	10 × 30		25
		Plywood	10 × 40 (kerf 0.118)*		36
The Fine Tool Shops Box 1262 Danbury CT 06810	Fine Tools	Rip	10 × 40 (kerf 0.102)*	Conventional, straight	35
		Combo	10 × 60		40
		Combo	10 × 80 (kerf 0.102)*		50
		Extra-fine	10 × 100		60
Freud USA 218 Feld Ave. High Point NC 27264	Freud	Combo-planer	9 × 40 (kerf 0.132)*	Conventional, straight	35
		Combo-planer	10 × 50 (kerf 0.132)*		39
		Fine-finish	10 × 80 (kerf 0.106)*		101
Vermont American Tool Box 340 Lincolnton NC 28093-0340	Laser X2	Combo	6½ × 20	V-groove, straight	11
		Combo	7–7¼ × 20 (kerf 0.103)*		11
		Combo	8 × 20		13
		Combo	9 × 28		19
		Combo	10 × 28		20
	Particleboard/plywood	Particleboard/plywood	6½ × 24	V-hook	12
			7–7¼ × 24 (kerf 0.114)*		12
	Handi-Duty	Cutoff/rip	7–7¼ × 18 (kerf 0.097)*	Conventional, straight	6
Woodcraft Supply Box 4000 Woburn MA 01888	Tsumura	Rip	7¼ × 8 (kerf 0.084)*	Conventional, straight	12
		Combo	7¼ × 36 (kerf 0.082)*		14
		Combo	10 × 50		48
		Extra-fine	10 × 80		62

*Blades tested; kerf width (in.) as measured by the author

index